# INNOCENT PASSAGE

# INNOCENT PASSAGE
## THE WRECK OF THE TANKER BRAER

# JONATHAN WILLS
## AND KAREN WARNER

*Foreword by*
# ALY BAIN

*Photography by*
TOM KIDD

*Additional Photography by*
JOHN COUTTS, *DAILY RECORD*, ADAM ELDER (*Scotland on Sunday*),
MIKE FORSTER (*Daily Mail*), DONALD MACLEOD (*The Scotsman*),
*THE SCOTSMAN*, GRAEME STOREY, JONATHAN WILLS

**MAINSTREAM PUBLISHING**

EDINBURGH AND LONDON

Other books by Jonathan Wills:

*A Place in the Sun – Shetland and Oil, Myths and Realities*, Mainstream, 1991

*Wilma Widdershins and the Muckle Tree* (illustr. by Gurli Feilberg), Bressabooks, 1991

*Bressay – A Visitor's Guide*, Bressay History Group, 1991

*Old Rock – Shetland in Pictures*, Shetland Times Ltd, 1989

'The Zetland Method', in Crawford (Ed.), *Essays in Shetland History*, Shetland Times Ltd, 1984

*The Lands of Garth*, Shetland Times Ltd, 1978

*Linda and the Lighthouse*, Canongate, 1976

*The Travels of Magnus Pole*, Chatto & Windus, 1975

Copyright © main text and research by Jonathan Wills, with additional research and interviews by Karen Warner, 1993

The moral right of the authors has been asserted

First published in Great Britain 1993 by

MAINSTREAM PUBLISHING COMPANY (EDINBURGH) LTD
7 Albany Street
Edinburgh EH1 3UG

ISBN 1 85158 542 7

A catalogue record for this book is available from the British Library

Typeset in Linotype Sabon by Servis Filmsetting Ltd, Manchester

Printed in Great Britain by Butler & Tanner Ltd, Frome

Frontispiece:
*Braer ashore on the western side of Garth's Ness, with Lady Holm and Scatness in the background, 5 January 1993*
(Photo: John Coutts)

To Stan Stephens of Valdez, Alaska, who had the courage to 'keep on keeping on at them'; to Lesley and Nessie Roberts, who held the fort at Sundside, Bressay; and to the anonymous friend who tipped us off at 6.40am on Tuesday, 5 January 1993.

*We consider this a heavy-weather accident. Whether the vents were damaged by the weather, we don't know. The waves were awesome.*

MICHAEL S. HUDNER, QUOTED IN *The Advocate* NEWSPAPER, CONNECTICUT, USA, FEBRUARY 1993

*The British Government is deeply concerned about the possibility of a major oil spill occurring off the Shetland coast . . . Shetland experiences a high frequency of gale force winds throughout the year, predominantly between south and west in direction. The coast in many places is 'steep-to', making it possible for large vessels to drift close inshore before grounding. It is likely that tugs would have to travel a long distance to assist an endangered tanker.*

LETTER WRITTEN TO THE UN'S INTERNATIONAL MARITIME ORGANISATION BY MS Z. ROBERTS, SECRETARY OF THE UK SAFETY OF NAVIGATION COMMITTEE, DEPARTMENT OF TRANSPORT, LONDON, 9 JULY 1990

*To those responsible, I can only say: 'You bastards.'*

CHRIS BUNYAN, SHETLAND JOURNALIST, *The Scotsman*, 18 JANUARY 1993

# ACKNOWLEDGEMENTS

We are grateful to the following people and organisations who helped us in various ways as we reported the story of the *Braer* and later, during the writing of this book. In the absence of a Freedom of Information Act and a 'Whistleblower's Charter' in our country, we also thank those sources who would probably rather not be named. We would like to thank Messrs Bergvall & Hudner for their full co-operation but we regret that we cannot. Without the information which they refused to give, and which they ought to release now in the public interest, we have done our best to establish the facts. We emphatically do not wish to thank Lord Caithness, John MacGregor MP and their predecessors in office, who could have made the spill and this book unnecessary, but chose not to.

*Jonathan Wills*
*Karen Warner*

Shetland, March 1993

Ken Adams and Julie Becker of Dickstein, Shapiro & Morin, Washington DC; Hazel Anderson, Chief Executive's Department, Shetland Islands Council; Julia Anderson, Quendale, Shetland; Tom Angus, Cunningsburgh, Shetland; BBC Radio Orkney; BBC Radio Scotland; BBC Radio Shetland; the Bressay ferry crew; British Airways' staff at Sumburgh, Aberdeen, London and Washington DC; British Telecom; John and Anne Bateson, Bressay, Shetland; Jeff Blackler at Rex Features; Mary Blance, Lerwick, Shetland; Kenny and Sylvia Bruce, Bressay; Alex Bruner at Frank Spooner; Captain Alvin Cattalini and staff, US Coast Guard, Washington DC; Ivy Cluness, Lerwick; Bill Coughlin, Boston, Massachusetts; John and Dennis Coutts; Jeremy Cresswell, *Press & Journal*, Aberdeen; Martin Dalziel, Shetland Islands Council Planning Department; Captain Jim Dickson, Oil Pollution Control Officer, Shetland Islands Council; Dunrossness Community Council; Bob Gibb, Clydesdale Bank, Lerwick, Shetland; Captain Graham Gilbey and First Officer Peter Walmsley, British Airways, Heathrow; Peter and Morag Gray, Bressay; Malcolm Green, Chief Executive, Shetland Islands Council; David Grimes, Cordova, Alaska; Councillor Leonard

Groat, Lerwick; Mr and Mrs Charles J. Hamel (and Muffin), Alexandria, Virginia; Martin Hall, Director of Environmental Services, Shetland Islands Council; Robert L. Hart, New York; Cecil Hughson and staff, The Camera Shop, Lerwick; Hydro Electric staff, Shetland; Lilian Jamieson, staff and pupils of Bressay Primary School; Peter Hamilton, Lerwick; Dave and Debbie Hammond, Skeld, Shetland; Ian Leask, Lerwick and Belfast; Lerwick Harbour Trust; Martin Heubeck, Skelberry, Dunrossness, Shetland; Andrew Jaspan, Will Peakin, William Paul, Euan Ferguson and Adam Elder of *Scotland on Sunday*; Dan Lawn, Valdez, Alaska; Marilyn Leland, Washington DC; Peter and Jane Manson, Bressay; Arthur McKenzie, New York; Tom Mainland, Bressay; Mercury Communications Newslink staff, London; Congressman George Miller and Jeff Petrich, US House of Representatives Committee on Natural Resources; Gene Minso, Lucas Control System Products, Hampton, Virginia; Jan Morgan, Hillswick, Shetland; National Farmers' Union, Shetland Branch; Keith Morrison; Northern Constabulary; Norwegian Meteorological Service (DNMI), Bergen, Norway; Dave Okill, Trondra, Shetland; Dr Riki Ott, Cordova, Alaska; John Prescott MP; Press Association, Glasgow; the *Press & Journal*; Procurator Fiscal's Office, Lerwick; Drew Ratter, Ollaberry, Shetland; Danny Renton, Lerwick; John Robertson, Bressay; Royal Society for the Protection of Birds; The *Scotsman* Picture Desk; The Scottish Information Office, Edinburgh; Scottish Natural Heritage; Sheriff Clerk's Office, Lerwick; Shetland Bird Club; Shetland Coastguards; Shetland Crofters' Union; Shetland Health Board; Shetland Hotel, Lerwick; Shetland Fishermen's Association; Shetland Islands Council members and staff; Shetland Islands Tourism Ltd; Shetland Salmon Farmers' Association; Charlie Simpson, Cunningsburgh, Shetland; Anne Sinclair, Fair Isle, Shetland; Rick Steiner, Cordova, Alaska; Scott Sterling, Wasilla, Alaska; Barry Stevens, Highlands & Islands Airports Ltd, Sumburgh, Shetland; *Sunday Times* Picture Desk; Captain George Sutherland, Director of Marine Operations, Shetland Islands Council; Televiradio, Lerwick; Councillor Edward Thomason, Convener, Shetland Islands Council; Times Newspapers Picture Library; Kay Tulloch and Hazel Anderson, Shetland Islands Council switchboard operators; Jim Wallace MP; John Waters, Lerwick; Dave Wheeler, Fair Isle; Mike Wilkinson; Andrew, Katy, Magnus and Tom Wills, Bressay; Linda and Dave Wood and staff, Maryfield House Hotel; Chris and Rose Young, Walls, Shetland; and Malcolm Younger.

# CONTENTS

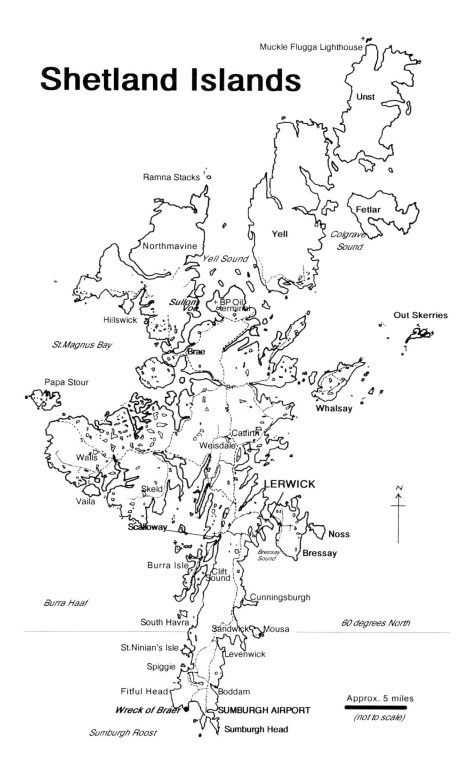

# Shetland Islands

Muckle Flugga Lighthouse

Unst

Ramna Stacks

Fetlar

Yell

Colgrave
Sound

Northmavine

Yell Sound

Sullom Voe

+ BP Oil
Terminal

Out Skerries

Hillswick

St.Magnus Bay

Brae

Papa Stour

Whalsay

Catfirth

Weisdale

Walls

LERWICK

Skeld

Vaila

Scalloway

Noss

Bressay

Burra Isle

Bressay
Sound

Burra Haaf

Clift
Sound

Cunningsburgh

South Havra

Sandwick

Mousa

60 degrees North

St.Ninian's Isle

Levenwick

Spiggie

Fitful Head

Boddam

Approx. 5 miles

Wreck of Braer

SUMBURGH AIRPORT

(not to scale)

Sumburgh Roost

Sumburgh Head

N

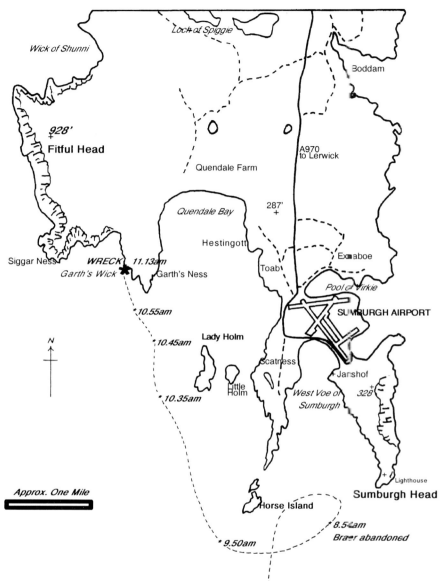

**TRACK OF THE BRAER, 5th January 1993**
*(Scale and distances are approximate.*

*Graphics courtesy of Martin Dalziel, SIC*

# FOREWORD

This is a nightmare come true. These were my thoughts and I am sure those of all Shetlanders as we watched on television the tanker *Braer* break up in the Bay of Quendale. Somehow in her death throes she reminded me of a stricken monster spewing up her poisoned entrails around and over our beautiful islands. The sight of Shetland children wearing masks shocked me. What would the consequences be? Would our islands ever be the same again? How many fears and dreadful thoughts went through our minds during those days as we watched the disaster unfold. It was as if a dark cloud had descended over our island never to rise again. Voices were filled with tension and anger.

I believe we should remember those fears well, for if the *Braer* had been carrying heavy crude or our old enemies, the wind and sea, had not come to our rescue, it might have been a different story. Faceless Government officials come and go but there is little doubt that Shetland people themselves would have been left to pick up the pieces.

Unless we learn from this disaster and begin to work with people around the world in order to keep our oceans clean, these same fears may come back and haunt us another day. Next time we might not be so lucky.

*Aly Bain*
*March 1993*

13

# INTRODUCTION

It was an international disaster. It could have happened anywhere. This time it was the turn of the Shetland Islands.

At 11.13 on the morning of Tuesday, 5 January, an American-managed tanker, built in Japan, registered in Liberia, owned in Bermuda by Americans, and carrying 84,413 tonnes of Norwegian oil to Canada, ran aground at Garth's Ness on the southern tip of Shetland, a hundred miles north of the mainland of Scotland. She also had on board 1,700 tonnes of heavy fuel oil and 125 tonnes of diesel. The *Braer* and all her oil became a total loss.

The ship, 89,730 tonnes deadweight, was two days out from Norway on a 'routine' voyage to Quebec. She had been drifting without power since at least 4.40am. Her engine room had been in trouble at least five hours earlier.

Within minutes, the first oil began to flow into the sea. Within six days, twice as much oil had been spilled as the official figures for the *Exxon Valdez* disaster in Alaska on Good Friday 1989 – probably about the same amount as the true figure.

This was the nightmare Shetland had dreaded since the first oil was shipped from the Sullom Voe oil terminal in November 1978. It quickly became a disaster for Dunrossness, the most southerly parish of the main island of Shetland. For eight days the wreck appeared to be turning into a catastrophe for the 22,500 Shetlanders and the millions of other living things which share this 567 square-mile archipelago. But Mother Nature meant the *Braer* as a warning, not the end of the world. On the morning of Wednesday, 13 January, it became clear that the devastation would be much, much less than feared. Something extraordinary was happening under the sea.

Six days of hurricanes smashed the tanker to pieces. But the storms that spilled the oil also helped to clean it up. The spill doctors and pollution experts had seen nothing quite like it before. Waves up to 100 feet high and winds gusting over 100 miles an hour churned the oil and the sea into a toxic broth. The tide carried much of the oil away – most of it diluted in the sea, not lying on top of it.

Islanders who had feared an *Exxon Valdez* catastrophe called it a 'miracle' when they escaped with a mere disaster. Only a few thousand dead birds, not three-quarters of a million, like Alaska. And only 25 miles of shoreline oiled, not 1,200.

15

It will take a long time for the shore (and the land) to recover fully – in the small part of Shetland which was worst affected. We will never know the full effects of the invisible, underwater oilspill but, thankfully, most of the islands and their fishing grounds escaped pollution.

The economic effects of the *Braer* spill may last longer and be more severe than the damage to Nature. Shetland jobs depend on 'green' industries like tourism, agriculture, fishing and fish farming. Even BP's terminal at Sullom Voe is the cleanest in Europe. After all those TV pictures of oiled birds, seals, fish and even Shetland ponies, the islanders are now fighting to restore their reputation for the clearest seas, the cleanest air, and the freshest food.

The owners of the *Braer* say the wreck was an 'accident', caused by a severe storm. They imply that it was an Act of God. We believe it was a crime, the latest in a series of assaults against the sea. We know of no intentionally illegal act by any individual, although reckless disregard seems possible. The real crime is Government neglect which allows these things to happen, even when captains, crews, shipowners and insurers stay within the law.

There has been much rumour and innuendo about the *Braer* disaster. There may be innocent explanations for what happened but until the full facts are published this speculation can only grow. Reading the various and sometimes inconsistent accounts of those involved, we have assumed that all parties have been telling the truth as they know it.

People need scapegoats. Plausible explanations range from human error to mechanical failure. More significant than either are the errors and failures of politicians. The saddest thing is that our rulers, who were ultimately responsible for this crime, have done so little since. If they had heeded the warnings they could have prevented the wreck, and many others. They chose not to. They have become serial killers of wildlife the world over.

This is our story of the nightmare, the disaster and the 'miracle'. Like most things written by journalists, it is only the 'first rough draft of history'. At the time of writing, the official inquiries into the wreck of the *Braer* are still in progress. We do not wish to pre-judge the work of the Marine Accidents Investigation Branch, nor of Lord Donaldson's inquiry into the wider lessons. But many facts are already known and the need for action to prevent another, much worse, disaster is urgent.

We have tried to explain why the *Braer* went aground, to describe what it was like to be in Shetland in January 1993, and to take part in the international debate on the only way to deal with massive marine oil spills – stopping them happening in the first place. We have some practical suggestions on how to do that – next week, not next year or next decade.

This is a book about Shetland, a place we love and cherish. It is also about something much more important – the fate of the global ocean. It is written in the hope that totally avoidable 'accidents' like the *Braer* may, one day soon, be consigned to the final draft of the history books.

*Jonathan Wills and Karen Warner*
*Shetland, March 1993*

16

*Chapter One*

# INNOCENT PASSAGE

*'Sumburgh Roost, a [tide] race of great violence . . . it is most dangerous during the West-going stream with a West or North-west gale, and during the West-going stream it is violent with any strong wind between West-south-west and North-north-west . . . the race is violent with winds between South-south-west and East-north-east.'*

North Coast of Scotland Pilot, PUBLISHED
BY THE HYDROGRAPHER OF THE NAVY.

The oil tanker *Braer* was 'not a happy ship', according to the International Transport Workers' Federation.

The federation has evidence of disputes between the crew of the Liberian-registered ship and her owners, the Bergvall & Hudner Group (B+H), of Stamford, Connecticut, USA. A year before the tanker was wrecked, there were complaints from the crew about 'unpaid standby pay, insufficient food allowance, unpaid excess overtime for deck- and engineer-officers (as much as 200 hours per month), inadequate manning in the vessel's deck department and inadequate compensation for Sunday and holiday work'. Two of her previous skippers were in legal dispute with B+H over unpaid wages.

For years the federation, which represents workers on 'flag of convenience' vessels like the *Braer*, has campaigned against 'inadequate maintenance or repairs, insufficient manning or training' and 'lack of communication between crew members' speaking three or more languages, with some crew not able to understand 'basic navigational English'.

The *Braer* had a Greek master, Captain Alexandros Gelis (46), from Piraeus. The Chief Engineer was also a Greek. The other officers and crew were Filipinos. Four Polish maintenance fitters and a Mr Khan, a B+H Engineering Superintendent, also sailed with the ship when she left the Mongstad tanker terminal, north of Bergen, on the morning of Sunday, 3 January 1993.

The crew was recruited by a Norwegian company, Singa Ship Management of Oslo, which specialises in supplying seafarers to flag of convenience ships. Coastguards and rescuers had difficulty understanding the basic navigational English of the *Braer*'s radio operator and others on board when they were rescued 48 hours after leaving Norway. But Captain Gelis told the official inquiry that he had 'no difficulties communicating with any of the Filipinos'. He said, in signed testimony: 'Such communications were in English and all the Filipinos, particularly the officers, spoke good English. Communications were never a problem on board.'

At the Fedje Pilot Station outside Mongstad on that Sunday morning, when Axel Sundøy left the tanker at 12.10 GMT after piloting her out to the open sea, he noticed nothing unusual. She was a 17-year-old tanker with a single-skinned hull, a single main engine and a single rudder, but so were most of the ships he took in and out of Mongstad. For her age, the *Braer* was in reasonably good condition, he thought.

In port there had been trouble with the steam boiler. Steam is needed to heat the ship's fuel oil and to keep her crew warm. With the main engine shut down during loading, the auxiliary burner had been fired up, as was normal. It produced exhaust gases which were pumped in to blanket the air spaces above the oil as it rose in the 12 cargo tanks. This kept the oxygen levels low enough to prevent fire and explosion. The *Braer*'s boiler was not making enough of this 'inert gas'. Engineers were called and the problem was apparently fixed. The terminal operator allowed the oil to flow onboard again, but at a slower rate than usual – just in case there was any more trouble.

It was not a serious incident. Such things happen, even on new ships. There had been another inert gas system problem on the *Braer*'s last trip to Shetland, on 18 and 19 October 1992. During loading, a small quantity of fluid – either oil or a mixture of carbon dust and water – spouted into the air and on to the deck from a vent pipe which was clogged with rust and dust, allegedly because of poor maintenance. Loading stopped immediately. The pipe, known as a 'mast IG riser', is used to vent the inert exhaust gases to the atmosphere after they have done their work in the cargo tanks.

That was on Captain Gelis' first voyage with the *Braer*. He had joined her in Wilhelmshavn, Germany, on 11 October. Captain Gelis refused to sign his copy of a 'letter of protest' issued by BP, operators of the terminal. A letter of protest is standard procedure at Sullom Voe when there is an incident of this kind, and is designed to record the facts in case there are any subsequent legal proceedings. Refusal to sign is unusual.

During the same visit, an inspection at the BP oil terminal by marine surveyors found a faulty gauge in the cargo control room. The instrument was designed to measure the oxygen content of the tanks, which has to be below eight per cent before a tanker is allowed to enter Sullom Voe. The level was well below the limit.

The faults repaired, the tanker sailed late, after being loaded more slowly than normal. Sailing late can cost a lot of money on a tanker.

That was the last call by the *Braer* at Sullom Voe, a port she had visited 99 times over the previous decade. On her next trip for a Shetland cargo she would be due for a 'gong'. When a tanker has made 100 calls at the port, they have a pleasant little social custom. An informal reception is held by Shetland Islands Council (harbour authority for Sullom Voe) and BP (operators of the terminal on behalf of over 30 other oil companies). Graceful and humorous speeches are made – perhaps alluding comically to minor incidents involving the ship – and then a commemorative plaque is presented to the skipper, a jolly photograph is taken, hands are shaken, and everybody enjoys a strictly off-duty refreshment. The *Braer*'s plaque had been ordered. It was never to hang in the captain's cabin.

Outside Mongstad, as the *Braer* sailed on her last voyage, the weather was bad. At 11.10am GMT, it was blowing Gale Force Nine (41–47 knots) from the south, according to records kept by the Norwegian Meteorological Service's district office. The Norwegian figures are for mean wind speeds. The gusts were stronger. At the port of Sullom Voe this would have been marginal for allowing a loaded tanker to sail. The outward-bound limit there is when the wind is gusting up to 50 knots. The limit for bringing a tanker in to Sullom Voe is 30 knots.

Soon after Pilot Axel Sundøy left the *Braer*, the tanker ran into even worse weather. It had been forecast. There is nothing unusual about heavy weather in sea areas North Utsire, Viking and Fair Isle, which the *Braer* would cross on the first 200 miles of her intended voyage to Quebec, particularly in the first week of January.

Captain Gelis described the conditions to the accident investigators: 'The weather conditions on sailing were very poor . . . I estimate the seas were 8–9 metres [26–30 feet] and they were hitting us on our port side. Waves were coming on deck as green water and breaking. The vessel was rolling about ten degrees to each side . . . The period of roll was five to ten seconds. The vessel was also pitching heavily . . . Although normal sea speed [propeller] revolutions are 107rpm, I had to order a reduction in revolutions to 90rpm . . . due to the bad weather conditions. On reaching the open sea off Mongstad the vessel was making very slow progress . . .'

Progress was so slow that 24 hours after leaving, the ship was still only 60 miles offshore, an average sea speed of 2.5 knots. Her average speed over the 200 nautical miles from Norway to the Fair Isle Channel would work out at between five and six knots, compared with a normal, fuel-saving, sea speed of about 12 to 15 knots for a mid-range tanker.

With the dangerous, rocky coastline of western Norway downwind, Captain Gelis would have had no doubt of the correct procedure – at all costs keep heading westwards, to increase the sea-room between his ship and the skerries and small islands around the mouth of Hjeltefjord. The name means 'The Shetlanders' Fjord'. For over a thousand years, after the Norse colonisation of Shetland in the eighth century, ships from the islands had come in by Hjeltefjord to trade with the Hansa merchants at Bergen's Tyskebryggen, 'The Germans' Wharf'.

The heavy weather was heavier than usual. A year before, a hurricane had raged in from sea area Fair Isle and on to the Norwegian coast. The January 1992 storm had gusted to well over 125mph. It caused widespread devastation in Shetland and Norway. It looked as if 1993's January storm was going to be almost as strong, only it would last a lot longer. Of the 31 days in the month, 25 would be 'gale days'.

The *Braer* was a solidly built ship, launched at the Oshima Shipyard in Oshima, Japan, in 1975. She was one of the last to be designed the old way, just before computer-aided design and high-tensile steels revolutionised tanker construction. With computers, the naval architects could calculate the exact gauge of the steel for the hull. They could build in just enough strength to survive the stresses of ocean storms, and no more. And they could do it with high-tensile steel, which was lighter, stronger, but more subject to sudden, catastrophic failure than traditional shipbuilders' steel.

Before computer-aided design, shipbuilders put in as much metal as experience had taught them to use, and then added some more, to be on the safe side. So the *Braer*, launched as the *Hellespont Pride* and later re-named *Brae Trader* before being christened for the third time as *Braer*, was probably a stronger boat than her more modern sisters. Just how strong would be proved when it took seven nights of North Atlantic storms to destroy her on the rocks of Garth's Ness.

Like most maritime communities, Shetland has its 'Pierhead Skippers' – nautical-minded pundits who do not go to sea much any more and maybe never did. They can always be relied upon for instant comment when something goes wrong afloat. The instant opinion of some Pierhead Skippers, eagerly offered to the Sunday newspapers, was that the reason for the *Braer* going ashore was that she was old – what is known as a 'rustbucket'. But she was not particularly old. There are many far older tankers hauling oil around the oceans. Arthur Mackenzie's Tanker Information Bureau in New York gave the *Braer* a four out of five star rating when potential charterers asked for her details. She had passed without difficulty her most recent inspections by Det Norske Veritas, a well-known Norwegian 'classification society' company which issues certificates of seaworthiness to tanker owners.

According to Captain Gelis, the ship was inspected by the US Coastguard in New York on 11 November 1992: 'Four Coastguard inspectors conducted a complete investigation into the safety aspects of the ship. They were entirely satisfied and gave her a clean certificate. In preparation for this inspection, Mr Siddhu from B+H head office sailed with the ship from Gdansk [in Poland] to Mongstad in October 1992 and conducted detailed inspections with me, the Chief Officer and the Chief Engineer ... these inspections included looking at the condition of all vent pipes on deck ... I know that various screens were replaced on some of the vent pipes. Any maintenance needed was also carried out.'

Given proper maintenance, particularly in the engine room and pipework, there was no theoretical reason why her hull should not last for another 20 years. With new 90,000 tonners costing $80 million, and freight rates low and staying low, it made sense to keep the older, stronger ships running.

On the port quarter (rear left-hand side) of the 260-yards long deck of the *Braer* there were some steel pipes. Sixteen feet long, they were lashed to steel racks outside the 'I.G. [inert gas] room' – the compartment where the ship's exhaust gases were cooled and pumped to the air spaces above the oil in the cargo tanks. The racks were new, as Captain Gelis explained to the investigation team: 'The Chief Engineer had built a steel rack, with the assistance of the Deck Fitter, to secure the pipes. This rack involved three brackets welded to the deck at their bases and to the side of the I.G. room at their tops. The brackets were also welded to the pipes themselves. This rack was built on a ballast leg [return trip without cargo] from New York to Mongstad in November 1992. I also inspected the finished rack at Mongstad and was satisfied that it was secure.' Secure it might appear, but the rack and its pipes were to be the *Braer*'s undoing.

Before leaving Mongstad, the deck officers had reported to Captain Gelis that the ship was 'secured for sea'. This meant that all hatches were closed and everything that could conceivably break loose in the winter seas of the North Atlantic at latitude 60°N was firmly fixed to the ship. The anchors, for example, had been checked, to make sure that the 'Devil's Claws', restraining clamps, were holding on to the studded steel anchor chains, and that the 'Guillotines', large steel bars, were in place to stop the chains running away with the anchors in very heavy seas.

On this grey Sunday afternoon, dusk fell well before four pm. For the next 16 hours the ship battered on in darkness, shouldering aside seas that rose and fell up to 50 feet. Even in the steam-heated, well-lit accommodation in the superstructure at the stern of the ship, the crew could hear the sound of the storm above the hum of the generators and the comforting rumble of the propeller shaft.

The waves were running the full length of the deck and thumping into the superstructure. Forward-facing portholes had been blanked off with steel plates. The *Braer* rolled and pitched, but her motion was slow and ponderous, punctuated by sudden shocks when particularly large waves slammed into the bows. At the stern, on the port side where the waves were coming aboard, the welds on the pipe rack were coming under unbearable pressure. This was not at all surprising. They had, after all, been made on a cold, clammy, open deck in mid-Atlantic, in mid-winter. Hardly ideal for welding steel, which is best done in still, dry, warm air. A cold, wet welding job may look all right, but it will not be as strong as a warm, dry one.

The trouble was noticed soon after dawn on Monday. Captain Gelis told the inquiry: 'Unfortunately, the pipes broke loose in the heavy weather encountered after sailing from Mongstad. I was informed by the Chief Officer on the morning of 4 January that the pipes were loose and rolling around on the port aft deck. Unfortunately, it was too dangerous for anyone to be allowed to go out on deck to resecure the pipes.'

By early afternoon, in normal weather, the *Braer* should have been approaching the Fair Isle Channel, between the island, famous for its bird observatory and knitwear, and Sumburgh Head, the southern tip of the main island of Shetland. At about this time, the officer of the watch may have had another look at the chart. It was his job to check the ship's position every hour or so. The course ahead looked easy enough. In the jargon of maritime lawyers, the *Braer* would be on 'innocent passage' through an international waterway. She had a perfect right to be there, in all weathers and tides. It was 20 nautical miles wide and deeper than the alternative route through the Dover Straits, with not much other traffic, but still a tricky place because of

*Sumburgh Head*
*Lighthouse*
(Photo: Jonathan Wills)

its reputation for bad weather and confused seas. In weather like this it was best to go through in daylight if possible, particularly with fishing boats around – and there might be other tankers too.

Well, at this rate it would be midnight before they got there. The ship was still only about half-way across to Shetland. Never mind, once they were past that gap in the string of islands north of Scotland they would reach the longer swells of the open Atlantic. The motion of the ship would be easier. Life on board would become more relaxed and everyone could catch up on the sleep they had missed during all that overtime when they were slow-loading at Mongstad. There would be no more land in their way until they raised the coast of Newfoundland on the way into the Gulf of St Lawrence. A pity it was still too rough to send someone down on deck to sort out that untidy jumble of loose pipes, either to stow them securely again or dump them over the side.

The heavy pipes were careering around the aft deck, bumping into things that stuck up through it. Things like the vents which let air out of the ship's fuel tanks when they were being filled, and let air in as the fuel was burned in the main engine and generators.

The air vents had patent ball valves on top, to prevent sea-water and rain from getting in. But when the pipes below the vents were bent, buckled and eventually punctured by repeated blows from those much heavier pipes now rolling around the deck, there was nothing to stop water pouring into the fuel tanks. Just a little at first but more and more of it as the weather worsened and the unseen damage spread into the heart of the ship.

From the moment the vents were damaged, probably sometime before dawn on Monday, 4 January, the *Braer* was doomed. A spiral of mechanical failure had begun.

The Pierhead Skippers say Captain Gelis could have stopped his ship or slowed her down, so that crew could go on deck and deal with the loose pipes. But even stopped, bows on to the waves, it is doubtful whether it could have been done in those seas without hazarding the lives of the crew. And the tanker might drift back towards the Norwegian coast, where people were still speaking about the fuel oil pollution from the Brazilian iron ore carrier *Mercantil Marica*, wrecked on a lee shore not far away, at the mouth of Sogne Fjord, back in 1989. There could be no doubt. Captain Gelis had to keep going, at least until he had enough sea-room to heave to.

But, says the Pierhead, he should have asked his engineers to make extra checks for water in the fuel. And, if they found a lot of it, he should have asked for a tug to stand by him. The Pierhead could have a point there. But Captain Gelis says he did not know about the water in the fuel until it was too late.

Captain Gelis knew the pipes were rolling around loose on the after deck; he also knew that the fuel tank vents were on the after deck, because he had inspected them before that US Coastguard workover in New York, back in November; but he didn't know about the water problem in the fuel until it was too late. It was all an accident, just as it had been an accident to do that welding at sea instead of in port.

The darkness came down again. As was his habit in bad weather, Captain Gelis had been on the bridge since leaving port 36 hours before, apart from 'the occasional trip to my cabin to make some coffee and to have some food and rest', as he told the investigators. At eight pm on Monday the 2000–2400 watch came on duty in the engine room, far below the bridge. It was going to be a difficult shift. But the weather had eased a little, from Gale Force Ten to Gale Force Nine and, according to Captain Gelis, 'it had been possible to increase the speed again to 107rpm [*top speed*]' at eight o'clock.

At about this time, the exhausted Captain Gelis went back to his cabin to try to get some rest. He was desperately tired. For years, the International Transport Workers' Federation had been demanding 'relieving masters' on big tankers so that the men in command could have enough sleep to keep their heads clear for dealing with the enormous responsibilities they carried – and to be wide awake when there was an emergency. The *Braer*'s owners had not supplied a relieving master. It was not company policy. Captain Gelis left on the bridge his 'Night Orders book'. His standing orders 'indicated that I should be called at any time the duty officer wanted to speak to me', he told the inquiry. 'In addition [they] listed specific circumstances in which the officer must call me. These circumstances included poor visibility, difficult navigational situations, closing radar targets and poor weather conditions.'

In seaman's language, the phrase 'difficult navigational situations' would include serious engine trouble which could threaten an imminent loss of power. That is what the *Braer* already had but, according to Captain Gelis' account, no-one had told him.

The ship was still taking green water right along her decks. And no-one had done anything about the loose pipes, which could only do more damage as the tanker speeded up. Perhaps they hoped the pipes would wash overboard. The main engine needed a good, hard run. It had been turning slowly for a very long time. Slow speed means that there is less waste heat than usual from the cooling water and exhaust gases. The ship uses this heat to raise steam and make her more energy-efficient. Steam is essential to keep a big motor ship running. It is used to heat up the heavy fuel oil, to make it runny enough to pump it through purifying plants and squirt it into the cylinders of the main engine.

Without steam heat, the oil will quickly become too sticky to pump and too thick to go through the atomisers into the combustion cylinders. The engine will stop.

Marine engineers have two ways of dealing with a slow-running engine that is clogging up: they can light an auxiliary burner, powered by fuel oil or diesel fed through nozzles; or they can switch over the main engine from heavy fuel oil to the much thinner diesel – which does not need to be warmed up before it will make the engine go. The trouble with diesel is that it is much more expensive. On most ships it is conserved 'like gold dust', as one former ship's engineer told us.

Between the ship's bunker tanks and the engine's fuel injectors, the fuel oil is heated, filtered to remove any lumps and put through centrifugal clarifiers and purifiers which take out any remaining solids and water. This is the ship's own miniature oil refinery. The waste sludge it produces is mixed with lubricating oil, bilge water and the remains of former cargoes, and ends up in the tanker's slop tanks. Getting rid of this toxic brew is a major problem.

The *Braer*'s main engine was a very conventional, old-fashioned and normally reliable plant – according to *Clarkson's Tanker Register* it was a seven-cylinder, two-stroke, single-acting Sulzer, designed in Switzerland and assembled under licence in Japan by Sumimoto Heavy Industries at the same time as the hull was built at Oshima in 1975. Ship's engineers affectionately refer to the old Sulzers as 'cathedral engines' or 'stone crushers' – because of their massive engineering and the noise they make – uncannily like a large piece of equipment in a roadstone quarry. They are very large and very tall – the height of a two-storey house – and they run very slowly. The *Braer*'s Sulzer was typical, turning only 107 times a minute, at most. This produced some 18,000 horsepower to drive the ship's vast bulk through the sea.

The ship also had two auxiliary engines, driving machinery but not the propeller. The auxiliary engines are all that lie between a big ship and a big disaster. They are conventional diesel-powered piston engines which are sometimes rated to run on heavy fuel oil as well. The *Braer*'s twin 800-kilowatt diesels powered the generators to produce the ship's electricity, run pumps for fuel, lubricating oil and cargo handling, air compressors and hydraulic systems to start and control the main engine and steering, and a great deal else on board.

Even a conventional plant like the *Braer*'s engine room is a very complicated piece of kit which requires constant attention by trained and experienced engineers. The trouble is that each part of the system is connected to the rest. When one bit goes wrong, a cascade of faults can rapidly put the whole ship out of action. Things which happen automatically in a car engine have to be done by people in a ship's engine room. A lot of people.

The engineer in charge on the *Braer*'s voyage from Canada to Mongstad in the last days of 1992 had complained that he did not have enough people to carry out all the routine engine maintenance that he should have been doing. Captain Gelis later testified that the four Polish fitters taken on board at Mongstad were 'to assist the engine department with general maintenance work'. Engineering Superintendent Khan was on the voyage to familiarise himself with the vessel, as the 'shoreside superintendent' looking after the *Braer*'s mechanical needs.

When auxiliary engines, generators and steam boiler fail at the same time as the main engine, you have very serious trouble. A common cause is contamination of a shared fuel supply. This can take some hours to become apparent because the fuel goes through settling tanks before it reaches the service tank which actually feeds the engines. In heavy weather, if the settling tank is not kept well topped-up, the motion of the ship may set the fuel sloshing around inside it. This can trip switches designed to cut off the fuel supply if the level is too low. The reason for the switches is that the bottom of the tank is where any water in the fuel will collect. In cold climates, condensation on the inside of a partly-filled fuel tank can produce enough water to cause trouble, even without the sea leaking in from outside. That is why part of the engineer's job is to check for water in the settling and service tanks every day, and to drain off any that has gathered at the bottom of the tank. Tanks have a little tap on them, and usually an inspection glass, to make this job easier.

If the contamination is severe, the fuel lines and fuel injectors must be taken apart, cleaned and re-assembled – a job that can take several hours on a large engine. If the main Sulzer engine has also stopped, you must get the auxiliary power back on before you can make enough compressed air to turn over the heavy crankshaft and make the beast fire again.

To start a cold Sulzer you use straight diesel, switching over to the heavy fuel oil once the engine has warmed up. If that diesel comes from the same, contaminated source as the auxiliary plant's fuel, then you are in a real fix. To start a warm Sulzer, one that has stopped during a voyage, for example, you have to be quick. After 30 minutes the fuel oil starts to thicken. One way to keep the fuel runny enough is to mix it with diesel. But again you must act quickly. And you cannot re-start it without generators to make electricity to run the fuel pumps, cooling pumps, fuel booster pumps, sea-water pumps and, most importantly, the lubricating oil pumps for the main engines. The spiral of power losses and equipment breakdowns often begins as a trickle of minor problems when a ship has to slow down in heavy weather. That is what happened to the *Braer*.

Sometime during the last four hours of Monday, 4 January, the engine room watch noticed that something was wrong with the auxiliary boiler. They shut it down, for what the shipowner later described as 'routine adjustment'. That probably meant they were cleaning the burner nozzles after they had become clogged up with water-contaminated fuel.

Then they tried to light it again. The boiler has to be lit, stopped and re-lit several times, because to fire it up to full heat all at once could cause metal parts to distort. 'After several sequences of shutting down and re-lighting, the boiler failed to ignite', according to a preliminary report from the shipowner's own investigation.

The *Braer*'s Third Assistant Engineer tried to find out what was wrong. He was still trying when the watch changed at midnight. Instead of going off watch, he stayed on with the Second Assistant Engineer to track down and correct the cause of the trouble. But time was running out. Around midnight the heavy fuel oil was getting too cool to run the main engine. 'Shortly before midnight', according to the shipowner, they had switched over to diesel. The diesel would have taken something like 15 minutes to work its way through the fuel pipes, until the engine was running on the pure 'gold dust'. She gradually built up to full speed again, making perhaps ten knots or more through the Force Eight to Nine gale which was still blowing on her port bow.

You cannot hear a sigh of relief in the incessant noise of a big ship's engine room but there must have been relief in the eyes of those Filipino engineers around midnight on Monday. They knew that they had enough diesel to keep the main engine going for two or three days – enough to take them well clear of the Fair Isle Channel and out into the open Atlantic, where hopefully the wind would ease, they could sort out that troublesome boiler and switch back to heavy fuel oil. Their troubles seemed to be over.

The relief did not last long. The *Braer*'s main engine was now running on the same fuel supply as the two auxiliaries. The engineers checked the diesel settling tank which fed the single service tank in the engine room. A slug of water came out of the bottom valve. They checked again. Another slug of water. And another, and another. Still apparently unaware of the damaged vent pipes on deck, which were letting the water in as fast as they could drain it off, they wearily plodded on with the trouble-shooting routine laid down in the engine room manuals.

For over two hours they tried. But the water was defeating them. According to the shipowner, at 2.30am on Tuesday the watch engineers finally called Chief Engineer Ionnis Vloutis from his bunk. Together they tried again to fix the boiler. But the ship was moving around so much that the water would not settle out of the diesel. The deadly emulsion which had clogged the burner nozzles in the steam boiler was now inching its way towards the service tank and all three engines.

According to the shipowner, 'eventually' Vloutis called Captain Gelis. Here we come to one of the unsolved riddles of the deep. In his evidence to the Marine Accidents Investigation Branch on 15 January, Captain Gelis said he was on the bridge most of the time from leaving Mongstad on Sunday lunchtime until 'evening' the following day when, presumably, he went to bed. But he must have got up again later on the Monday night, for in his statement he also said he 'went to bed at 0200 on 5th January'. If he was wakened after going to bed in the evening, why? And if he was awake during the 2000–2400 hrs watch when the boiler trouble started, how could it be that, as he told the inquiry, when he finally turned in at two he was 'unaware of problems in the engine room'?

'I first became aware of a problem at 0410 on 5th January when Mr Khan came into my cabin. I had already been woken by the Second Officer, who was on bridge duty, a few minutes earlier, to report a reduction in the revolutions [*of the main engine*]. I was washing and preparing to return to the bridge when Mr Khan arrived. He reported a problem with the generators. He said they had found water in two diesel oil service tanks. He said the boiler was not functioning and the main engine was being run on diesel oil because there was insufficient heat to use heavy [*fuel*] oil. He suggested I consider altering course to a calm anchorage so the engineers could drain the water out of the service tanks.'

Captain Gelis' statement on 15 January described what happened next: 'I laid off a course and at 0436 I ordered a change of course. At that time we were in position 59° 41.5'N, 001° 13.7'W which was fixed from Sumburgh Head, about 10.5 miles distant. The weather at this time was south to south-west Force Nine, with nine metre [*30 feet*] seas. The anemometer showed wind speed of 55–60 knots with gusts in excess of this figure. After the alteration of course I went back to my cabin to change from my pyjamas into some day clothes.'

He planned to anchor near the Beatrice oilfield in the Moray Firth, a hundred miles or so to the south. The course change at 4.36am was more than two hours after Vloutis was called to the engine room and about five hours after the boiler failure forced the engineers to switch over the main engine to diesel.

The new course put the *Braer* broadside on to the gale. As she turned, rolled heavily and steadied up on her new heading, the water in the fuel pipes reached the Sulzer. Then the contaminated fuel hit the auxiliary engines: 'A few minutes after our alteration of course when I was still in my cabin, the vessel's main engine stopped and a short time later we suffered a blackout at 0440,' Captain Gelis said. There was no back-up generator and no duplicate fuel supply. The *Braer* was a dead ship.

Captain Gelis switched on the two red lights at the masthead which signal 'Not Under Command' to other vessels. In the glow of the ship's battery-powered emergency lights, Captain Gelis went into the radio operator's 'shack', immediately behind the bridge. He did not call the Coastguards first. Instead, he asked the radio operator to get him a ship-to-shore call through Wick Radio to a number in Stamford, Connecticut – 0101 203 967 7300.

Bergvall & Hudner have offices in many places around the world – including Bermuda where some of their companies are registered, Connecticut where Michael S. Hudner lives, and a nameplate office in Liberia, where they register their ships to avoid paying US and even Liberian taxes. But when a B+H skipper has engine failure, he calls the B+H office in Stamford, and asks to speak to Mr Makrinos, the B+H Technical Director. Captain Gelis wished to 'advise him generally of our difficulties', he said.

Captain Gelis placed the call 'at about 0500'. 'I also asked the Radio Officer to make contact with the Coastguard to advise them of our situation. That call was made to Aberdeen Coastguard at about 0508 . . . At about 0513 the connection was made to Mr Makrinos in Connecticut.'

But Captain Gelis did not speak to Makrinos. Superintendent Engineer Khan did. The Captain could not hear Makrinos' side of the conversation: 'The call lasted only a few minutes. Mr Khan said he was going back to the engine room to re-assess the situation and was to call Mr Makrinos again in about ten minutes. He left for the engine room. In the meantime I was called by Lerwick Coastguard on VHF, Channel 16. This was at about 0519. I advised them of our position and the power failure.'

The Radio Officer's call to Aberdeen Coastguard was on 2182 kilohertz, the international calling, safety and distress frequency. He did not say he was in distress. He sounded quite calm and matter-of-fact. Aberdeen Coastguards passed the information on to Shetland Coastguards in Lerwick as a non-urgent transmission.

Thirty-nine minutes had gone by since the engines stopped; 69 minutes since Captain Gelis was told of the problem; and 169 minutes since Vloutis had been called to help with the problem of water in the only fuel supply left to the ship. Rather a long time, the Pierhead Skippers would say.

The Pierhead Skippers say (and this time they are absolutely right) that, not later than 4.50am, Captain Gelis should have sent out an urgent distress message, a 'Mayday' call, not asked for an ordinary link call so that he could speak to someone on a telephone on the other side of the Atlantic. They say he should perhaps have done this at about 2.35am, when the Chief Engineer should have woken him, as soon as he realised there was a dangerous amount of water in the diesel fuel.

The Pierhead thinks Captain Gelis should have said this on the radio:

> 'Mayday, Mayday, Mayday. This is Liberian oil tanker Braer, Liberian oil tanker Braer, Liberian oil tanker Braer. My position is one eight zero, from Sumburgh Head ten miles. I have lost all power and require immediate assistance. Total crew 34 on board black-hulled tanker with yellow funnel. I have cargo of 84,500 tonnes of crude oil. Drifting north. Over.'

That message would have had an instant effect. Within 20 seconds the Shetland Coastguards would have replied and asked the Braer to switch her radio to the VHF distress frequency, Channel 16. They had a VHF aerial at Sumburgh, just 10 miles from the Braer. They would have asked all ships in the area to alter course to go to the Braer's assistance. They would have alerted the Lerwick lifeboat and the Coastguard rescue helicopter at Sumburgh Airport, just ten minutes flying time from the tanker. And they would immediately have called out a tug. There was a big North Sea oilfield anchor-handling tug, the *Star Sirius*, lying alongside the wharf at Lerwick. She could have reached the *Braer* by 6.07am, had she been called out at, say, 2.40am.

If Captain Gelis had delayed sending a Mayday until 4.55am, the *Star Sirius* could still have reached him by 8.07am. A vital hour and a half's delay could have been avoided.

It is not only the Pierhead Skippers who think this. When a candidate for a United Kingdom Class I Master Mariner's licence has finished the written part of his examinations, the final stage is a verbal grilling by a Department of Transport examiner. This is one of the few professional qualifications where everything depends on the oral examination. It can last from one to three hours. The purpose is to find out if candidates can apply their technical knowledge in different situations.

Questions usually include something like this: 'You are the master of a loaded tanker carrying 80,000 tonnes of crude oil. You break down and lose all power in a shipping channel, ten miles from land. Your chief engineer tells you the engines cannot be re-started. The weather is bad. The tides will tend to drive you closer to the shore during the next few hours. What should you do?'

The correct answer, according to the head of studies at one of Britain's major nautical colleges, is: 'Send a Mayday signal; lower the anchors; and ask for a tug.' If you replied: 'Phone the owners, discuss the costs of ordering a tug, delay telling the Coastguards and avoid putting out a distress signal for as long as possible,' you would fail the examination.

'Mayday' comes from the French 'M'Aidez' ('Help Me') and it means, in the Standard Marine Navigational Vocabulary, that 'a ship or person is threatened by grave and imminent danger and requests immediate assistance'.

When he spoke to the Shetland Coastguards at 5.19am, Captain Gelis said his ship had no engine power but was in 'no immediate danger'. About half an hour later, the Fraserburgh fishing boat *Philorth* reported the tanker's position to the Coastguards. Captain Gelis had no means of fixing his position without power. Visibility was only about a mile and it was still dark: 'The Second Officer plotted the position reported by the fishing vessel. It was clear we had drifted northwards by about two miles in the hour since the power failure,' Captain Gelis said. But not until 6.26am, when he realised that he was only six nautical miles from Sumburgh Head, did he put out the 'Pan' message that the Coastguards had urged him to transmit at 6.11am.

Pans are one step down from Maydays. If you say 'Pan, Pan, Pan' at the beginning of a radio transmission, it means you have a 'very urgent message to transmit concerning the safety of a ship, aircraft (or other vehicle) or person'. And if you have put out a Mayday, you can always downgrade it to a Pan if matters improve. No-one will blame you for erring on the side of caution, not even the lifeboatmen and helicopter crews who may have risked their lives to come to your aid. They would much rather be called on a false alarm than arrive too late and have to fish out drowned corpses.

To anyone with any nautical knowledge, Captain Gelis' plight certainly sounded more like a Mayday than a Pan. 'Grave and imminent danger' was putting it mildly. The *Braer* had broken down in 'The Hole', the name on the chart for the middle of the Fair Isle Channel, just south of the tide race of the Sumburgh Roost.

The direction of the tidal stream in The Hole changes rapidly, in a clockwise movement. The tides here are not 'unusual', as Hudner told the world's media in a statement on 25 January. They are predictable, and described in some detail by the British Admiralty's publication the *North Coast of Scotland Pilot*. Captain Gelis was familiar with that volume, or he should have been, because – as he told the inquiry – he had taken the *Braer* through The Hole four times since he took command in October 1992, on two round trips from Mongstad to New York, chartered by Exxon.

If the *Braer* had been in The Hole at 2.30am on 5 January, the tide would set her north-north-west, towards the island of Foula, on the west coast of Shetland. But the south-westerly gale would be nudging her towards Fitful Head. Two hours later, just before the *Braer* finally broke down, the tide would drive her north-north-east, going with the storm towards Sumburgh Head. As the ship moved north she drifted out of the main tide and into the much stronger Sumburgh Roost, which runs like a river several miles wide.

The tide seas were breaking clear across the *Braer*'s deck and bows. They are known locally as 'tide lumps' – unpredictable, huge waves up to 100 feet high. They can rise out of nowhere and dump hundreds of tonnes of water on your deck. Since the days of the Viking longships, sailors have dreaded the Sumburgh Roost. In the North Sea they are called 'freak' waves, often by skippers who have been caught out by one and have some explaining to do. In the Sumburgh Roost they are not freak waves. They are normal, whenever high winds, swells and tides meet. The Roost's tide lumps are the sea's way of dissipating the massive energy of irresistible forces contending with irresistible forces.

The other thing a master in Captain Gelis' situation ought to do, after sending out a Mayday, is to lower the anchors. Anchors are bigger and have changed shape in the nine centuries since the Norwegian Earl Rognvald was wrecked in this part of Shetland, but the principle remains the same.

The *Braer* had two 15-tonne anchors, one on each side of the bow. A tanker of her size, 792 feet long, would normally carry about 990 feet of studded chain in her starboard chain locker and 810 feet in the port locker. The sea between Fair Isle and Shetland is around 300 feet deep in mid-channel, shoaling to 100 feet within a few hundred yards of the shore. The bottom is covered in shifting sand ridges, created by 12,000 years of storms since the ice melted. It is not what mariners call 'good holding ground' and the anchors would certainly not have stopped her, but the combined weight of anchors and chain dragging along and through the sand on the seabed could have slowed her drift, particularly in the last half mile to the shore. If she had slowed enough to be driven ashore on the sands of Quendale Bay, she might have lasted long enough for much of the oil to be salvaged. And with her anchor chains out, the anchor-handling tug *Star Sirius* might have been able to get hold of them and tow her, even without assistance from the ship.

The only way to anchor was to send men to the bows and release the chains manually. There is a manual brake on the windlass, or anchor winch, allowing the crew to control the speed at which the chains run out down the hawsepipes and through the bows. The fatal design flaw on the *Braer*, and on nearly every large tanker in the world, was that the anchors were out of reach in heavy weather. Captain Gelis and his owners knew that, years before the *Braer*'s fatal voyage. Lowering the anchors is a dangerous and tricky business in calm weather. In the Fair Isle Channel on the morning of 5 January 1993 the job was impossible.

The crew could not reach the bows. Not alive, anyway. The 200-yard route to the bows from the accommodation block at the stern of the ship was like a snakes and ladders board, winding around and over the big loading and discharging pipes mounted on the deck. Even with hand-rails, anyone trying to reach the bows would have been swept overboard long before he got to the twin masts called 'Samson Posts', only half-way to the anchors. The designers of the ship had not included an all-weather, sheltered catwalk above the cargo piping from the accommodation to the bows.

Nor could anyone reach the towing cables – heavy-duty wires also stored in the bows – to make them fast to a line fired by rocket from a salvage tug. And no-one had thought to carry a spare towing wire on the stern.

There was no emergency anchor at the stern either, although such anchors are common on the ageing 'rustbucket' ships used by the Russians as fish factories around the Shetland coast. A stern anchor can almost always be released by hand, whatever the weather. It may turn the ship's stern into the full force of the sea and cause the waves to rip her rudder off, but that is hardly a major concern when the vessel is powerless anyway.

So the *Braer* might as well not have had any anchors. In those seas and that wind, the tanker was in serious trouble as soon as the auxiliary burner in her composite boiler could not be re-lit. And she was in 'grave and imminent danger' from the moment her engines stopped. Captain Gelis told the inquiry that, broken down in a Force Nine and 30-foot seas, he was 'not initially too concerned about the proximity of Sumburgh Head because I thought we would, under the influence of the south-westerly wind, drift to the north-east, past the Shetlands into open seas'.

Hudner, in a statement released on the day after the wreck, said the *Braer* had requested a tug at 5.19am. Nine days later, Captain Gelis' statement said he asked the Coastguards at 5.45am 'to despatch the tug urgently'. There were language difficulties with the tanker's radio operator, who spoke execrable English, so the Coastguards may not have understood. But the Coastguards' published log shows that they again asked Captain Gelis at 5.53am if he wanted one. He replied that he would speak to the insurance underwriters on the phone and call back within five minutes. According to this log, the captain did not in fact ask for a tug until 6.09am, over an hour after he lost all power. Anticipating the rapidly deteriorating situation, the Coastguards had already alerted two tugs at the Shetland Towage Ltd jetty in Sullom Voe, 50 miles north of Sumburgh, and were trying to find one nearer.

The B+H Technical Director, Makrinos, was ordering a tug, too. But his tug was the Dutch salvage tug *Smit Lloyd 121*, berthed in Aberdeen, 150 miles south of the *Braer*. He signed a 'no cure, no pay' contract with the tug owners. Aberdeen looked quite near to Sumburgh on an office wall map.

At six am, with the crew of the Coastguard helicopter *Rescue 117* already on standby at Sumburgh, they asked the RAF rescue helicopter *Rescue 137* to fly north from Lossiemouth to help. Four minutes later, Lerwick Harbour's port control office had alerted the tug *Star Sirius*, berthed at Shell's Holmsgarth oilfield supply base. Within half an hour her crew had been woken up and were making the ship ready for sea.

Off-duty crew on the *Braer* were woken up too. Captain Gelis recalled: 'at 0610 I ordered one of the duty ABs [*Able Seamen*] to wake all crew and for them to assemble on the bridge . . . The crew assembled with their life-jackets. There was no panic, but obviously the crew were nervous. Mr Khan, the Chief Engineer, First Engineer, Second Engineer and one Motorman remained in the engine room at this time, trying to re-start the engine.'

Their desperate efforts failed. The *Braer* was drifting rapidly northwards with the tide and the wind. By 6.32am she was less then seven miles from Sumburgh Head. Captain Gelis asked for 20 of his 34-man crew to be taken off. He said, at long last: 'This is dangerous.' The crew of *Rescue 117* were already airborne. Seven minutes later they were hovering above the stern of the *Braer*, in winds gusting to Storm Force Ten.

*Rescue 117* is a Sikorsky S61N, on contract to the Coastguards from Bristow Helicopters, who have a major commercial operation at Sumburgh to service the offshore oilfields in the East Shetland Basin. The aircraft is fitted with sophisticated devices for search and rescue work, including an 'auto-hover' system. On this wild, black morning the rescue crew's skills and bravery would be tested as rarely before. They had risked their lives many times in dramatic rescues around the Shetland coast, but this was the most spectacular and hazardous job yet.

Flying a helicopter within a few feet of a wildly gyrating mast and funnel, while lowering a winchman on to a deck which is lurching, plunging and rolling 50 feet in all three dimensions, has to be one of the most demanding jobs in the world. The pilots of *Rescue 117* and *Rescue 137* are cool customers. Throughout the terrifying flights to rescue the crew of the *Braer*, their voices on the radio sounded icy calm, as though they were on a routine training exercise.

It was still dark. To lift the frightened crewmen from the stern of the tanker, *Rescue 117* had first to lower winchman Friede Manson on to the ship, to show them what to do and to keep them calm. He landed badly and hurt his back as he was flung against a steel stanchion. It was not the first injury he has suffered in his job. The crew had no idea how to get into the sling which was to lift them. Their grasp of English was so poor that it took Manson many minutes to explain, clinging on to the rail of the ship in a whirlwind of chilling spray.

Captain Alexandros
Gelis, *master of the*
Braer, *shortly after
being landed at
Sumburgh, 9.30 a.m.,
5 January 1993*
(Photo: *Daily Record*)

At 6.54am, when BBC Radio Scotland was about to broadcast a telephone interview with the ship's radio officer, who assured listeners that all was well aboard the *Braer*, the first of them was ready to leave her. The job took over an hour. Each lift was a potential catastrophe but by 8.07am *Rescue 117* had 16 of the *Braer*'s crew on board. *Rescue 137*, the RAF helicopter, had arrived half an hour earlier. At 7.41am the RAF pilot had reported that the *Braer* was only 2.5 nautical miles from Sumburgh Head. She had drifted seven and a half nautical miles in two hours and 50 minutes – a mean speed of 2.6 knots. It did not take a nautical expert to fear that the tanker would hit either Sumburgh Head or the offlying Horse Island within an hour.

*Rescue 137* was hovering nearby, ready to move in as *Rescue 117* pulled away and headed for Sumburgh to land the first batch of rescued crewmen, wash the salt water off the fuselage and refuel, after almost two hours in the air. From the cockpit of *Rescue 137*, the situation now looked desperate. Like the Coastguards, the RAF rescue service's prime consideration has to be the safety of life. The risk of pollution, even massive pollution, comes second. To the RAF pilot and the Coastguards controlling the rescue from their headquarters in Lerwick, it was not unreasonable to suppose that the *Braer*'s crew were all now in grave and imminent danger of death.

At 8.11am *Rescue 137* asked Captain Gelis his intentions. Did he wish to abandon ship? If so, he should immediately gather the remaining crew at the stern because there was little time left. It would take an hour to lift them all in these conditions.

Four minutes later there were still no crewmen visible on the stern. *Rescue 137* was running low on fuel and *Rescue 117* had not yet returned from refuelling.

At 8.18 *Rescue 137* radioed: 'The sea is getting bad. You must get all on deck.'

| | |
|---|---|
| *Braer:* | 'This is second mate. Will call you back.' |

At 8.23am:

| | |
|---|---|
| *Braer:* | '*Rescue 137*, this is *Braer*. Captain asks if you can wait longer.' |
| *Rescue 137:* | 'No. You must abandon now. It will take us all the time left to lift off the crew.' |
| *Braer:* | 'I will tell the Captain.' |

At 8.25am:

| | |
|---|---|
| *Braer:* | 'Is it possible to leave eight persons on board? I intend to anchor.' |
| *Rescue 137:* | 'There is a rock close to the starboard side. It will take one hour to winch.' |
| *Braer:* | 'We abandon. Eighteen persons on board.' |
| *Rescue 137:* | 'Commencing to winch.' |

Eight minutes earlier, at 8.17, 'The Still' had begun, according to the tidal predictions for 5 January. The Still is the name given by the Sumburgh inshore fishermen to the period of slack tide off Sumburgh Head. It only lasts for half an hour, from when the flood tide stops running eastwards until the ebb, the 'West Shot', begins to pour back to the west. Lobstermen take a great interest in The Still because on many days, even in summer, it is the only chance they have to round 'The Heads' of Sumburgh and Fitful, to reach their creels on the west coast.

As the *Braer* edged northwards into The Still, something odd happened. She slowed down and began to move clockwise, in a circle on the southern edge of the West Voe of Sumburgh. The wind was now reaching 60 knots, still blowing from the south-west, and for a while it looked as if Shetland, and the men still aboard the ship, might get away with it after all.

'It's fifty-fifty whether she goes east of Sumburgh Head,' a Coastguard told us at the time. 'But if she goes west, that's it, I'm afraid.'

She went west. At 8.47am the *Braer* drifted out of the West Voe of Sumburgh and the first rush of the west-going ebb tide caught her massive hull, three-quarters of a mile west of the Sumburgh Head Lighthouse. The force of the tide on the ship's port side – 30,000 square feet of steel below the waterline – was much greater than the windage on the 10,000 square feet or so above it. The tide began to push her westwards, against the storm.

In the grey gloom of dawn, the first car-loads of horrified islanders were beginning to jam the single-track road up to the lighthouse, for a grandstand view of the melodrama. From the local radio reports, they already knew that the *Braer* had twice as much oil aboard as the amount officially spilled by the *Exxon Valdez*, four years before and 4,000 miles away on the other side of the North Pole.

At 8.45am, Captain Gelis radioed that there was now no time to anchor. During the brief respite of The Still the waves had no longer been breaking green over the deck, but only a desperate man would have gone to the bows to release the anchors. There was still a danger of being blown overboard.

Squadron Leader David Simpson, the pilot of *Rescue 137*, reported that there were 14 of the *Braer*'s crew on the helicopter, and four still waiting to be lifted. He again insisted that all the crew should leave, as the rocks were very close and he was very short of fuel. *Rescue 117* was still on the tarmac, preparing for take-off.

Squadron Leader Simpson later told the local newspaper: 'The important point before hitting Horse Island was rescuing the crew . . . it seemed more than likely, given his fast drift rate, that he was going to hit the rocks before we had time to lift off the crew.' In his view, later disputed by some fishermen who knew the coastline better, it was impossible to anticipate what the tides were going to do. He advised Captain Gelis to abandon ship because he feared that the *Braer* might explode, just as the tanker *Aegean Sea* had done off northern Spain when she had run aground with a load of Sullom Voe crude oil a month earlier.

At 8.50am there were still two men left aboard. At 8.54am Captain Gelis, the last to leave his ship, rose slowly from the heaving deck, swinging on the end of a steel wire. Shortly before he was bundled in through the open door of *Rescue 137*, *Rescue 117* returned to the scene with a full load of fuel. But there was nothing for it to do but 'monitor the drift', as the radio message put it.

The Lerwick lifeboat, the fishing boat *Philorth* and the local trawler *Sette Mari* of Out Skerries were standing by, despite the continuing violence of the weather. There was nothing they could do either, except radio to the Coast-guards that it still looked as if the tanker would hit Horse Island. A tug might even now prevent a disaster but that was a forlorn hope. The *Star Sirius* was still 44 minutes away. Aboard the abandoned ship, the anchors were still locked in place. The heavy towing wires were still stowed in their lockers at the bows.

No-one knew that the tide would take the *Braer* clear of Horse Island, with half a mile to spare, and clear of the Lady Holm, a little to the west, by about the same distance. No-one knew that it would be another two hours and 19 minutes before the rocks in Garth's Wick pierced the single layer of steel plate between the crude oil and the sea.

The crew of the *Braer* had been saved from death by fire or drowning, in a rescue that deserved several medals. That was a consolation. It was Shetland that was now in grave and imminent danger.

On the shore behind the dunes, a ruined mansion house overlooked the clear waters of the West Voe of Sumburgh. A hundred and seventy-nine years before, Sir Walter Scott had dubbed the old ruin 'Jarlshof', the hall of the Viking Earls of Shetland. He used Jarlshof as a location in his book *The Pirate*. The name stuck. In the late 1950s it was given to the prehistoric settlements clustered around the old hall house, when archaeologists disco-vered that Jarlshof had been inhabited for over 5,000 years. The earliest people had gathered shellfish from the shores of Quendale Bay, hunted seals and otters on Horse Island, the Lady Holm and Scatness, and gathered seabirds' eggs from the cliffs of Sumburgh Head, Fitful Head and Garth's Ness.

Sir Walter included a witch called Norna in his cast of characters for *The Pirate*. Norna's lair was high on Fitful Head, where she had lured ships to their doom for hundreds of years. At nine o'clock in the morning of 5 January, Norna was waiting to claim her biggest prize. Not just the death of another ship, but the death of almost every sea creature for miles around.

# CAPTAIN JIM DICKSON, SHETLAND ISLANDS POLLUTION CONTROL OFFICER

HE HAD been expecting the call. As Shetland Islands Council's Pollution Control Officer, Jim Dickson had been working towards this day for years.

It was 6.38am. At the other end of the telephone, he heard the head of his department, Captain George Sutherland, say a vessel had broken down and was heading towards Sumburgh Head.

'We both shot into port control, got out the charts and plotted the ship's position. We used the famous book *Perils At Sea – A Shipmaster's Guide* to work out where the wind might take the tanker.

'It was kind of obvious to everybody that it was a case of "when", not "if", she went ashore.'

A much rehearsed plan went into action: 'We set up an incident room at Sullom Voe and called in the troops.

'At first light we got the helicopter out and headed off to Sumburgh, where I think they had just got the last of the crew off. We watched her drift and saw the ship wasn't going to go on Horse Island after all.'

Another call then came from Captain Sutherland. Jim ordered the helicopter to land at the Bristows hangar nearby, where he was told two marine pilots were being sent down from Sullom Voe on the offchance that they could drop the anchor on the *Braer*.

'By the time they arrived, the crew of the tug *Star Sirius* were shouting that they wanted to put a line aboard and we decided that was a better idea.'

The Coastguard helicopter flew the team back out to the *Braer*, and lowered them aboard the poop deck.

'I followed the winchman down and thought everyone was coming behind me. I got on to the deck and headed for the bridge to see if I could speak to the *Star Sirius* on the VHF radio.

'I couldn't go through the accommodation deck because it was in darkness, so I had to go along the outside. The ship was rolling severely – at times I had to hang on for grim death.'

He made it to the bridge, where the emergency lights and the radio were still working. The tug crew told him they would fire a rocket line across the deck. Jim made the perilous journey back to his colleagues as the sea and wind thrashed the ship.

'When I got there there was just me, the winchman and two of the ship's crew. The others had decided it wasn't worth coming down.'

The first line was fired and missed. The second hit, but became tangled in the port side lifeboat. Coastguard winchman Friede Manson managed to untangle the rope. With the ship's winch out of action because there was no power, the men had to haul the thick, wet mass aboard by hand.

'We got the messenger rope half-way across, but then the friction of the sea tore it out of our hands. We just couldn't hold it. There was a 40-foot swell. One moment the *Star Sirius* was way above us and the next moment she was way below.

'Next thing there was a hell of a big swell and the *Braer* rose quite remarkably and came down on the rocks with a big bang. Everything was vibrating – the deck, the funnel, the mast were all shaking as she came down.'

The ship was ashore. As Jim had hauled the line aboard, he had hoped the backwash of the drift would hold the *Braer* off the rocks, like a piece of driftwood.

The helicopter, still hovering above them, winched up the two crewmen before lifting Jim and Friede to safety.

'As I was going up, I could see the brown oil coming out already. And on the port side one whole section of rails on the poop deck was missing and the others were all bent outwards.'

This fitted in with later reports that spare pipes, which had been lashed to the deck, had gone over the side, breaking not only the rails but also the vent pipes to the ship's diesel tanks.

Jim spoke matter-of-factly. His department was well prepared for the scenario. The only difference in a real situation was the amount of help that flooded in from other agencies. In the weeks after, everyone involved was going over what they did right, what they did wrong, what they might have done differently.

'To be honest, I can't for the life of me see what we could have done better. The thing now is to stop it happening in the future.'

He added it was 'unfortunate' that the shipowners were getting all the criticism, when others had to take part blame for the situation.

'The Shells and BPs of this world will have to start paying better rates for chartering these ships, so the owners can invest in better ships and better crews.

'A brand new ship of, say 100,000 tonnes, costs $80,000 a day to run. The present charter rate is $30,000 a day.

'The poor old Filipinos are the cheapest crews just now. In a few years it will be the Red Chinese, and I can't think who will be cheaper than them.'

*Chapter Two*

# THE NIGHTMARE SCENARIO

*13th January 1993*

*Dear Mr Major,*

*There was an oil slick last Tuesday. I want you to do something about this oil slick. We would need more radars! I am very angry because you are not doing anything about it. So get to work! All the oil is killing the animals.*

*Yours sincerely,*

*Eileen Paton*
*Bressay Primary School*

The Pierhead Skippers, including one of the authors of this book, had a field day with the tug *Star Sirius*. It was whispered – shouted, even – that she seemed to have taken her time reaching the *Braer*. We were wrong. In fact, the *Star Sirius* was made ready for sea in only an hour, a very fast time for a ship berthed in port and shut down for the night after an arduous voyage from the offshore oil fields.

*Star Sirius* left Holmsgarth Quay in Lerwick around 7.15am. At 7.25am she passed Bressay Lighthouse, the southern limit of Lerwick Harbour. Even before she reached the open sea, her bows were disappearing under the breaking waves. Those who watched from shore could only marvel that there were men willing to put to sea on such a morning. For the Lerwick lifeboat, a much smaller vessel, sailing in such weather was even more astonishing. Just to reach Sumburgh Head, 25 miles to the south, was an extraordinary feat of seamanship.

Despite the pounding from the sea, *Star Sirius* actually reached the *Braer* half an hour before her first estimated time of arrival. The problem was not that the tug was late but that she was called out late.

It is tempting to blame the Coastguards for the delay but they were dealing with a man who said he was not in any immediate danger, did not broadcast a Mayday and did not even transmit a Pan message until after the tug had been asked to make ready for sea. If the Coastguards had sent the tug earlier and the *Braer* had subsequently got under way again and steamed out into the open Atlantic, the Pierhead would have accused them of over-reacting. And there could well have been an argument over who was liable to pay for the tug.

Responsibility for the delay in summoning a tug must lie with the captain of the *Braer* and/or the shipowner. Ten days after the wreck, Captain Gelis received support from an unexpected quarter. In an interview with *The Shetland Times*, published on 15 January, the Coastguards' District Controller for Shetland, Ken Lowe, surprised some local seafarers when he was reported as saying: 'There was no need to put out a Mayday. He had broken down and wanted tug assistance ten miles south of Sumburgh Head . . . He was not doing anything wrong. His ship let him down.' Lowe then said a curious thing, which did not make sense to local people who knew the tides around Sumburgh Head much better than Lowe, a relatively recent arrival in the islands. He said the tide turned about two hours earlier than marked on the tidal charts and the tanker moved in a completely unexpected way after being abandoned.

It may have looked like that but in fact what happened was that the *Braer* had drifted into an eddy on the edge of the Sumburgh Roost. The tide here runs nine hours to the west and only three hours to the east, instead of the usual six and six. On the morning of 5 January the slack tide off Sumburgh Head, 'The Still', happened exactly at the expected time, between 8.17am and 8.47am. And then the 'West Shot' began – as the tide began to ebb to the westward.

When *Star Sirius* appeared out of the murk off Sumburgh Head at 9.30am there was renewed hope among the spectators on the shore. 'Thank God, here comes the cavalry,' as one Shetlander said. That view was not shared by District Controller Lowe, who doubted if the *Star Sirius* would have been able to pull the heavily-laden tanker, even if she had got a line aboard her. 'It was just a dream,' he was quoted as saying.

Before ten am the Coastguards were telling the press that the plan was to put some of the *Braer* crew back aboard by helicopter, along with two marine pilots from Sullom Voe. Hundreds of onlookers waited to watch the operation. And waited. And waited. For over an hour the *Star Sirius* stood by the tanker but could do nothing. It was far too rough to risk putting a salvage crew aboard from the tug. At times the *Star Sirius* was riding waves 50 feet higher than the *Braer*'s decks.

The Coastguard helicopter *Rescue 117* is always refuelled, checked and made ready for flight as soon as it returns from a mission. It is the same with the RAF rescue helicopter. They never know when the next call may come. On a morning like 5 January, it was quite likely that some other ship would be in distress off Shetland, or that the helicopter would be called to one of the outer islands to act as an air ambulance, because ferries and fixed-wing aircraft were stormbound – that happened on the weekend following the wreck.

*Rescue 117* was airborne again before the last of the *Braer*'s crew were taken off by Squadron Leader Simpson and his crew in *Rescue 137*. This led the Pierhead to wonder why there had been such urgency in abandoning ship, even if the RAF aircraft did have to return to Sumburgh immediately to refuel. At 9.38am, when *Star Sirius* was as close alongside the *Braer* as her skipper, Captain David Theobald, dared take her, *Rescue 117* still had enough fuel to land again at Sumburgh, pick up a salvage crew and lower them on to the tanker. *Rescue 137* would have been refuelled and ready to stand by and take over if necessary. The *Braer* was still half a mile from the 'rock on the starboard side' (in fact it was not a rock but Horse Island).

It was not only the Pierhead Skippers who wondered. Three days after the wreck, much more knowledgeable people asked the same question. An emergency meeting of the Shetland Fishermen's Association put out a statement saying that they were 'astonished' at the decision to abandon ship so early. 'Shetland fishermen are experienced seamen and have intimate knowledge of the seas and tides in the [Sumburgh] Roost,' the association said. In their view the stranding 'could have been avoided' if someone had still been aboard the *Braer* at 9.40am to make fast a towline. It had not occurred to these thoroughly professional sailors that anyone would go to sea in a tanker without at all times keeping handy a towline strong enough for the job.

According to the published summary of the Coastguards' log, the *Star Sirius* radioed at 9.44am that she could fire a line aboard the *Braer* if there was someone aboard to catch it and make it fast. The tug skipper reported that at this time there was 'no green water on bow or aft' – meaning that the seas had temporarily abated and it could be possible to work with a towline on the bows of the ship (where the anchor winches were also) or on the deck immediately behind the superstructure. It might have been possible to work on the bows but to hover over them in a helicopter and attempt to lower crew there would have been suicidal. The *Braer*'s foremast was in the way of the rotors. So any attempt at salvage had to be made at the stern, where there was a little more room.

The *Braer* had only ordinary mooring ropes attached to the winch on her stern. It would take a heavy duty towing wire for a tug to pull a laden tanker in a Force Nine gale – and a lot of luck. A mooring rope, designed to hold the ship alongside her berth in harbour, would certainly have snapped like a thread as soon as *Star Sirius* put on any power. Captain Gelis did release the brakes on the winch before he left the ship, so that the mooring rope could be pulled out if salvage was attempted. But there was no heavy duty towing wire kept at the stern. And, because there was no power to the stern winches, it was impossible to haul a towing wire across to the tanker from the *Star Sirius*. Whatever the tug's owners would later say (and they said plenty) there never was any realistic hope of getting the *Braer* under tow in those seas. It was indeed 'just a dream'. The game was already up.

Meanwhile, Captain Gelis was in the operations room set up at Sumburgh Airport, talking to the police and the emergency team. They were all uncomfortably aware of the fatal problem of the missing towing wire. While everyone outside waited and wondered, the talking went on. Captain Jim Dickson, Oil Pollution Control Officer for Shetland Islands Council, was at the airport, ready to fly to the tanker. So were crewmen from the ship. One of them told reporters he was ready to go back: 'I don't mind. It is my job,' he said.

Captain Gelis told the Marine Accidents Investigation Branch his recollection of the long wait: 'At about 0930 I received a call from . . . the Lerwick Coastguard asking if I would go back to the vessel to attempt to drop the anchors . . . I immediately agreed to return with a boarding party to assist the two pilots he [*Ken Lowe*] said were coming from Sullom Voe . . . Between the time I received the call from the Coastguard at about 0930 and 1030 when the taxi arrived to take us to the helicopter base, we were awaiting the arrival of the marine pilots from Sullom Voe. I was told by . . . Lowe of the Coastguard that they were travelling by road.'

A witness to that long discussion in the operations room at Sumburgh Airport has told us that the delay was partly caused by Captain Gelis having difficulty in persuading enough crewmen to go back to the *Braer* with him. At first he wanted to take ten men but was told that the helicopter would only be able to take five, then four.

Captain Gelis, as reported to *The Shetland Times* by Lowe, had no hesitation in going back. He had been 'most reluctant' to leave the ship in the first place. In retrospect, Lowe's criticisms were of himself: 'I bitterly regret jeopardising four lives, not once, but twice, by asking Captain Gelis to go back aboard. I asked him if he would be willing to go back and he said he would. It was fine for me in the warm operations room, but when I saw the 'copter trying to take off the crew later, I wondered what on earth I had done . . . But in the agony of the moment we were grasping at straws.'

Not until 32 minutes after the *Star Sirius*' skipper had said he was ready to fire a rocket line to the *Braer* did the Coastguards radio to the pilot of *Rescue 117*, by that time back on the tarmac, that the police would deliver him 'five [*Braer*] crew plus two [*marine*] pilots' to be taken to the tanker. At that time, 10.16am, the *Braer*, driven by the tide, was on course to pass over half a mile west of Horse Island and was moving directly towards Garth's Ness.

After another 26 minutes, *Rescue 117*'s base at Bristow Helicopters' hangar (just five minutes across the main runway from the airport terminal where the *Braer* crew were waiting) told the Coastguards that the police had still not delivered the salvage crew to the helicopter.

It was 10.51am, almost two hours after the *Braer* was abandoned and over an hour after the *Star Sirius* arrived on scene, before *Rescue 117*'s pilot could report that he was airborne and heading for the tanker with the four-man salvage crew. Time was desperately short. The *Braer* was only half a mile from Garth's Ness. Unless a towline was secured within ten minutes there was no chance that she would miss Garth's Ness, as she had missed Horse Island and the Lady Holm in Quendale Bay.

The islanders watching the ship were praying that the tide would carry the crippled tanker clear of the rocks at Fitful Head and out into the Atlantic. That might give time to catch her before she drove on to the Shaalds of Foula, a reef west of Shetland which claimed the White Star liner *Oceanic* in 1914. But the tide had slackened west of Horse Island and the wind had risen, driving the *Braer* inexorably towards Garth's Ness.

And then there was one last hope. They saw the helicopter lifting off from Sumburgh. At that moment, on the other side of the Atlantic, the phone rang in a Stamford bedroom. Makrinos had decided it was time to wake up his boss, Michael Hudner. It was three in the morning, Connecticut time.

Within nine minutes of take-off, the pilots of *Rescue 117*, Captain Tony Brewster and First Officer John Rawlings, were lowering Captain Dickson, helicopter winchman Manson and Engineering Superintendent Khan down on to the stern of the tanker. There was no time to lower the *Braer*'s Bosun. Captain Gelis also remained aboard the helicopter. He was puzzled. They had asked him to go back to lower the anchors, so that the *Star Sirius* could try to grapple them and tow the tanker out, but the chopper was over the stern: 'It was too noisy in the helicopter to discuss what was to happen,' he would tell the inquiry. 'I do not know who decided to lower the men at the stern rather than the foc'sle. I saw Mr Dickson go to the bridge.' But it was much, much too late to lower the anchors. The stern was only about 150 feet from the rocks.

The wind had risen to 80mph and the waves in the little bay of Garth's Wick were between 20 and 30 feet high. Manson later told reporters what

*'In the agony of the moment we were grasping at straws': the Coastguard helicopter* Rescue 117 *moves in to land four men on the stern of the* Braer, *minutes before the tanker grounded. The tug* Star Sirius *stands by, ready to fire a line aboard in huge seas. It was all in vain*

(Photo: Graeme Storey)

happened. At 11.07am the first line fired from the *Star Sirius* missed. They got hold of the second line but it was too heavy to drag through the water from the tug. 'We had the rope pulled out of our hands,' Captain Dickson said. He had severe rope burns on his palms to prove it.

And then, at 11.13am, the *Braer* struck the first of the rocks sticking up through the sand in Garth's Wick: 'I've never been so scared in my life,' Captain Dickson said. 'A big swell came up and we fell upon a rock with a tremendous thud. It was just a huge judder.' He thought: 'Oh, oh! Time to leave.'

Manson said: 'It was going through your mind – "What's going to happen? Is the tanker going to break and blow up?" '

The rescue of the salvage crew from the wreck was the most heroic performance yet. Hovering with their rotor blades a few feet from the heaving smokestack of the dying ship, pilots Brewster and Rawlings knew that the slightest error would kill them, their winch operator Bob Taylor, Captain Gelis and the four men clinging to the stern. And at any moment the *Braer* could explode, destroying them all in a fireball. The inert gas above the oil in her holds was very probably all gone.

It was a long eight minutes but at 11.21am *Rescue 117* could report that everyone was off the ship. They turned for the airport and safety. Six minutes later, the horrified crowd on top of the cliff saw the first of 84,413 tonnes of crude oil rising to the surface.

Martin Heubeck, a biologist who for 15 years had monitored Shetland's wildlife for the Shetland Oil Terminal Environmental Advisory Group, was one of those peering out through the roaring gale. He was not the only one to feel sick, long before the first oil fumes reached him.

Magnus Flaws, the councillor for Dunrossness South, had been out since before dawn, working on Sumburgh Head as an auxiliary Coastguard. Flaws is a former seaman who now manages an office supplies shop in Lerwick. He lives in a house by the shore of the West Voe of Sumburgh. He watched the *Braer* go ashore: 'Having been at sea, you feel hellish when you see a ship on the rocks . . . What worried me was that the whole south end of Shetland was going to be black with oil . . . I just couldn't believe it '

Everything that could go wrong had gone wrong. Shetland's nightmare scenario had arrived. As the news came out on the local radio station, people all over the islands hugged each other, shook their heads in disbelief and cried. Some were incomers, some could trace their Shetland families back to the time of the Vikings. Others were just visiting. In every house, school and workplace there was despair and a numbing, helpless grief. And the first television pictures, by local cameramen John Waters for the BBC and Malcolm Younger for Grampian TV, were still waiting for a plane to take the video cassettes south from Sumburgh. When they hit the screens, the grief and bewildered anger would circle the globe.

For many islanders there was no time yet for tears. Years before, an emergency plan had been drawn up by Shetland Islands Council, the Northern Constabulary, the Coastguards, the Fire Brigade, BP, the Shetland Health Board and other organisations. There had been regular exercises and it had

been tested during the Chinook helicopter disaster at Sumburgh in 1986 and the Cormorant Alpha helicopter crash, 100 miles offshore, in March 1992. Over 50 people had died in those tragedies. Thanks to the heroism of the RAF and Coastguard helicopter crews, there were no human fatalities this time, but the *Braer* already looked like being the biggest test of the emergency plan. Four hours before the tanker hit the rocks, the plan was activated. It was the job that the council's emergency planning staff had rehearsed over and over again, the job they had hoped they would never have to do.

One of the first tasks was to look after the frightened crewmen who had been airlifted from their ship in the most alarming circumstances imaginable. Local GP Dr Chris Rowlands was one of the first to reach the operations rooms at the airport, along with the south of Shetland's lone policeman, PC Colin Gunn. Dr Rowlands, himself a veteran of many helicopter rescues and medical evacuations with *Rescue 117*, checked that the crew were all unharmed and reassured them. Cups of tea appeared. Assistant Airport Manager Barry Stevens and his staff began to arrange free phone calls so that the men could tell their families they were safe. Calls to Athens and Manila were not too difficult but lines to Warsaw for the Polish crew caused some problems. At last everyone got through. Then the Royal National Mission to

*Crewmen from the* Braer *leave the Brae Hotel after questioning by the police and accident investigators*
(Photo: Tom Kidd)

45

Deep Sea Fishermen took over and ferried the shipwrecked crew to Lerwick.

Contrary to some press reports, local people did not threaten the men from the *Braer*. Whatever opinions might be of Captain Gelis and flag of convenience ships, this traditionally seafaring community had sympathy for the crew. Filipinos living in Shetland would prepare them special meals when they moved into a hotel near the Sullom Voe oil terminal for their interviews with the MAIB. Ironically, it was called the Brae Hotel. The village of Brae, where many oil terminal workers live, has a North Sea oilfield named after it. The oilfield once had a ship named after it; the *Brae Trader*, now the *Braer*.

If the tanker disaster had to happen in Shetland, it could not have picked a better spot for communications. Sumburgh Airport is not exactly a quiet rural backwater at the best of times. As the forward base for the northern North Sea oilfields, the airfield, run by Highlands and Islands Airports Ltd (HIAL), is a transit station for about 10,000 oil workers a month. Fleets of helicopters fly shuttles out to the production platforms and rigs, a hundred miles or so to the north-east. Every day, squads of North Sea 'bears' arrive from the mainland on Viscounts and other planes, change into their survival suits and head off on the choppers – or sometimes have to sit around for hours when bad weather shuts down the oilfields. Sumburgh is also busy with daily scheduled flights by British Airways and Loganair to Orkney, Aberdeen, Edinburgh and Glasgow, plus inter-island flights in Shetland, air ambulance work and occasional charter flights to Scandinavia. Annually, it handles about 25,000 take-offs and landings and 400,000 passengers.

Barry Stevens had dealt with disasters before. By 7.30am, before the *Braer* was abandoned, an operations room had been set up, including a press centre. Regular meals would soon be just a memory for Stevens, his boss Tudor Lewis and the two HIAL office staff, Mrs Sunniva O'Brien and Mrs Frances Wiles. For 12 days they would live mostly on 'coffee and sandwiches on the hoof' as over 600 journalists, TV presenters and crews from all over the world descended on Sumburgh. For the Dan Air crash at Sumburgh in 1979, when a plane ran off the end of the runway and killed 17 people, there had been 40 visiting reporters; for the Chinook, which killed 45 in 1986, there were 105.

The main airport building has been called a 'white elephant', too big for present needs. It was designed to cope with the boom-time of North Sea aviation, during the late 1970s and early 1980s when oilfield production platforms, submarine pipelines and the £1.3 billion Sullom Voe oil terminal were all being built at the same time. So there was some spare space, on Day One at least. By Day Two the place was packed. Somehow, the airport staff, the airport security company Securiplan and catering/retail firm Sports & Leisure Foods Ltd managed to find offices, food and facilities for the national and international press corps, for CNN, CBS, Sky News, the BBC, Channel 4 and all the other TV stations who would fly and ferry their mobile satellite dishes to Shetland.

The first effect of the *Braer* was to jam every phone and fax line in the airport. The HIAL office staff quickly lost count of the calls. Every time they put a phone down, another call for Sumburgh 60654 came through. Stevens told how, in the first three days (and nights), Richard Watts, Bob Brandie and their local team of British Telecom engineers put in two new telephone exchanges, an optic-fibre link right around the airport perimeter and 140 extra phone lines. They ran out of Sumburgh numbers and borrowed 40 from Lerwick.

'Their contribution was immense,' Stevens said. 'We couldn't have coped without them. They were very cheerful, very tired, running on pure adrenalin and never once did they turn round and say to somebody, "I'm sorry, we can't do that." Nothing was too much for them.'

An oil workers' transit lounge became the press centre, half of the canteen was turned into a newsroom with open-plan radio and TV studio, and more offices were found to house the operations room and the 'Joint Response Committee' set up by the islands council, police, Coastguards, health board, shipowner and insurers.

The hordes of visiting reporters were astonished when they arrived at what many imagined to be a remote outpost of civilisation and discovered a fully equipped press centre, complete with phones, faxes, photocopiers and free coffee. They were delighted when they found that Shetland Islands Council had set up a press bureau staffed by local people who gave them hard information, arranged press conferences for times to suit deadlines, helped them find hire cars and accommodation, and treated them as gentlemen and ladies of the press rather than despised tabloid hacks.

Some were so moved by their reception in Shetland that they later wrote fulsome letters of thanks to the council and to Lewis, Stevens and their staff.

*David Bedborough (second from left) takes a question at a cramped press conference in Sumburgh on day two*
(Photo: Tom Kidd)

The sheaf of thank-you letters from the media became a news story in itself. The RAF were so impressed that they started using the *Braer* incident as a case-study in training their public relations officers in how to get along with the press during a major emergency. The detailed planning for how the council would react to a disaster had paid off handsomely.

The airport would not close for 12 days and nights. There were 500 emergency centre staff to look after as well as the 600 media visitors. Catering workers were in at six am and getting home after 11pm. Cleaners were busy from dawn to dusk (and later) as hundreds of people produced vast quantities of litter and brought muddy oil into the terminal on their boots. Securiplan staff found themselves making coffee for cat-napping journalists on the night shift and shifting furniture into makeshift offices, as well as doing their routine airport security and passenger/baggage searches. On top of that, they had to process a 74 per cent increase in charter flights.

A local contracting company in the parish of Dunrossness, Ness Engineering, turned out literally at a moment's notice and soon had a power supply rigged to the press centre. Flying in equipment from Aberdeen, they had everything ready by the time the main influx of media folk arrived on Day Three.

Airport firemen were spending a lot of time in their vehicles, wearing full rescue kit and with their engines running, a normal precaution when planes are landing in very high winds. In the first three days of the disaster they also had to deal with four other serious emergencies. On Day One a British Airways ATP plane suffered an engine failure while coming in to land in a Force Nine gale with a full load of reporters on board. Fortunately for British Airways and the manufacturers of the ATP, the *Braer* kept the story off most front pages. The plane landed safely. Thursday, Day Three, brought alerts for two of Sumburgh's North Sea oilfield helicopters. Both landed without incident after lights warning of mechanical failure had come on in the cockpit. On the same day the engine of a DC3 dispersant-spraying aircraft burst into flames on the tarmac.

It was a stressful time for all the airport workers, most of whom live in and around Sumburgh. Hard-pressed at work and on duty around the clock, they had the extra anxiety of worrying about their families at home as the oil pollution spread, plus the feeling of shock and horror at the damage to one of the most beautiful districts of Shetland. Perhaps it was a good thing to be so frantically busy. It kept their minds off the enormity of what had happened.

'They were all absolutely brilliant,' Stevens said. To show their appreciation, HIAL were to throw a huge party for everyone working at the airport, complete with free beer, when things eventually quietened down a little, five weeks after the disaster.

The emergency plan worked so well that, when the British Government's Marine Pollution Control Unit (MPCU) team flew in from London on Day One, they found that almost everything they had thought they would have to set up was already there. And there was no doubt about who was in control – Shetland Islands Council. Chief Executive Malcolm Green and the

*Malcolm Green, Chief Executive of Shetland Islands Council and Co-ordinator of the emergency response team*
(Photo: *The Scotsman*)

council's political leader, Convener Edward Thomason, made it plain that they had no intention of handing over to the men from the ministry.

The council had responded to over half a dozen disasters and near-disasters involving ships, aircraft and helicopters during the previous 14 years. Mistakes had been made and lessons learned. This time it was well prepared, organised and staffed to deal with the situation. Green told the MPCU and the UK Government's Scottish Office that they were more than welcome to help, advise and take part in the decision-making, but control would rest very firmly in the hands of the council.

The civil servants found that the local police, Coastguards and health board officials were of the same mind. After all, they had been involved in the design of the plan from the start. The MPCU had to accept a *fait accompli*. A formal agreement was drawn up, committing the Government, the ship insurers, the council and others to co-operate in the Joint Response Committee. What clinched the council's argument, and ensured that Green would remain as co-ordinator of the effort, was that it knew the local area and the local people better than anyone else. And its officials had studied what had happened in Alaska with the *Exxon Valdez*, where control was taken out of the hands of the locals and fought over by two corporations (Exxon and Alyeska), the state authorities and the federals. It had led to delay, confusion and worse. That would not be allowed to happen in Shetland.

The Shetland public might rail against the council in normal times over parish pump issues, but they were more likely to accept information in good faith from their local councillors than from a London bureaucrat who had just flown in. Once that was reluctantly agreed, everyone got along as well as could be expected. The MPCU's representative was one of their senior scientists, David Bedborough. He would soon earn respect at the press conferences with his frankness, scientific knowledge and, above all, his natural, plain-speaking way of answering questions. In cutting through the gobbledegook, indeed, he could show some council officials, policemen and health board staffers a thing or two.

Shetland's oil spill contingency plan was only prepared to deal with a spill of up to 2,000 tonnes of oil, and one inside the port of Sullom Voe at that. This was deliberate policy. The council had realised years before that there was little they could do on their own to tackle a major spill, although in April 1991 the local MP had suggested to the Transport Minister, without success, that the Government should have larger stockpiles of clean-up gear in the islands.

The emergency plan, which backed up the oil spill plan, called for materials, equipment and people to be brought in from the south. By mid-morning on Day One things were moving. Containerloads of floating booms to corral the oil, skimmers to suck it up, various vessels to contain it, and stocks of oilskins, boots, rubber gloves and black plastic bags for those who would have to shovel it up, were trucked south from BP's pollution response base at Sullom Voe. In Aberdeen, P&O Scottish Ferries' terminal became a marshalling yard for much larger amounts of gear heading north from various depots in Britain. The three roll-on/roll-off ferries on the Aberdeen-Shetland route, *St Clair*, *St Sunniva* and *St Rognvald*, would keep running throughout the storms, discharging more oil-spill equipment at Lerwick every day.

There were 150 tonnes of oil dispersant chemicals in Shetland. A Hercules cargo plane was standing by to fly in more. A flight of six elderly Douglas Dakota DC3 planes was scrambled at an airfield near Coventry in the English Midlands and flew north on a mission to spray dispersant on the oil slick for the MPCU. Operated by a firm called Air Atlantique, the DC3s looked ridiculously out of place, like something from the pages of a 'Biggles' book. There were jokes about 'Air Antique' until it was pointed out that no modern aircraft of the right size could fly low and slow enough to do the job. On Day One the DC3s got as far as Inverness, where they were stormbound.

Everything was stormbound. Compared with the chaotic response to the *Exxon Valdez* four years before, this was a superbly organised, well-equipped, thoroughly professional reaction to a major tanker disaster. Inside the Sumburgh Airport operations room, and at the council's emergency control centre in Lerwick, everything was ready to go. But there was nowhere to go. As Malcolm Green said in the council's first press release, rushed out less than half an hour after the *Braer* grounded: 'The weather is of such severity that no containment or clean-up action can be contemplated.' At lunchtime the wind was still blowing at Storm Force Ten. The police cleared sightseers and even Coastguards from the clifftop next to the wreck, for fear of an explosion. As darkness fell, soon after three pm, the weather reached Violent Storm Force 11. Hurricane Force 12 was imminent. Going outside became a major effort, and dangerous with it. Unwary reporters driving hired cars would be blown off the road before daylight.

For four hours the ship had been heaving up and down on the rocks which stuck up from the sand. Crude oil was leaking from the bows and fuel oil from the stern. The sea around her was full of oil. Most of it was trapped by the south-westerly wind in the bay where the *Braer* had gone ashore but some had started to spread into Quendale Bay on the east and around Fitful Head on the west. Seas up to 80 feet high were burying the tanker's deck and bursting over the superstructure. The sea smoked with spindrift. There was nothing to do but wait, impotently, for the dawn, 16 hours away.

At 2.30pm, Shetland time, a British Airways Concorde took off from New York, bound for London. On board was Michael Hudner, Chief Executive Officer of the B+H Group. He had an open-dated return ticket through to LSI – Sumburgh airport.

At 3.25pm Green's second press release said the tanker was 'expected to break up rapidly'. In answer to countless phone calls asking what was happening, Green was his usual blunt, forthright self: '. . . mechanical booms are useless and the only preventative will be to spray dispersant . . . whilst the council is mobilised and ready to act, it cannot.' Green had already been advised by his Director of Marine Operations, Captain George Sutherland, to expect the worst. Captain Sutherland, the boss of the council's tanker harbour at Sullom Voe, knew the *Braer* well. He had every reason to fear that she would become a total loss. He decided to keep his thoughts to himself and concentrate on the job that now had to be done.

Two hours later a press release announced that there would be no more press releases until ten am the next day: 'The reason for this is that during the hours of darkness nothing much can be seen or indeed done except to hope that the present severe weather abates.'

Nothing much could be seen but something could be smelled. Airports always have a whiff of kerosene. At first no-one inside the main terminal at Sumburgh had noticed the slightly different stink of the Gullfaks crude from the *Braer*. By teatime there was no escaping it. Whirled into a frenzied cloud by the screaming wind, an oily fog 200-feet high was streaming across the two-mile-wide southern tip of Shetland and away over the North Sea to the east. The homes of crofters, farmers, fishermen, airport workers and heli-copter crews were standing in the path of a downpour of crude oil, moving at over 70mph. The air was saturated with oil, as if someone was spraying a giant aerosol can over 15 square miles.

Those Dunrossness folk who were not working at the airport shut their doors and windows against the poisonous cloud. But not many slept well that Tuesday night in the houses of Scatness, Exnaboe, Quendale, Hues-breck, Scousburgh or Boddam. The housing estate of Hestinsgott, next to the ancient hamlet of Toab, was worst hit. Even inside the houses people breathed vapours from the oil. Children and old people especially began to cough, feel sick and have headaches. No-one issued breathing masks. They would come later, after most of the oil had blown away. And no-one on that first, appalling night of the spill thought to take the folk away to the north, where the air was just salty, not oily. No-one had ever thought that a tanker wreck might poison the air as well as the sea. It was one of the few things not in the plan.

In the dark fields and along the Dunrossness shore, sheep and Shetland ponies stood with their patient backs to the hurricane, breathing oil, nibbling contaminated grass and seaweed and getting soaked to the skin with Gull-faks crude.

Unseen in the sea, the first seabirds, fish and shellfish were struggling, suffocating and beginning to die. Out on the Lady Holm, Little Holm and Horse Island, seals were hauling ashore to escape the stinging poison burning their eyes and making them sneeze, itch and retch. A few otters, setting out for a night's fishing along the rocks, sniffed the air, tasted the spray and turned back towards their holts for a moment. But they had cubs to feed and they were hungry themselves. So they swam out into the strangely brown water.

The Dunrossness Disaster had begun. And Michael Hudner was on his way to look at it. Two years before, his company had carried out a 'desk-top' training exercise which involved an imaginary tanker getting into trouble off Shetland. Hudner would later tell the Connecticut newspaper *The Advocate* that this 'spill drill' had prepared B+H for the *Braer* wreck and helped to ensure that the response was 'correct and immediate'.

# BARRY STEVENS, SUMBURGH AIRPORT ASSISTANT MANAGER

THE AIRPORT was quiet again. A few oil workers in leather jackets sat waiting for their flight to be called. The security man in the corner leaned wearily on his desk.

Just two weeks before, over 1,000 extra people descended on Sumburgh Airport over the course of a few days. The place had never been so busy. Now all that betrayed that hectic past were a few extra phone lines.

Barry Stevens, the airport's assistant manager, was sitting at his huge 'L'-shaped desk. The walls of the office were decorated with pictures of oilrigs, aerial views of Sumburgh and maps. He picked up a new telephone.

'This was left over from it all. British Telecom had to put three complete extra exchanges into this building for the press. And when all the Sumburgh numbers were used up they managed to transfer a batch of Lerwick numbers down here.'

His admiration for the local engineers was limitless. 'During the first night they dug in cables right around the airfield from the sub-exchange. They were marvellous . . . But we still needed even more phones.'

Barry talked on, happy to recount each new step, each new decision he and his staff had to take that first week. He'd been over it all before, of course, at the stress counselling sessions.

'I was still in bed at five to seven in the morning when I got a call from the police saying there was a rescue in operation and could I get in quick.

'I was in here at 7.30 to receive the crew off the *Braer*. We got them health checks and fed them and let them phone their homes in Manila, Warsaw and Athens. We got the international operator to keep a continuous line open for the calls and found out later that they were all dealt with by one little lady sitting in a room in Grimsby.'

The next few hours passed with Barry working on automatic pilot. He was acting as airport manager while the manager, Tudor Lewis, attempted to catch a flight back from Glasgow.

Shortly before the tanker hit, Barry was in the Shell lounge with the crew. They wandered about anxiously from window to television. Then the oil began to spill out.

'I felt quite emotional underneath but I couldn't let go. I had a job to do.' Barry leaned back in his chair and considered. 'This may sound dramatic, but I felt it was almost akin to being raped. There was a time I nearly lost it when I was talking to Greenpeace. I had to cut the conversation short because I could feel it bubbling up.'

For the first few days, though, there was so much to be done that personal feelings had to be brushed aside. The morning the *Braer* hit there were just a couple of local reporters in the airport, taking turns on a public phone upstairs. By the afternoon the first planes of journalists had arrived. But numbers were still manageable. The next day and for the days following, every flight that managed to defy the stormy weather was packed.

'As soon as they started to arrive I had to try to find rooms for them and straight away they were asking for permission to site their satellite dishes.

'By Day Three there were over 350 press at the airport and the only place we could put them was in the restaurant area.'

By the end of the week over 530 press passes had been issued, and that didn't include all the technicians. Shetland had never seen anything like it. The media list embraced the world. The Italians flew into the isles in their private jet. ITN had their own helicopter. There were three teams from Japan, crews from Canada and Europe and from North America came ABC, NBC, CNN, CBC and CTV.

'My job was not only to work on the airport management side,

*Barry Stevens,*
*Assistant Manager of*
*Sumburgh Airport*
(Photo: Tom Kidd)

53

but if we left the press to fend for themselves it would cause problems for us as well as them.

'They had a story which we wanted them to get out and if the best way of doing that was to make their lives as easy as possible then that is what had to be done.

'Whatever they asked for, within reason, we tried our hardest to give them. Some of them were sleeping in the airport so we let them use the shower in the fire station; or we took them home for meals.

'It was wonderful because everybody in the airport worked together. We were making it all up as we went along, but nothing was a problem and nobody had any groans about working. In a strange way, it was probably one of the most satisfying ten days I've ever spent here.'

Barry moved to Shetland from London with his wife Janice and their son and daughter 14 years ago. He was in the army for 16 years before joining the Civil Aviation Authority, who shifted him north after just 20 months. Now he is embroiled in island life and says he will never leave: 'I'm not a Shetlander but I am fiercely proud of Shetland.'

Outside his work at the airport, he chairs the Shetland Telecommunications Advisory Committee, is vice-chairman of the Shetland Oil Industries Group and is a branch training officer for the Red Cross, lecturing in first aid.

'If you are on a high all day, performing almost like an ignition spark plug, then you can't unwind quickly. I found I was going home and wasn't able to sleep.

'At three am on the Monday when Prince Charles was supposed to arrive I was up ironing my suit.'

The health of his family suffered too, with daughter Victoria (22), who lives in nearby Toab, complaining of a sore throat and sore eyes. Barry himself came out in a crop of cold sores. 'It was horrible and I'm sure it wasn't psychosomatic,' he said.

In the weeks following the disaster all the airport staff were to be given stress counselling – a chance to talk about how they felt.

'I've already spent an afternoon in Lerwick going through our own technical and stress debrief. It really helps talking things through – what upset people, what pleased them. You have got to get rid of it, to come to terms with it all.

'At the end of the Chinook disaster, staff here had gone through some pretty horrible things but nobody came to talk to us. Years later some people are still suffering. This time, it will be different.'

Barry stood up and smoothed down his grey beard. It was five o'clock and time to go home. The fact he could leave the office at the right time showed life was slowly getting back to normal.

He walked along the corridors to the large, empty restaurant. Just a stray sticker on a pillar identified it as the press village.

# Chapter Three

# THE MOORIT SEA

*The message of course is – let's keep our heads down.*

BP PRESS OFFICER, 6 JANUARY 1993

Long before first light on Wednesday, 6 January, the Coastguards and police struggled out to the cliffs above the wreck. The *Braer* was still there but she had moved about 140 yards to the north. Her stern was under the sea, with the accommodation, bridge and smokestack sticking up through the surf. She was so close inshore that her smokestack could no longer be seen from a distance, only from the clifftop. Islanders monitoring the crackling radio messages heard the words 'breaking up'. A rumour spread, and panic with it: the *Braer*'s back was broken; the tanker was breaking up. She would, but not yet. It was the radio transmissions that were 'breaking up'.

The wind was still blowing a gale from the south-west, driving heavy seas into Garth's Wick. Training searchlights on the wreck, Coastguards could see the deck bending as the ship was lifted and dropped, lifted and dropped on to the rocks. Oil was coming from amidships as well as from the bow and the stern. At least three of her 12 cargo-carrying tanks seemed to be leaking on the starboard side, nearest the shore.

A helicopter went up at dawn. Quendale Bay was full of oil. The pollution had spread around the cliffs of Fitful Head and four miles north to the grazing isle of Colsay, the magnificent beaches of Spiggie and Rerwick, and as far as St Ninian's Isle. On the east side, the oil was streaming along Scatness, round the Lady Holm and Horse Island, and past the mouth of the West Voe of Sumburgh to the lighthouse. There were patches of oil a mile east of Sumburgh Head.

On the beach at Scatness, Black Guillemots, Shags and Eider Ducks were flapping ashore, soaked in oil but still alive. Dead fish littered the tideline – Ling, Cod, Sandeels, Lumpfish, Wrasse, Saithe and Octopus. After 20 minutes down there, humans found their throats sore, their eyes running and their skin burning. The air was full of vapours. At Robin's Brae, three miles downwind of the wreck, drivers going south noticed an odd smell in their cars, as if the engine had a serious oil leak. Windscreens suddenly became

*The morning after she went ashore, the* Braer's *stern had sunk, but the ship would last for another six nights*
(Photo: Tom Kidd)

Opposite:
*Measuring oil vapours in the* Braer *wind, Dunrossness, January 1993*
(Photo: Graeme Storey)

smeared. The sickly-sweet stench became stronger the nearer they came to Sumburgh.

Children in the playground at the Dunrossness Primary School in the village of Boddam could smell the oil. They were quickly taken inside again. Some were off school that day, feeling unwell after the pollution had sprayed over their homes all night. At Hestinsgott, Scatness and Quendale, the windows of the houses were smeared with oil. Over 15 square miles of Dunrossness, oil lay on puddles of salty rain in the sodden fields. The grass was sticky with it. Fields of turnips and winter cabbage, grown to feed livestock or for sale in the Lerwick grocers' shops, had a thin film of oil.

On the shoreline, islanders who had woken expecting to see horrific scenes reminiscent of the Persian Gulf oil spills and the *Exxon Valdez* were surprised, and at first relieved, to find that this spill was very different from the ones on TV. The birds were not coated in a stifling black mess. They were soaked, shivering but still breathing and able to preen. Instead of being suffocated in the oil they were dying of cold as they lost their insulation, or of poisoning as they tried to clean their feathers and swallowed the oil. Most of the seabirds were still lively enough to peck and draw blood from the wildlife rescue volunteers who tried to catch them and take them away for cleaning.

For the television crews this was less than satisfactory. They had come to film an oil slick, but it did not look right. They needed pictures of birds looking as if they had been dipped in chocolate. These birds just looked wet and, annoyingly, they would flap back into the polluted sea just as the cameraman got them in focus. It took a while to find a spot where the birds had been hit by the heavy fuel oil and looked the part. Those were the pictures flashed around the world, attracting attention to Shetland's plight but subtly overstating and misrepresenting the extent and nature of the disaster.

This was a very strange oil spill. The oily water ran up the beaches but, when it ran down again, the beaches did not look oiled. The pollution sank down through the sand and hid under the pebbles, where some of it will remain for months, if not years. The oil was *in* the water, right through it from seabed to surface, rather than on top of it. The breaking waves were brown, the colour of milky coffee. No, not quite that colour, more like the unusual hue of those brownish sheep grazing in the fields nearby. Shetland's small but sturdy native sheep come in many colours. Most are white, some are black or grey, but a few are what the islanders call 'moorit' – a warmish chocolate brown. The surf which ought to be white on this Wednesday morning was pale moorit. Hardly any black oil was to be seen, except in Garth's Wick where the fuel oil from the tanker was ponded by the wind, and round on the sheltered side of Sumburgh Head, where the oil surfaced to form dark slicks on the steely-grey winter sea.

Oil this light had not been spilled in large quantities into the North Sea since the Ekofisk oilfield blow-out in 1977, half-way between Scotland and Norway. The huge slicks from Ekofisk were disappearing from the surface even before 'Red' Adair, the Texan well-fire fighter, arrived and capped the wild well. The weather in April 1977 had been bad, but nothing like the night of 5/6 January 1993.

Unlike heavy Alaskan crude oil or the even stickier Arabian crudes, North Sea oil is almost as runny as water. The Gullfaks oil from the *Braer* is one of the lightest and runniest crudes of all. Scientific tests done in Norway in 1991 had shown that up to a third of it would evaporate in the first five days. It responded well to dispersant chemicals for about the same length of time. It took two or three days before it began to form thicker, emulsified patches with sea-water, but these emulsions were unstable and soon broke down. Gullfaks was also unusually susceptible to being broken down by bacteria. If you had to have an oil spill, Gullfaks was much less unpleasant than almost any other kind of crude oil. But it was still very damaging to most forms of marine life, as Shetland was to find out.

When the lightest oil ever spilled in a major tanker wreck met the roughest seas and highest, most sustained winds, blowing from the same direction for 14 days, unprecedented things happened. Churned up by incessant waves between 50 and 100 feet high, the oil and the water formed a sort of toxic salad dressing in Garth's Wick and Quendale Bay, both a hundred feet deep. The oil became suspended in the water. Because Gullfaks crude contains very few of the waxes and tars found in Middle Eastern and Alaskan crude, the oil slicks on the surface were surprisingly thin. A few miles from the wreck, only light sheens were formed, by films of oil a few thousandths of an inch thick.

With the oil in the sea as an underwater cloud, the tides rather than the wind dictated which way it would move. Because each ebb tide runs westwards around Sumburgh Head and Fitful Head for three hours longer than the flood goes east, most of the oil went along the west coast of the south Mainland of Shetland. The prevailing ocean current, which is very slow at the southern tip of Shetland, tended to move some of the oil south-eastwards, out to the North Sea where the herring would spawn in late summer. In the open sea, the oily cloud was very quickly diluted by hundreds of cubic miles of sea-water, leading one council official to remark that 84,500 tonnes of oil was 'bugger all in the Atlantic Ocean'. He was right but his timing could have been better.

On the west side, the tide and the wind would slow down the rate of dilution and, as generations of Shetland beachcombers knew so well, would concentrate the oil in rocky geos (coves) and on some beaches but not others. In the days immediately after the wreck, some of the highest (and therefore strongest) tides of the year were predicted. Intense low pressure areas passing west of Shetland made the tides the highest ever recorded in the islands.

As the first of the helicopter surveillance missions made its report on Wednesday morning, worried salmon farmers and fishermen on the southwest coast of Shetland (and their bank managers) began to panic. How on earth were they to protect their floating fish cages, anchored in bays and between the islands? What would happen to the rich inshore fishing grounds

*Getting it just right. A photographer adjusts reality on Quendale Beach*
(Photo: Tom Kidd)

*A salmon is sacrificed for science as testing for contamination begins*
(Photo: Tom Kidd)

known as the 'Burra Haaf' – the mainstay of a dozen small trawlers and seine-netters in the early months of the year? It was much too windy to use floating booms to trap the oil, let alone skimmers to collect it. The equipment would just blow away. And there was no technology at all to deal with a cloud of submerged oil, suspended in the sea and moving with the tides, nothing to stop it sweeping through the cages and contaminating millions of pounds' worth of prime salmon, growing in 'the cleanest seas in the world'.

Chris Young, the Chairman of the Shetland Salmon Farmers' Association, put a brave face on it. He told reporters: 'The situation is potentially very serious.' Young, who has a salmon farm at Vaila Sound, 25 miles north-west of the wreck, said: 'What works on a fine day is useless in bad weather. In some cases it may be possible to move fish farm cages but it all depends on the local geography. It's all very problematic.'

Even more problematic was the threat of damage to Shetland's image for producing fresh, clean food from a pristine environment. One TV picture of a polluted fish was enough to destroy a commercial reputation built up with years of expensive marketing and underpinned by some of the strictest quality controls in Europe. The Shetland seafood industry was unsure whether to scream blue murder about the tanker on the rocks or to play down its effects in the hope of reassuring the customers. By the afternoon of Day Two, there were rumours that supermarket chains in the south were cancelling orders for all Shetland seafood. Some of the rumours would soon be confirmed.

The local tourist industry, which had been expecting a record 1993 season for foreign visitors because of the recent 15 per cent devaluation of the pound, had similar concerns. Things would have to be 'put into perspective'. There would soon be locals talking down the spill, as well as the shipowner's 'crisis management consultants' and the charming chaps from the insurance companies.

John Goodlad, Secretary of the Shetland Fishermen's Association, was quick to condemn 'alarmist' statements about the possible effect of the spill on stocks of wild fish. He admitted that it could be 'catastrophic' but said no fish stocks had yet been harmed. That was an optimistic statement for the morning after the wreck. Harm was already being done. Neither Goodlad nor anyone else yet knew how much.

Similarly upbeat comments would come from Frank Odie, a director of Framgord, the company handling most of Shetland's farmed salmon sales. He said one chain store had stated it would continue buying the fish, 'confident that we will not sacrifice standards even in the face of this adversity'. He pointed out that the fish being harvested that week were from farms in the north-west and east of the islands, many miles from the wreck and completely unaffected. Odie admitted that the future was uncertain. He added that media coverage had 'not been positive for the industry'.

Blaming the messenger had begun. No-one would explain, however, just how the mass media were supposed to keep secret the fact that a tanker was spilling 84,500 tonnes of oil and 1,700 tonnes of fuel oil.

The fishermen had another fear – the indiscriminate use of chemical dispersants to treat the oil. In a joint statement with the salmon farmers and the fish processing factories, they announced that they were 'totally opposed' to spraying dispersants close to fish farms, shellfish grounds and herring spawning areas which were not in immediate danger.

Unfortunately, spraying dispersants from the air was the only possibility on Day Two. Dutch salvage experts had already arrived and their tug *Smit Lloyd 121* was standing by the wreck but there was nothing they could do except guess how badly the tanker was holed. The seas were still running very high although the wind had briefly eased to a modest Force Seven. It was spraying or nothing. And spraying was the British Government's standard policy for dealing with oil slicks where booms and skimmers could not be used.

The dispersants caused the first major row in the Joint Response Committee, which was formally set up early on Wednesday morning. The JRC was to be run by a management committee, chaired by Captain Sutherland from the council. The vice-chairman, Martin Hall, was council's top environmental official. Other organisations represented on the committee included the Coastguards, police, the oil industry's Oil Spills Service Centre, the Government's Marine Pollution Control Unit (MPCU), the tanker insurers Assuranceforeningen Skuld of Oslo and the International Tanker Owners Pollution Federation (ITOPF).

All these bodies were now bound to reach and abide by joint decisions. The council might be in the chair but it could not impose its will – there had to be consensus. Some were surprised that the representatives of the spill's victims should be sharing effective control of the operation with ITOPF and Skuld, whose clients had caused the problem. But there they were, Dr Brian Dicks from ITOPF and his colleague Michael Thorp from Skuld, and there they would stay. According to one insider, as soon as the two landed at Sumburgh they just walked into the operations room, found themselves desks and chairs, and sat down. No-one asked them to leave. Some but not all council officials were pleased to see them. The insurers were the only way to get access to the International Oil Pollution Compensation (IOPC) funds. IOPC was picking up the bills. Their price for doing so was a slice of the action. This slice did not amount to a veto on the JRC.

The JRC immediately set up three sub-committees – Environment, Technical and Procurement. David Okill, an Environmental Services official from the council and a prominent member of the Shetland Bird Club, chaired the Environment group. Dr Chris Goodman from MPCU was in charge at Technical, advising on what could be done and how. Procurement – whose job was to get the right kit to the right place at the right time – was run by MPCU, the Oil Spills Service Centre and the oil companies' UK Offshore Operators' Association (UKOOA). Council officials were delighted to find immediate and full co-operation from the oil industry, which supplied most of the equipment. The Sullom Voe oil terminal sent tonnes of gear on the first day. It was returned to the terminal – where it was needed in case they had an oil spill – as soon as replacement equipment arrived from the south.

The Government supplied the air power. Just after nine am the first of the

DC3 sprayer planes came in to land at Sumburgh. Council Chief Executive Malcolm Green was uneasy about them. The MPCU wanted to start test spraying at once. Green demanded assurances that the dispersants had been tested for human health hazards and were no more toxic than the oil itself. He got them. He was told that all the dispersants had been passed as fit for use. The assurances would turn out to be less than accurate. For a while, the dispersant controversy would occupy more column inches than the causes of the spill.

It was Shetland's best flying display since the great air show to celebrate Sumburgh Airport's 50th anniversay, back in 1986. The pilots of the DC3s were a bunch of characters and obviously delighted to be using their old crates on a real mission. With great skill they flew 20 feet above the waves as they sprayed over Quendale Bay and around the Lady Holm. They weaved and banked and turned. As one landed another took off. From a spotter plane high above, the flying circus was co-ordinated and the results filmed. Even at shore level it was soon clear that the dispersants were working, sweeping grey-blue lanes though the moorit sea. The test spraying was judged a success. By nightfall over 120 tonnes of dispersant had been dumped on the oil.

In the early afternoon the DC3s put on a wonderful show for Shipping Minister Lord Caithness and Scottish Fisheries Minister Sir Hector Munro MP. The old Dakotas, skimming the wavetops and trailing clouds of dispersant, silhouetted against the jagged rocks of Fitful Head, made splendid television, particularly when there were so few oiled-looking birds around. Better still, the film could be shot in comfort from a convenient road at the end of the runway, handy for a quick dash back to the airport terminal where satellite dishes were waiting to beam the pictures to the studio in London, complete with sound-bitten commentaries from reporters on the spot and intercut with clips of the MPCU control room in London, where staff were busily answering phones and shifting pieces of paper around crowded desks.

It was very good public relations for the Government and particularly for the MPCU, even if some of the spray did fall on a French TV crew and local teenagers out collecting dying seabirds, and make their eyes sting. Ministers had rushed to the scene and had their pictures taken in helicopters flying over the wreck. The subliminal impression was given that the Government was in charge of the situation. Everything possible was being done. The fact that what they were doing was dangerous, partly illegal and almost totally ineffective would only come out later, when the old crates were again grounded by the weather.

The DC3 action shots were much more interesting to the television news editors than views of the afternoon press conference at Sumburgh, when Lord Caithness exposed his total ignorance of radar in the Fair Isle Channel and Sir Hector Munro publicly disagreed with him, saying that Captain Gelis had run a risk taking the route he did. That footage was severely pruned.

B+H also had reason to thank the DC3 pilots. They ensured that Hudner's grilling by the reporters, who forced him to admit that he might not, after all, send another tanker through the Fair Isle Channel in a storm, received minimal TV coverage. The impression was given of a nice man whose ship had met with an unforeseeable accident and who had rushed across the Atlantic to Shetland to express his condolences to the islanders and to do everything he could to help. On television, Hudner sat as an equal at the same table as the council officials, the MPCU's David Bedborough and the local police chief. He looked part of the team. He was courteous under pressure. His crisis management consultants were delighted.

Only Councillor Willie Tait, a crofter who represents Dunrossness North, rocked the boat. Tait was bitter and angry: 'I cannot say whether it was bad seamanship or not. I don't think the tanker should have been there,' he had told the morning press conference. 'We try our best to make Sullom Voe safe but we need an exclusion zone around Shetland so that a tanker of this size can't go between Fair Isle and Sumburgh Head . . . You might get a 300,000-tonne ship coming through that channel – which is ludicrous – and we need to convince the Government that there must be an exclusion zone.'

Tait's demand was taken up by MPs of all parties in the House of Commons. Transport Secretary John MacGregor announced an immediate inquiry and promised that it would look specifically at whether it had been safe to take the *Braer* so close to the islands. Two investigators were already in Shetland, he reported, and would look at action taken to prevent the 'accident', steps taken after the event, the seaworthiness of the vessel, the competence of the crew and the safety of navigation.

A Department of Transport press officer dismissed suggestions that the inquiry could take up to 18 months: 'Our aim is that we complete the inquiry as quickly as possible. We're talking about a few months, with a preliminary report to the Secretary of State for Transport within a few weeks.' If nothing much could be done on Day Two to limit the damage to the environment, it was clear that the political damage-limitation was going well.

At BP's offices in London and Cleveland, Ohio, the public relations people were having a busy day. BP had an image problem, thanks to Mr Hudner's tanker. As the constructor and operator of the Sullom Voe oil terminal since the mid-1970s, BP, Shetland and oil were synonymous in the public mind. The *Braer* might not be a BP ship; BP might have helped the islands council to pioneer the best tanker safety scheme in the world; and BP might be helping now with equipment and labour for the stalled clean-up (to the tune of £200,000 in the first two days) – but Joe Public Esq, driving into his local filling station, did not necessarily know that. BP was painfully aware of how hard the US consumer boycott had hit Exxon, its junior partner in the Alaska pipeline, after the *Exxon Valdez* disaster.

The media had remembered that the *Exxon Valdez* would have spilled much less than she did if she had had a double hull, that the new US Oil Pollution Act made double hulls mandatory for all new tankers, and that the shipowners had been dragging their feet because of the 20 per cent higher building costs of safer tankers. On the not wholly sensible assumption that a double hull might have saved the *Braer*, journalists were asking questions of BP, a major owner and hirer of tankers.

By 11.49am the public relations people had agreed a line on the problem. BP's Pamela Mounter sent a telex to the company's Brussels office:

*'Following a press request for information on BP's policy on double hulls, BP Shipping does not, repeat not, want BP to become involved in a debate about tanker safety, etc., arising from the tanker disaster off the Shetlands [sic]. We must keep our heads down on this one.*

*'Allan Carter, BP Shipping's press chief, reminds us that questions from the press about the incident should be directed to the Shetland Islands Council. If the press persists in asking BP-related questions, then direct them to the corporate BP press office in London.*

*'For your information, and for your use only as background information in case you are asked by any of your associates, the following is the BP Shipping policy on double hulls. It is not, repeat not, for the press:*

*' "BP notes that legislation requiring the phasing in of double hull ships for US port deliveries has been introduced, although [not] the precise nature of the . . . ship design and construction. We believe that more attention should be paid internationally to the prevention of accidents and action should be taken in the areas of better traffic control, better ship navigation and improved training programmes for personnel. There are considerable benefits to be derived from such improved operational measures aimed at avoiding tanker accidents and reducing the scope for human error." '*

Mounter went on to list the very considerable help that BP had already given to the council. The reticence about BP's policy on double hulls was curious, because BP's London office had released an almost identical and equally anodyne statement in response to a request for information from one of the authors two years before. Perhaps BP did not think it would be helpful at this time for the public to be reminded that, when faced with simple questions about its policy on double hulls, BP spokespersons invariably changed the subject to matters such as vessel traffic systems which are not BP's direct responsibility.

Someone leaked Mounter's telex to Greenpeace, whose campaign ship *Solo* had arrived in Lerwick late on Tuesday night. Greenpeace went to town on it, of course, accusing BP of speaking with forked tongues. Not unreasonable, perhaps, but in BP's view extremely unfair when the *Braer* was not their problem and they were doing all they could. There was a vitriolic exchange of press releases and legal threats, this time with a request for publication by the London newspapers.

Six hundred miles north of London, the weather cleared enough for a weak, midwinter Shetland sunset on that Wednesday afternoon. The silhouette of Fair Isle could be seen dimly on the south-western horizon. No more tankers were going through The Hole, not yet. The wind began to rise again. The evening weather forecast was for another hurricane. The main slick on the surface, a mixture of crude oil and heavy fuel oil, was now seven miles long. Ahead of it, fingers of oily sheen passed roofless croft houses on the uninhabited island of South Havra, pointing straight at fish farms in the narrow sounds between the islands of West Burra, East Burra, Trondra and the Shetland Mainland.

Fresh water lochs were also affected. The morning high tide at Spiggie sent oily waves driving up the little burn between the beach and Spiggie Loch, an RSPB nature reserve famous for its wintering Whooper Swans and ducks. The JRC sent a plastic boom to stop the oil spreading into the loch but it was not enough. Later, mechanical diggers were sent in to block the channel. Even after a month had passed, the sand on Spiggie beach would smell of oil.

Oil was coming ashore on the beautiful strand of St Ninian's Ayre, which had always featured prominently in the glossy, sunlit brochures mailed all over the world by the Shetland tourist board. Shetland Islands Tourism Ltd would have to reprint a 1993 leaflet. One of their magnificent sunset shots, all dark sea and orange sky, now looked unfortunately like a black tide. The sheep grazing around the ancient chapel on St Ninian's Isle – the place where a famous eighth-century Celtic silver hoard had been found – would have to be evacuated, and fast.

Many oiled seabirds had been picked up during the day. The dead ones went into a freezer truck for scientific research and, possibly, as evidence for court proceedings. Those still alive were taken to a Scout Hut at Boddam, where a team of volunteers was working with the Scottish Society for the Prevention of Cruelty to Animals (SSPCA), the Royal Society for the Protection of Birds (RSPB) and the Shetland Bird Club. Of the first 126 birds brought in, only 18 were judged strong enough to survive the shock of being handled by humans and cleaned with detergents. The weaker casualties were humanely killed, out of sight of the TV cameras. The survivors were put in boxes to be shipped to a wildlife rehabilitation centre at Inverkeithing on the mainland of Scotland. Already there was talk of up to 10,000 bird casualties. Ornithologists generally reckon to find along the shore about one in ten of the birds killed by an oil spill. The continuing south-westerly winds made it likely that a rather higher proportion of the Shetland casualties would be picked up.

The estimate would have been higher but in midwinter Shetland's famous seabird breeding colonies were mostly empty. Hundreds of thousands of birds – Common Guillemots, Razorbills, Puffins, Gannets, Arctic Terns, Kittiwakes and Arctic and Great Skuas – were still foraging far out on the ocean. Had it been March or April, the *Braer* would have killed at least a hundred times as many, just as the *Exxon Valdez* had caused havoc among the very similar bird species of Prince William Sound, Alaska, in the spring of 1989.

The birds taking the brunt of the damage were those who stayed in the islands all year round – particularly the Eiders, Black Guillemots, Shags and various gulls – and the winter visitors from further north. They included rare, beautiful Long-tailed Ducks ('Old Squaw' in North America) and Great Northern Divers ('Loons') from Iceland, Greenland and eastern Canada. Small wading birds from northern Norway and the Siberian tundra, such as Purple Sandpipers and Turnstones, were also being splashed with oil as they hunted for worms and larvae in the piles of seaweed along the tideline. Their neighbours, Rock Pipits, Starlings and tiny Shetland Wrens, were similarly at risk.

Some birds escaped at first because the south-westerly storms of the first days of January had driven them to the sheltered east side of Dunrossness. But soon the sheens of oil were spreading along that coastline too, up to ten miles north of Sumburgh Head. Some of the oil was surfacing from the underwater slick and some had been blown straight across the land, back into the sea.

The deaths among Eiders and Shags worried the ornithologists most. Both species had been declining for several years in Shetland. No-one knew why. One theory was that hundreds of them were drowning in salmon cage nets when they dived to feed on the mussels clinging to the cages and became entangled. Discarded offcuts of fishing net floating in the sea were another possible explanation. It is not only some tankers who have too little regard for the environment. The southern peninsula of Shetland is too exposed for salmon farming and here there were large flocks of Eiders and Shags. Probably much more than half of the Shags were killed.

Shetland's seals had also endured persecution from fish farmers who were allowed to shoot a few on licences from the Department of Fisheries but killed many more illegally. Salmon farms were supposed to have anti-preda-

*On parade, Quendale Bay. RSPB workers and some of the day's catch of dead Tysties and Shags*
(Photo: Tom Kidd)

tor screens – heavy, close-meshed nets which kept inquisitive seals away from the cages. One or two had taken to setting deadly single-filament nylon nets, with meshes invisible to seals but just big enough to trap their heads and drown them. Headless seals had begun to wash ashore around the Shetland coast. Like the Alaskan fishermen who regularly shot Sea Otters before the *Exxon Valdez* disaster, Shetland's salmon farmers and trawlermen had no reason to regret the killing of their competitors, the seals, as long as it was done without ruining their own livelihoods. But even the seals' worst enemies would not have wished an oil slick on them.

Some of the Quendale Bay seals saw the oil coming and escaped. But a group of about 60 Common and Grey Seals was trapped on the Lady Holm, surrounded by oil, unable to feed in the moorit sea. It made them ill and lethargic but did not immediately kill many. Unlike Otters, they had a thick layer of blubber to keep them warm.

Fortunately, Dunrossness is not a stronghold for Otters, which thrive better in Shetland than anywhere in Europe. Of the estimated 700–900 animals in the islands, only a dozen or so were thought to be in the danger area. How many of them crawled into their holts to die, no-one will ever know.

Sheep were oiled, as they had been by the *Esso Bernicia* spill in the north of Shetland 14 years earlier, but farmers and crofters managed to move most of them away from the shore to less heavily oiled land. Those who had room took their flocks inside the barns and byres, along with pedigreed Shetland ponies such as 'Doddles', a star of the London Horse of the Year Show. All had to be fed valuable hay which their owners had been saving for the lambing in April and May. Imported feedstuffs for livestock would be high on the council's shopping list.

On Wednesday night Council Convener Edward Thomason gave a pep talk for the media. He was proud of the council emergency team who had responded so quickly to the disaster; everyone at the Joint Response Committee in Sumburgh was co-operating well; morale was high; and, with Jim Wallace MP, he had already told Sir Hector Munro that the islands expected the Government to meet the bills of those directly affected by the spill – and to pursue those responsible.

At the end of Day Two the Joint Response Committee (JRC) reviewed the situation. The ship was still intact but with every hour that passed the damage to her bottom must be getting worse. No-one had managed to board her. Arjen Hoekstra, the Salvage Master from Smit Tak, and his colleague Geert Hoffeman reckoned they might be able to pump off the remaining cargo from the *Braer* if the weather eased. A dumb barge to hold the oil was under tow from Rotterdam but was already being delayed by gales. Alternatively, they might be able to pump the oil over Garth's Ness and into the barge, moored in more sheltered water.

Locals who knew what Fitful Head was like in a normal January doubted if it could be done. And this was proving to be the windiest Shetland January in living memory. Even if the wind fell away, it would be several days before the swell subsided enough to put salvors aboard the wreck, let alone a large tug alongside. The wind was not going to fall away. A low pressure system with a centre of only 937 millibars was tracking north-west of Shetland towards the Norwegian Sea. That would bring violent winds from the south-west. And an even more menacing depression was heading for the Faroe-Iceland gap. It would eventually bottom out at 916 millibars, the lowest pressure ever recorded in the north-east Atlantic. The wind had not fallen below Gale Force Eight for more than a few hours in the first six days of January. In fact, it would be 19 January, two weeks after the wreck, before the Coastguards would be able to tell inshore fishermen: 'There are no gale warnings in operation for sea area Fair Isle.'

The sense of frustration was palpable. The JRC's only hope was more of the controversial spraying but the DC3s could not be used in gale force winds or close to the cliffs. Helicopters could spray the heavier oil nearer the rocks but could not carry as much dispersant as the DC3s. It was going to be a bucket and shovel job by the look of it, just like the *Esso Bernicia*. Within hours of the first alert, the council and BP had squads of men kitted out in oilskins and rubber gloves, ready to gather oiled debris from the beaches and put it in plastic sacks. But the smell of oil was still so severe that the workers feared their health could be at risk, even wearing the breathing masks which had been rushed to the scene. Much of the oiled coastline was inaccessible

*The salvage tug* Smit Lloyd 121 *stands by the wreck during the lull in the storms on 6 January, unable to put men aboard because of the swell* (Photo: Donald MacLeod, *The Scotsman*)

anyway and heavy plant could not be driven on to the worst-affected beach, Quendale, for fear of destroying prehistoric archaeological remains believed to lie under the dunes.

The awful truth was that this one was out of control. With what later looked like the gift of prophecy, John Scott, owner of the Noss National Nature Reserve and Shetland's representative on the board of Scottish Natural Heritage (formerly the Nature Conservancy), summed up his feelings on Day Two; the best thing would be another two weeks of westerly storms to break up the wreck and disperse the pollution. Members of the JRC were beginning to think the same. The gales might not be such an enemy after all.

All through Wednesday night the wind increased. The aerosol of salty oil again blew across the southern tip of Shetland. People could smell it in Lerwick and Bressay now, 20 miles downwind, even as far away as Burravoe in the island of Yell, over 40 miles from the wreck. And still no-one from the authorities came to measure the oil level in the Dunrossness air. They were measuring oil vapour and the levels were low – but most of the flying oil was in the form of droplets, not vapour, and the instruments did not register it. Face masks were not yet available to the general public. Some families moved their children north. Most stayed put, trusting the Shetland Health Board to say if they should be evacuated or not.

As the wind crept up the Beaufort Scale to touch Force Ten again, Shetland's evangelical Christians were praying for an Act of God to save the islands. Other denominations were on their knees too. A theological puzzle, that if God was responsible for clearing up the mess then He must also have had a hand in causing the wreck, was lost in the devotional fervour of the crisis.

*Chapter Four*

# DAYS OF DISTRESS

*'If we're at risk, what are we doing here?'*

JOHN JOHNSTON, SCATNESS, SHETLAND, 8 JANUARY 1993

The Thursday morning was what Shetlanders call 'A Day o' Distress'. The gale howled worse than ever, bearing showers of sleet. It was the sort of day when the wise crofter finds something to do about the house or sorts out seed potatoes in the barn. Just going outside to feed the sheep or fetch in peats for the fire was an ordeal.

In Lerwick, the shipchandlers were doing a roaring trade in full oilskin suits and rubber boots, as visiting tellypersons and members of the mediability decided that, fashion or no fashion, they had better get some serious protection on if they were to stay in Shetland much longer.

This third day of the spill brought the first sick jokes. A rabbit found dead and covered with oil on the dunes near Quendale Bay was promptly dubbed '*Braer* Rabbit' by the press corps. Another nasty tale, never officially confirmed, was that a visiting journalist had run over an otter in his car and, seeing a good photo opportunity, had dipped the corpse in oil and taken its picture. In a school playground on the mainland of Scotland, grinning pupils leaned at a 30-degree angle and asked: 'Who am I?' Answer: 'A TV reporter in Shetland!' Indeed, it was something of a miracle that no newshound had yet been blown over the slippery cliffs above the *Braer* while emoting on camera. Intrepid reporters had given up trying to evade the police cordon to get near the tanker. Recognising the danger, they were now allowing themselves to be shepherded to the cliff by the constabulary.

At daybreak the helicopter found the *Braer* still in one piece, impaled on the rocks and continuing to leak oil but apparently less of it than in the previous 36 hours. No-one knew yet if she had spilled most of her cargo or just some of it, or what would happen when she broke up, which now seemed inevitable. The salvage tug could get nowhere near the tanker. Yet the Joint Response Committee's morning press release looked on the bright side: 'Despite worsening weather conditions . . . the vessel remains firmly wedged on the rocks . . . and as yet has shown no signs of breaking up.' The

71

weather had 'prevented salvage experts from boarding the tanker' to see how much oil was left in her but, the media were told: 'This task will be given a high level of priority once weather conditions improve.' They would try if they could.

The press release spoke of 'massive air, sea and land operations to contain the spillage'. Well, there were a few helicopter flights but the weather had grounded the planes. Spraying from the DC3s was out of the question but about a tonne of dispersant was dropped from a helicopter before the weather intervened. The weather was doing a better job of dispersing the oil anyway. At sea there was an attempt to place heavy booms around a salmon farm. It failed because small boats, intended to help lay out the booms from the trawler *Adonis* in Clift Sound, could not manoeuvre safely in the gale. Efforts to deploy lightweight absorbent booms to soak up the oil also failed. The booms worked but they blew away. On land, truckloads of booms and other equipment from Sullom Voe were being stockpiled on the pier at the fishing village of Scalloway, 20 miles north of the wreck. The rigid booms were useless for the open sea. And all booms were useless in winds that blew oil over them and tides that carried it under. Besides, most of the oil was in, not on, the 'water column' (as officials had begun to call the sea).

A massive operation; but it was not 'containing' anything. Nothing could contain the oil that day and the JRC knew it. They also knew now that nothing could contain an underwater oil spill, even in a flat calm. But they did not say so. Perhaps the insurance men were just trying to keep everyone's spirits up.

While the weather worked away at the *Braer*, the humans kept busy. Inside the emergency centres at Lerwick and Sumburgh Airport, staff wrote press releases, kept logs, recorded statistics, briefed and debriefed each other, debated salvage strategies, answered phones, typed memos and tried to find beds and hire cars for even more reporters. It was valiant, well organised and almost but not yet quite hopeless – particularly finding beds and cars.

On the beaches and in the Boddam Scout Hut, volunteers continued collecting, killing and trying to clean oiled birds, while dozens of BP and council men worked at the disgusting task of bagging oily muck on the beaches. The weather soon became too vile for beach work, even with the newly issued face masks, and many had to give up. Now that the shock of the wreck and the adrenalin of the initial response had passed, lots of people were just plain miserable at the helpless pity of it all. Maybe that Up-and-at-'em, Dunkirk-Spirit press release from the JRC was not such a bad idea after all. It helped to contain the growing sense of panic and despair.

The gale was steady in the south-west. The unstoppable oil underwater moved steadily north. The JRC brought in earth-movers to dam up the narrow channel between East and West Burra, trying to save cages of salmon. By now, 16 fish farm sites were immediately threatened around Burra and Scalloway. Between them they produced about £10 million worth of salmon a year, over a quarter of the Shetland total.

On Friday, the International Oil Pollution Compensation Fund and the Skuld company opened an office in Lerwick, ready to hand out compensa-

*Body bag, Quendale Beach*
(Photo: Tom Kidd)

tion claim forms and advise claimants. People were already being advised by council lawyers not to put in formal claims, which could mean signing away their rights at law, but only to notify the 'Braer Office', as it became known, of their intention to claim. Most folk took the advice. Only a handful of completed forms were handed in.

John MacGregor, the Transport Secretary, arrived at last, rejecting suggestions that his absence indicated indifference or worse. He had been too busy dealing with the London end of the response to the spill, he said. MacGregor found it 'extremely distressing' to see the wreck from the air. 'We have to do absolutely everything to minimise the effects,' he said. After a press conference where he paid tribute to the emergency planning team at the JRC – 'There has been a tremendous commitment from everyone involved' – he flew back to London. Parliament would resume after the weekend, following the Christmas recess, and MacGregor had a lot of work to do before he faced some very angry MPs in the House of Commons. One of the assurances he would give was that all the dispersants used had been properly approved.

Shetland's Director of Public Health, Dr Derek Cox, had been away in the south when the spill happened. Now he was back and in charge again. Health officials again took sampling instruments out to check the air. They found that hydrocarbon vapour levels in the Dunrossness air were lower than in a busy city street, a petrol station forecourt or downwind of a plane warming up its engines on the Sumburgh tarmac. Assurances were issued that there was no immediate threat to human health from the fumes. Some thought it patronising when explanations were given about how the human nose was a very sensitive instrument, much more so than the experts' measuring devices.

Dr Gerald Forbes, Director of the Environmental Health Unit at the Scottish Office, told reporters that tests inside homes near the wreck showed no measurable hydrocarbons: 'There is no human health risk, either acute or chronic,' he said. People might feel nauseous because of the smell but that was not regarded as a health problem. He conceded that things might change and he could not be certain about the future: 'You can never say there is no risk. But in this situation I would say there is no measurable risk to anybody living within a mile and a half of the ship.'

Dr Forbes, Dr Cox and the team from the Scottish Health Department working with them were using scientific method, not noses. The results told them not to worry, as would the detailed health studies carried out over the following month. They meant what they said when they reassured the people living near the wreck. But the people had smelled the awful stench. They had tried to sleep with crude oil raining on their bedroom windows. They knew it was making them feel sick. They had their common sense if they had no science. And many of them refused to believe the experts.

It emerged that the council had had an evacuation plan on Day One. Martin Hall, the council's Director of Environmental Services, said: 'If it became necessary, families living in the area would be evacuated. Plans had been drawn up three days ago and the council were confident they could cope with any contingency.' But it had not been considered necessary to move people from their homes. Mr Hall's and Dr Cox's problem was that there had been no attempt to measure the oil droplets pollution when it was at its worst, when the measurements could have told the health board and the council whether evacuation was necessary. Some householders believed they should have been evacuated as a precaution, in the absence of early scientific information. Some of them still wanted to leave. A few were now very, very angry. The air which had been brown was becoming blue. Many were afraid and showing signs of stress, even if they had no symptoms of pollution poisoning.

Dr Rowlands, the local GP, shared some of their worry. He, after all, was seeing Dunrossness patients. The air pollution experts were not. His concerns, and his apparent differences with Shetland Health Board, became public at a crowded meeting of local people in Dunrossness Primary School on Friday night. The meeting was called by the MP, Jim Wallace, and Dunrossness councillors Magnus Flaws and Willie Tait.

Dr Rowlands had already warned teachers at the school not to let pupils go outside at playtime. He told the meeting of almost 100 people that the oil contained three chemicals known to cause cancer. One of them was an 'exceedingly dangerous chemical', benzene. It could cause leukaemia. The others were butadiene and naphthalene. He recommended that parents should keep their children indoors but confirmed that his own four children were still at home in Sumburgh and going to school: 'Obviously I would not have them at home with me if I considered they were at risk from pollution.'

The GP caused some consternation when he advised his patients not to drink water from the public supply. He thought it likely that the reservoirs had been contaminated with oil and dispersants. Only after his boss, Dr Cox, had assured the meeting that tests on the water supply were negative did Dr Rowlands agree that he would drink tap water after all. This did not satisfy some of the audience. Sales of bottled water from local shops continued to rise.

The meeting in the Dunrossness School was where the truth about the dispersants came out before the local public. David Bedborough of the MPCU had earlier in the day admitted to the press that the dispersants sprayed on Day Two had included 15 tonnes of something called Dispolene 34S. According to the Norwegian environmental pressure group Bellona, who were taking a keen interest in the Shetland spill, Dispolene 34S had some years before been 'replaced by Dispolene 36S, which is half as poisonous'. Bellona said Dispolene 34S had never been allowed for use on rocky shores because it was so toxic. The Norwegians also criticised the use of the dispersants Dasic and BP Enersperse 1037, both of which had been used at Quendale Bay.

Several days later, Bedborough would release some but not all of the details that the public had demanded. By the end of the first week, he said, the MPCU had sprayed '95 tons of Dispolene LTSW, ten tons of BP Enersperse 1037 and 15 tons of Dasic 34S'. He insisted that 'a lot of nonsense' had been talked about dispersants. Asked why their chemical composition

*Captain George Sutherland, Marine Operations Director for Shetland Islands Council, addresses the issues with David Bedborough (left) from the Marine Pollution Control Unit and Council Convener Edward Thomason (right)*
(Photo: Tom Kidd)

was still a secret, he told the local press: 'I've got to give you a policy line on this. This information was supplied to the Government in commercial confidence. That was an undertaking that was given. Therefore we have to maintain that – without the supplier's permission we could do no other.' The stuff included solvents. It was not 'Fairy Liquid' washing-up detergent, he said. He confided that the chemical composition had been given to Dr Cox and his colleagues, again in commercial secrecy.

'These are the guys who needed it and it will obviously help them in their monitoring,' he said. 'So the people who are going to look at it and assess it have the information.'

But not the people who had breathed it and got it on their skin. The public were being asked to trust the experts. The 'trust, but don't verify in public' line, and the patter about commercial confidentiality, came as no surprise to those who for years had attempted to find out full technical details of the plant which is supposed to separate oil and other chemicals from dirty ballast water in tankers calling at BP's Sullom Voe oil terminal. Assurances, assurances, assurances, but never specific details. That is BP's way of doing things and also the British Government's. The same line would emerge, but for different reasons, when the time came to keep secret the detailed results of tests for contamination of fish in the path of the brown tide.

Dr Rowlands refused to toe the policy line. At the Dunrossness public meeting on that wild Friday night, he charged that the MPCU had made 'a determined effort' to keep the details of the dispersants secret: 'The situation is that they are using up old stock of chemicals that probably would not be manufactured for that purpose now,' he said. 'They are not sure of the exact

76

composition of the stuff they are putting on the water because they're using a mixture and are not sure what is in which barrels.'

It was true. And some of the barrels were so old and rusty that they had begun to leak on to the ground where they were stored at the airport. This created a bizarre situation where the very substances designed to control the oil pollution at sea were causing a serious pollution problem on shore. The drums of chemicals were kept on a site used by the airport firemen for practice drills. Now it was off-limits to them as the authorities tried to work out what to do with concentrated dispersants leaching into the sandy soil. Bury it, was the answer they first thought of.

It took another 13 days for Jim Wallace MP to force the Government to admit the deception. A junior Agriculture minister, David Curry MP, said on 21 January that all three dispersants had passed general tests for use in British waters. But one had failed the specific test for spraying on rocky shores. Another had passed and the third had not been tested for rocky shores because it had never been intended for them. Jim Wallace is a kind and soft-spoken man. He commented: 'The disclosure of this information underlines that residents in the south Mainland of Shetland were well justified in expressing misgivings about the use of these dispersants.' Friends of the Earth called the revelation 'shocking'. Greenpeace were also outraged.

*A DC3 aircraft from Air Atlantique makes a low pass over Quendale Bay during the controversial spraying of chemical dispersants the day after the wreck*
(Photo: Tom Kidd)

What had happened was that because some of the dispersants were no longer manufactured in that form, their Government licences had been allowed to lapse. So it was true that they were unlicensed chemicals. But they had been properly licensed and certified as fit for their purpose when they were manufactured and purchased. These older dispersants were quietly laid aside.

Trevor Redfern, a vociferous local critic of the spraying campaign, had made an emotional appeal to the public meeting: 'It's not doing any damn good at all, so stop it. It's just throwing it over all the land and making it ten times worse. For God's sake stop it before any more damage is done!' Redfern referred to a TV report of tests on a piece of Dunrossness turf, saying the dispersant Dasic had been found and it could cause mouth ulcers and burning of the lips and tongue on sheep. If inhaled it could lead to liver and lung complaints.

'This is sheep,' Redfern said. 'And a minute before this [was on TV] a man from Shetland Islands Council said it's perfectly all right for anybody to inhale this stuff and it's perfectly all right for anybody to drink the water. But if it's not all right for sheep it's not all right for human beings.' Again, Dr Cox assured him on behalf of the health board that no detectable amounts of the spray had been found.

Dr Rowlands nonetheless advised people who had to work outdoors to wear protective clothing — and the face masks which were being issued through a local shop. Any contamination should be washed off the skin at once and oiled clothing not used again until it had been cleaned. He invited patients to come in for health tests if they thought the dispersants were affecting their health. Such symptoms as sore eyes and sore throats were 'transient' and not unduly worrying. But patients who suffered headaches, nausea, stomach trouble and diarrhoea — these were 'far more significant' symptoms — should see a doctor. These symptoms had already been reported by many people in the path of the oil and the dispersant. They had not been considered significant by Dr Forbes of the Scottish Office Environmental Health Unit. It appeared that the local doctor was departing from the agreed script again.

One Dunrossness resident had such misgivings about the dispersants that on Saturday, 9 January, he made an anonymous phone call to the airport, threatening to organise a human barrier across the runway to prevent the sprayer planes taking off. The DC3 flights were grounded again, amid mutterings about 'loonies' and 'headbangers' from the frustrated authorities.

When flights resumed there were new guidelines, copies of which were distributed to every house in the area. Public pressure was having an effect. By then the Joint Response Committee had decided not to spray the slicks and sheens north of St Ninian's Isle, because of worries about what the chemicals might do to farmed salmon, commercial white fish and shellfish. Dr Rowlands had noted that this was 'rather ironic' when humans living near the wreck had already been exposed to the dispersants blown inland.

That public information notice distributed on Sunday, 10 January, was the second one signed by Malcolm Green, the council's Chief Executive. It was an intriguing document, cobbled together as a face-saving compromise after disagreements behind the scenes at the Joint Response Committee. Green felt that his council had been misled and made to look evasive by the MPCU's initial assurances. He could not say that publicly but in the notice he made it absolutely clear that responsibility for the spraying lay with the MPCU, not the council:

> 'They [the MPCU] acknowledge that on Wednesday 6th January, some dispersant may [sic], during particularly difficult weather conditions, have drifted outside the target area. Since that time the spraying method has been refined and further modified following spraying on Saturday.
>
> 'The refinements include measures to prevent residual dispersant in the system being discharged during the climb-out, and in addition the crew have undertaken to fly at 15 feet, which is half the normal operation height. The spray will be switched on as late as possible and switched off immediately on reaching the edge of the oil to be treated, following which the aircraft will remain at low level before turning away to sea. As standard practice, every spraying run will be carefully directed and monitored by the controlling aircraft.'

This was odd. For that last bit was what the media had been told would happen when the first spraying began on the day after the wreck.

In syntax which showed the strains of writing by committee, Green added: 'The composition of the dispersants used has been made known to the medical authorities and it is considered that, if used by correct methods, the risk to the public is so low as not to be measurable and, even if an amount of the dispersant did affect land close to the wreck, the levels of dispersant would be well within occupational exposure levels.' He then said: 'In fact, what people have been suffering from is the effects of oil in the air and the use of dispersants would reduce the problems.' Public concern continued to rise, encouraged by the Greenpeace campaigners who had now waded into the controversy with both feet. Dr Cox was incensed at their intervention. His view of Greenpeace was that they had caused ill-health through stress – worrying the people of Dunrossness unnecessarily.

Public trust had been shaken – the Government and, by association, the Joint Response Committee (which meant the council), had been caught telling what looked very like a fib. To that charge could be added another – causing grievous bodily harm to the English language. What some worried elderly and frail residents of Dunrossness made of the Dickensian pomposity, technical jargon and circumlocution in the public notice has not been recorded, and would probably not have been printable. Dr Cox himself said: '. . . lots of people, when they get these long letters, just throw them in the bin'.

As further evidence of the JRC's determination to have the public concern 'properly addressed', comprehensive health check-ups were offered to everyone in the area. The authorities were pained when there were complaints that it was no use taking blood and urine samples more than 36 hours after people had been exposed to the oil. By that time the stuff would probably have lodged in their body's fatty tissue, according to one critic.

*Oily rain spatters the window of a Dunrossness family's home*
(Photo: Tom Kidd)

And still Dr Cox could not quite understand why the dispersants had caused such worry and anger, why people would not believe the kind, concerned, competent 'authorities' who were doing their best to look after them. With hindsight, six days after that Dunrossness School meeting, he would say that perhaps the health board had been 'naïve' when it imagined that the daily press conferences at the airport would get the message across to the public. He admitted that bulletins pinned to shop noticeboards had not been read by many people either. Only when local community workers, social workers and church volunteers were enlisted, to visit families in their homes, did the public concern begin to subside. 'Maybe we've found a method that is right,' Dr Cox told *The Shetland Times*, 'and I'm just sorry that we didn't find out about that four or five days ago.' He noted that no-one had been admitted to hospital and only 'dozens', not hundreds, of people had been to see their doctor about the oil spill symptoms.

The affair of the dispersants would be a big talking point at the de-briefing sessions after the spill. But it had a wider significance: the media coverage of the row left the British Government's standard policy for dealing with large marine oil spills looking distinctly suspect. Spraying might be acceptable over the open sea, if the chemical composition of the dispersants was made public, but spraying close to rocky shores and human settlements would probably not be done again without some very serious re-thinking.

Apparently no-one in Whitehall had read the extensive literature on the very similar rows over dispersants during the first three days of the *Exxon Valdez* disaster. The Shetland controversy also left the very strong impression that the air show on Day Two had been a Government-sponsored stunt for the media.

It had taken only three days to open the first cracks in the widespread public support for the initial spill response by Government and Shetland Islands Council. What salmon processor David Hammond had described on local radio as 'constructive anger' was in danger of diverting its energies from the main target – those responsible for causing the spill – towards the public's representatives who were trying to deal with it. On Friday night JRC officials were wondering how much worse it would get.

An alarming report came from the salvage team hired by the tanker owners: Geert Koffeman of Smit Tak said it looked as if the stern section of the tanker was starting to split away from the rest of the ship. The break-up had begun. There was now no hope of towing the *Braer* away in one piece. All they could plan for was how to get the remaining oil out of her. But the barge to receive the oil had still not arrived and was not now expected until Monday. It would be a desperate race against time, even if the swell ran off over the weekend.

Privately, the salvage men shook their heads. If the damage to the stern was that bad, what on earth must the state of the tanker's bottom be like? Once the cargo tanks were opened up below, it was only a matter of time before the pressure of the sea, surging in and out with every swell, would destroy the hull. Tankers are built to resist pressure from the outside. Transfer that pressure to the inside and eventually the waves would burst the ship apart. Then everything would be in the sea. How much, though? That was the question no-one could answer.

Anticipating what was to come, Shetland's fishermen and salmon farmers had been in talks all day with Government Fishery Department officials. They agreed a voluntary ban on catching and harvesting fish inside an exclusion zone. It had been inevitable that they would, ever since Tuesday morning. The zone covered 400 square miles, from a point just west of Skelda Voe right around the south Mainland of Shetland, around Sumburgh Head and up the east coast as far as Bressay. The ban and exclusion zone were made law by the Government the following day. The area closed was less than a twentieth of the fishing grounds around the islands but the news shocked the seafood industry and its customers.

The ban brought the *Braer* back to the very top of the TV news bulletins, where the story was jostling for position with Saddam Hussein's latest posturings in Iraq. Salmon farmer Agust Alfredsson hit out at the media. This Icelandic giant of a man, who also had interests in shellfish processing, was well known for his robust plain speaking. He said: 'The media coverage will do more damage than the oil. The whole thing is bloody ridiculous!' Alfredsson revealed that it was true that the supermarket chain stores Sainsburys, Tesco and Marks & Spencer had cancelled orders for Shetland salmon, even though just one farm out of 63 had so far been affected. But French customers were taking 'a very sensible attitude' and resisting the 'media hype'. Salmon prices had not dropped and demand was still high, he said.

The fishermen's secretary, John Goodlad, said: 'We want to provide a guarantee that no tainted or polluted product will leave Shetland in the coming weeks and months. The name of Shetland products is at risk and we are determined to make sure that it is preserved.' Goodlad said the problem was not that the fish were affected by the oil but that there was a risk of contamination when they were hauled up through oil lying on the surface. Like most other people, he had not yet fully appreciated the significance of the underwater cloud of oil.

Surface sheens had now reached Scalloway and Whiteness Voe, 20 miles north of the wreck. The pollution, patchy and mostly very light so far, was affecting about 30 miles of Shetland's convoluted, 900-mile coastline. No-one knew it yet, but that was about as far as it would go.

While the humans argued and worried over compensation, exclusion zones and dispersants, and wondered how much more oil was yet to come, the birds and animals continued to suffer. Most significant ecologically was the holocaust among the tiny creatures at the bottom of the food chain, on and under the bottom of the sea. In the plankton, minute single-celled animals and the miniature monsters who ate them writhed as the shock-wave of pollution crept northwards. Molluscs pumped in dirty sea-water and sieved out poisonous particles of food. Fish and shellfish larvae, the size of

*Sheens of oil reached Scalloway within a week. The village became a depot for oil spill recovery gear that could not be used during the storms*
(Photo: Tom Kidd)

*Polite notice,*
*Wildlife Rescue*
*Centre*
(Photo: Tom Kidd)

pins, wriggled and died. The sandeels who ate them, and the bigger fish who ate them, sickened as the oil entered their insides and inflamed their gills. Like the Dunrossness humans on the first night of the wreck, they were breathing oil.

Ten days later, when the weather at last allowed biologists to dive in Quendale Bay, Garth's Wick, the Wick of Shunni, Muckle Sound, the Bay of Scousburgh and St Ninian's Bay, they found a dead seabed. Nothing writhed and wriggled, except a few sluggish worms buried in the sand. Curiously, what sealife there was would be concentrated on the sand very close to the upwind side of the wreck, where the relentless surge of the North Atlantic had swept the pollution away.

On the surface, 443 oiled birds had been picked up by Friday night, 326 of them dead. They may have been the lucky ones if a *Scotsman* newspaper report of the 'treatment' of an oiled Shag was to be believed. Reporter Alison Daniels had visited the SSPCA animal welfare centre near Inverkeithing in Fife. Staff helped by well-meaning volunteers were trying to rehabilitate some of the livelier oiled birds which had been flown over 300 miles from Shetland.

Shags are tough birds. They live all year round on the exposed, rocky coasts, roosting and nesting on cliffs and in sea caves. They generally avoid humans and become agitated at the approach of a boat. In the breeding season, the instinct to stay with their eggs and young will overcome their fear, and delay their flapping down into the sea and diving for cover. Occasionally a young one who knows no better will hang around a harbour for a while, appearing to be tame, but rarely for long. Capture a healthy Shag and it will panic, stabbing at anything within range of its vicious beak. Naturally enough, it thinks it is about to be killed and eaten.

For such wild, nervous birds, being handled at all by humans is a terrifying ordeal. The shock alone can kill them. This is what the bird-lovers did to them in Middlebank, Inverkeithing:

> '*Having been rehydrated [by forced tube-feeding] with a specially-formulated liquid containing salts, minerals and vitamins, the birds had already been placed in a darkened room to recover [sic] from the stress of being handled and transported.*
>
> '*A Shag was brought into the cleaning room where two people, a cleaner and a handler, were needed to keep the bird firmly held down in a sinkful of warm, soapy water.*
>
> '*The inside and outside of the beak were cleaned using a toothbrush and detergent and then the toothbrush was put in the bird's beak and secured with a rubber band to immobilise it.*
>
> '*Using washing-up liquid, the next task was to remove oil from the obviously disoriented bird's plumage, belly and feet. The wings were spread out and neat detergent worked into the feathers.*'

The report explained how the cleaned birds were then waterproofed: 'That is done by blasting the feathers with very hot water.'

After drying out, the birds were kept for a week or so while they preened

*An oiled Shag gets the Macleans treatment*
(Photo: Tom Kidd)

*Great Northern Diver, Shetland, January 1993*
(Photo: Tom Kidd)

themselves and recovered as best they could. Then they were released into the wild. Well, into the polluted waters of the Firth of Forth, to start with. Free flights back to Shetland were laid on for the casualties later on. The night that some of the first Eider Ducks were slipped into the Forth from their cardboard boxes, the birds were just in time to see a loaded liquefied petroleum gas tanker careering past the rocks after a gale blew her off her moorings at Braefoot Bay. That ship, unlike the *Braer*, did not get away. The tugs stopped her in time. The Eiders (and all the humans in Dalgety Bay and Aberdour) were saved from a holocaust.

The humans who flocked to the wildlife centres in Shetland and Fife, and sent money and materials to help with the work, meant so well that they would be shocked and upset to think they could have been unconsciously cruel to the victims. It is true that some lightly-oiled birds which have not had time to swallow or breathe much oil have a reasonable chance of survival. Sadly, the heart-warming efforts of the would-be rescuers sometimes did more for them than for the birds. The kindest and most heart-breaking thing to do, particularly for local people who felt that they knew the birds personally, was to take an Eider Duck or a Great Northern Diver round the back of the shed, while the TV crews were having a cup of tea, and put it out of its misery. By Friday night 12 Great Northerns had washed ashore, all but two of them dead.

In the case of the Great Northerns, magnificent, primitive birds which breed on the lakes and swamps of eastern Canada, Shetland birdwatchers like Martin Heubeck, and Pete Ellis of the RSPB, probably did know them personally. Great Northerns are long-lived creatures, and creatures of habit. Generations of the same family of birds had been coming to Quendale Bay for hundreds, perhaps thousands, of years. The bones of their ancestors were found in the prehistoric middens at Jarlshof. Quendale was where they always went for the winter, because they knew it was a good place to fish. It was just as much their home as the nesting grounds on the other side of the Atlantic. They brought their young with them, year after year.

There are not many Great Northerns in Shetland each winter and, when a pair both die, it may take decades before new ones come along and find the empty place. That is what happened in Sullom Voe and Yell Sound in the *Esso Bernicia* disaster, when just 1,174 tonnes of heavy fuel oil wiped out the Great Northern Divers who were there in January 1979. Most of their winter quarters are still empty.

*Esso Bernicia* was a spill on top of the water, not in it. That tanker's fuel oil probably killed more birds than the *Braer*, which spilled 72 times as much oil. Like the Great Northern Divers, all oil spills look the same — until you are close to them.

*Chapter Five*

# WAITING FOR THE END

*To get to know the Shetland Islands and some of their people during these past days of crisis and concern has been an enriching experience. On behalf of all of us connected with the m/t Braer, I thank you from the bottom of my heart.*

MICHAEL S. HUDNER, LETTER TO *The Shetland Times*, 15 JANUARY 1993

Word was getting around. From all over the world, Shetland's 'exiles' were phoning and writing home to express sorrow, sympathy and to ask for news. The open letter to Shetlanders from the Shetland Society in Wellington, New Zealand, was typical: '. . . we would like to convey to you our shock and disbelief . . . Although living on the other side of the world our thoughts are never far from home, especially now when . . . images of Shetland are brought to our living-rooms on the TV news and we can see for ourselves the havoc which is being wrought.'

People who had only been on holiday in the islands felt the same. Alison Martin of St Ives, Cornwall, was one of dozens who wrote to *The Shetland Times*: 'I am writing this with tears streaming down my face. My family and I have been to Shetland . . . and it has become a very special place for us. When I saw that the slick has reached St Ninian's Isle I was very distressed . . . I just had to write, as many will, to say we feel so much for you and pray that your special place will come through this terrible ordeal . . .'

Islanders who had emigrated in the hard times before the oil boom, in the days when Shetland's exports had been fish, lambs, educated people and empty beer bottles, called from Australia, Germany, France, the Middle East, Hong Kong, Japan, Canada and the United States. The Shetland diaspora may be far-flung, but they keep in touch. They sent cuttings from their local papers, names of people they knew who might be able to help, and suggestions for how to clean up the massive black oil slick which, they had been told, was smothering their old home.

At the Shetland News Agency that Saturday morning, we heard from an old school friend who had lived in London for 20 years; she faxed us a cutting from the *Evening Standard* which she found 'objectionable in tone

*St Ninian's Isle, 1*
*February 1993*
(Photo: Jonathan Wills)

and very offensive'. The *Standard*'s man in Shetland, Geraint Smith, had filed a story about islanders 'quietly . . . rubbing their hands and banking the profits' from the oil spill. The article, headlined 'Silver lining for islanders swamped by black gold', was good knockabout stuff:

> '*Shetlanders thought that they knew all about money, but they were wrong. In the days since the accident, a touch of the Klondyke has come to the scattered community.*
>
> '*The wind that blows the black oil has brought with it a huge cast of extras, thronging the airport . . . and spreading out across the island.*
>
> '*Hotels were overflowing within hours of the grounding.*
>
> '*Now, the proprietor of the nearest one to the disaster area, the Sumburgh [Hotel], says he would be happy if he had a hundred rooms rather than 30.*
>
> '*Desperate pleas broadcast on local radio for accommodation have been answered – but not in sufficient number. Beach-cleaning crews, after a hard day picking up oiled birds and trudging through the drizzle of fossil fuel, now mixed with snow, are having to make do with hard floors.*
>
> '*Understandably, they are not happy – less so because journalists are sleeping in comfort . . . The hard truth is that salvage crews don't pay like journalists. With short supply and huge demand, prices have mysteriously changed.*
>
> '*The Shetlanders are making hay for the few brief weeks of economic sunshine . . . A couple of weeks ago a bed-and-breakfast here would have been begging guests to stay for £12 a night. Now they are charging £45 plus breakfast, which is an extra £5 . . . Overwhelmed by the demand, the hire [car] company at the airport ran out of vehicles, at rather less than £40 a day, by the evening of the accident . . . Private cars are now being pressed*

*into service in an economy which has always had a healthy contempt for such things as the Inland Revenue.*

*'There are tales of camera crews paying as much as £250 a day for a single car, while the going rate for a battered pick-up truck is £50 at least.'*

Our London reader said she hoped that Smith's expenses sheet and tax return would be carefully scrutinised, and wondered why he had not given up his own bed to a beach-cleaner if he felt that strongly about it.

Smith ended his piece by warning that when the media, the men from the ministry and the 'do-gooders' moved out, there would be a large hole in the local economy, because of the damage to the image of Shetland tourism and seafood. This was a fair point. However, his final sentence was particularly infuriating to Shetlanders at home and abroad: 'But, of course, there will still be the terminal at Sullom Voe.'

The implication here, made explicit in some other press coverage at the time, was that an oil spill now and again was the price Shetland had to pay for enjoying all that oil wealth from Sullom Voe. Islanders were used to laughing off ignorance on the part of visiting metropolitan chauvinists – the sort of people who called Shetland 'the Shetlands' (rather like talking about 'the Londons' or 'the Glasgows'). But this charge stuck in the craw.

Now that there was not a lot new for the camera crews to film, except visiting dignitaries gazing at the *Braer* lying lower in the water each day, the locals set about educating the world media village at Sumburgh.

The more learned barflies, bartenders and bed-and-breakfast hosts told them that Shetland was singular, not plural, because the islands are so close together that, when Norwegian colonists first saw them from their longships, 1200 years ago, they thought the place was one big island. Hence the Norwegian name 'Hjaltland' – probably referring to the fact that the archipelago is shaped like the hilt of a sword. If their new friends from the media doubted this, they were referred to a famously brief pronouncement by Professor Gordon Donaldson, the Queen's Remembrancer and Historiographer Royal for Scotland and a Shetlander himself, who had said: 'The phrase "The Shetlands" is a solecism.'

It was explained that, far from being a rednecked backwater, Shetland was a cosmopolitan community from the start. The islanders were descended from Pictish, Viking, German, Dutch, Scots, Irish and even English settlers. Their dialect was a mixture of Scots, Doric and English, with thousands of Old Norse words still in daily use. They had not spoken Gaelic since 800 AD, had no intention of taking it up again, and resented every word of the Gaelic which BBC Scotland insisted on transmitting to them (Broadcasting House in Glasgow being one of the world's main centres for metropolitan chauvinism). And they were not part of the Hebrides.

Shetland was never as isolated as it looked – it had been used as a staging post on the Viking voyages to North America long before Columbus, a trading centre for the German merchants of the Hanseatic League, a rendezvous for the great Dutch herring fishery of the 17th century, a British naval base in the wars against Napoleon, the Kaiser and Hitler and, more recently, as the main life-support system for the huge North Sea oil industry which produced the diesel for *Evening Standard* journalists' taxis, generated huge profits for the oil companies and gave the British Government enough tax revenue to subsidise the London Underground and maintain three million unemployed in near-destitution for ten years.

So there: as for Shetland's fabled wealth from the oil industry – through property taxes (rates), a local tax on every barrel of oil, rent for the oil terminal site and profits from the council-run tanker harbour – it was just 'a peerie drap' (a small drop) in the ocean of money pumped from beneath the Shetland seabed.

What was more, islanders had endured a decade of housing shortages, overcrowded schools, chaotic roads, petty crime and social disruption during the construction of the terminal and the pipelines. Yes, islanders had got jobs in oil and they did now live in a miniature welfare state of almost Scandinavian opulence, with the best education system in Britain, but they had worked for every damn penny of it and they were not going to be patronised by a bunch of spill jockeys on fat expense accounts.

Oh, and by the way – the Dunrossness folk might be crofters (and some of them very up-to-date and efficient farmers) but that did not mean they were rustic simpletons. As well as the part-time croft, they were quite likely to have full-time jobs as teachers, electrical engineers, helicopter maintenance fitters, computer operators or office managers. Most of them had travelled widely and not a few had nautical qualifications just as good as Captain Gelis'.

*The Cabinet arrives – Scottish Secretary Ian Lang MP (right) and English Environment Secretary Michael Howard at Sumburgh after a flight over the wreck. Immediately behind them is Magnus Magnusson, Chairman of Scottish Natural Heritage*
(Photo: Adam Elder
*Scotland on Sunday*)

Once they had got all that off their chests, the Shetlanders found that these roving reporters maybe were not such a bad bunch after all. The feeling was mutual. Many friendships were struck up during the spill, which had the paradoxical effect of bringing more journalists to the islands than all the years of painstaking media promotions by the local tourist board. The journos mostly said yes, thank you, they would come back and see the place in the summer, when there is no night for two months and nobody bothers to watch satellite TV.

The reporters and camera crews who did trudge up to the clifftop on Saturday morning found that a walk does wonders for the head after a few beers with the locals on a Shetland Friday night. They also found that something odd was happening to the now familiar hulk of the *Braer*: the stern was no longer attached to the rest of the tanker. It was definitely moving around on its own. The salvage men's fears were justified. The weather had eased a little and the salvage tug was almost alongside the wreck – but it was still too dangerous to go aboard.

Using infra-red cameras to look through the steel plates into the wreck, Smit Tak came back with disturbing news. It seemed that up to half of the cargo might still be aboard.

The morning helicopter flights reported that the oil continued to spread, with sheens now as far as Mousa, Reawick, Skeld and Weisdale Voe. Scalloway Harbour was oiled and the fishmarket closed, but the heaviest oil was still trapped in Garth's Wick and Quendale Bay, churning up with the sea to make that submarine toxic soup.

There were some more Very Important Passengers for the choppers, including Scottish Secretary of State Ian Lang, the Conservative Government's 'governor general' in Scotland (a country ruled by a party which had won only a quarter of the popular vote). He flew in with his right honourable friend Michael Howard, the English Environment Secretary. They made the ritual overflight and had their pictures taken looking out of the helicopter window down on to the wreck, wearing appropriate and no doubt genuine frowns of concern. Lang said what a marvellous job everyone at the emergency centre was doing and how the Government would do all it could to alleviate the problems. None could argue with that. But the council wanted more than votes of thanks and fine words. Malcolm Green wanted cash.

Green explained to Lang the details of the council's compensation scheme for farmers and crofters in Dunrossness. The council would either borrow the money or take it from its own reserves. But Green had no intention of picking up the bill – in the long term he expected the Government to pay and then to pursue the polluter at law.

Green had experience in this business. One of the first jobs he did when he joined the council was to work on immediate compensation for crofters whose flocks had been heavily oiled in the *Esso Bernicia* disaster during that other oily January, 14 years before. Although he is no orator and not a man for the grand gesture, Green's quiet, relentlessly determined manner left the Scottish Secretary in no doubt that the council meant what it said. The Government had already proclaimed that the polluter must pay. Well, then, let us see you do it, was the message. Lang, clearly shocked by the extent of the disaster on land, let alone at sea, agreed to help. He was well aware of the adverse publicity and nationalist sentiment that would be provoked in his Scottish fiefdom if he refused. With the media backing Shetland as David against Goliath, Green had him over a barrel of oil – until the TV satellite dishes moved on to Baghdad. Within a week, the first instalment of the money would be promised from a 'bridging fund' set up by the Government.

It would take a little longer before they worked out how to dispose of the turnips, carrots and cabbages standing oiled in the fields. Every field crop in the worst affected area, some three square miles, was condemned. Meanwhile, crofters who could show that they had suffered could go to the agricultural supplies depot in Lerwick and collect the fodder they needed for their livestock, free of charge. There were complaints when it was found that there were not enough vets and officials to get round all the 200 affected crofts to certify the damage in time for the deadline, but the scheme worked, and earned new respect for Green, who had been embroiled in various local controversies and had been less than popular before the emergency began.

Before the Scottish Secretary flew back to Edinburgh, Green told him what he had wearily told every other Government VIP; long before the wreck, the council had organised a conference on managing the marine

*A sheep farmer prepares to move his flock away from oiled pasture, Dunrossness, Shetland, January 1993*
(Photo: Tom Kidd)

*Peter Poland,*
*Cornish volunteer,*
*with boxes of oiled*
*birds to be sent*
*south for cleaning*
(Photo: Tom Kidd)

environment, scheduled for the end of March. Ministers had so far refused invitations to attend, although senior civil servants were coming. Part of the conference was about tanker safety. 'It's important. You should be there,' Green said quietly. And then he said it again.

Other visitors were arriving with less fanfare. The *St Clair* docked at Lerwick on Saturday after her 14-hour overnight voyage from Aberdeen, discharging another load of seasick backpackers – young people from all over Britain and Europe who had come as volunteers, often with no idea of where they would stay or how they would live when they reached Shetland. Some signed on at the Boddam wildlife centre, collecting oiled creatures, patrolling shorelines that had not yet been checked, making tea and running errands. Others joined the Greenpeace campaigners who were helping with the work – using the *Solo*'s fast inflatable boats to visit inaccessible islands and check the damage.

Some of the young volunteers hitchhiked 36 miles north of Lerwick to the tiny village of Hillswick and The Booth bar, Shetland's oldest (and, many say, best) pub. The publican, Jan Morgan, had run a seal rescue centre in her back garden for years. Her family really could lie in bed and hear seals bark, as in the famous James Thurber cartoon. Jan and her seals were a Shetland institution. There was never enough money. She did the work for the love of it. Somehow she had always managed, rescuing sick and injured seals – and abandoned baby ones – and nursing them until they were well enough to return to the ocean. Unlike many birds, seals adapted well to the proximity of humans. The success rate was high. But now Jan and her helpers were overwhelmed, the pens and ponds in the garden overflowing, and money running out.

Local musicians who had enjoyed the famous hospitality of The Booth over the years decided this was the time to do something for Jan and the seals. The following Saturday dozens of them, and hundreds of their fans, would descend on The Booth for an all-day and most-of-the-night benefit concern to raise funds. Some oil spill compensation cash would follow, official recognition of what Jan Morgan had achieved.

The article in the local paper, previewing the benefit bop at The Booth, was opposite a full-page advertisement from a firm of Aberdeen lawyers, touting for business in Shetland's newest growth industry – suing the polluters in the American courts, where the compensation pickings were richer than in Scotland. For once, Frank Lefevre's 'Quantum Claims' firm was slow on the heels of disaster. A Glasgow rival had beaten him to it and taken the whole back page of *The Shetland Times* a week before, just three days after the spill. 'No cure, no fee' was the tempting offer – rather like the 'Lloyds Open Form' for marine salvage which the *Braer*'s owners had reportedly not signed with the tug *Star Sirius*. Most claimants decided to stick together in a 'class action' instead.

That benefit bop for the seal sanctuary was a joyful occasion. Everyone needed a party, to try for an hour or two to forget the spill and have some old-fashioned fun. In Lerwick, it was announced that the town's annual Up Helly A' fire festival would go ahead as scheduled on 26 January, complete

*A Common Seal recovers at Hillswick Wildlife Centre, Shetland, January 1993*

(Photo: Tom Kidd)

with 800 men marching through the streets bearing flaming torches (soaked in best North Sea paraffin) and the burning of a replica Viking war galley, as usual. The last time it had been postponed was in 1964, for Winston Churchill's funeral, and there had been a bit of a row about that. No-one was going to let an oil spill wreck Up Helly A'.

Up Helly A', which happens in many parts of Shetland besides Lerwick, is a 24-hour party to end all the parties that have been going on for a month – the climax of the ancient tradition of 'holding Yule'. People had been in the middle of the Yule visiting, dancing feasting and drinking when the *Braer* spoiled it all on 5 January, a day which – it was suddenly remembered – had been 'Old' Christmas Eve. In some parts of the islands the folk had never accepted the Papal astronomers' decree of 1752, which amended the calendar and cut out 11 days – to bring the human year back into line with the earth's orbit round the sun. No Pope of Rome was chopping 11 days off *their* allotted span, thank you! Accordingly, Christmas and New Year could be celebrated on the old dates or, in many cases, on both old and new dates. In Russia they still hold Christmas Eve by the old calendar. And in the Greek Orthodox Church. Poor Captain Gelis really had had a rotten Christmas.

There were more worshippers than usual in the Dunrossness kirk on Sunday, 10 January, and among congregations of all denominations throughout Shetland.

Prayer seemed all there was left. There was oil spurting out of the deck of the *Braer* with every wave that hit her. There was heavy pollution at the beautiful beaches of Banna Minn and Meal on the west coast of Burra Isle – favourite picnicking and beachcombing spots for island families.

Sunday trading or not, a director of the Safeways food stores chain arrived to meet his suppliers of Shetland seafood. He made a welcome statement, saying that fish from outside the exclusion zone were as good as ever. Safeways would continue to buy. The local quality control company announced the strictest testing programme in the world to ensure that nothing contaminated left the islands. But several fish farms were now running dangerously near their credit limits at the banks.

The official estimate of the land affected by the oily spray rose to 20 square miles. More than ten per cent of Shetland's agricultural holdings now had to move their sheep off contaminated pasture, and fast. They had nowhere to put them. Offers of help poured in from crofters and farmers in unaffected districts. Even Aberdeenshire farms offered to look after the Dunrossness sheep until the crisis was over. Shetland was grateful but reluctant to accept – the islands were certified free from a sheep disease common on the Scottish mainland. Crofters feared that their flocks could return from the south carrying it.

The Sabbath it might be, but the Joint Response Committee and the council were as busy as ever. Green announced that the council had hired Pennington's, a firm of London lawyers who specialised in marine and environmental damage cases, to negotiate details of an immediate payment

*Reassuring the supermarkets: testing for traces of oil in water samples from the polluted zone*
(Photo: Tom Kidd)

Opposite:
*'Fair Isle: south-westerly Severe Gale Nine to Violent Storm Eleven, occasionally Hurricane Force Twelve . . .' A freak wave soaks two photographers trying for a different view of the wreck (Tom Kidd on left)*
(Photo: Mike Forster, *Daily Mail*)

of £200,000 offered by Asssuranceforeningen Skuld. Green, hoping to keep the insurance men in Shetland with their chequebooks, said he was 'grateful' to them for the offer. The word jarred on local ears but the council's Chief Executive could not afford to antagonise Skuld. If the atmosphere turned nasty, they could easily catch the next plane out and say they would see him in court. That would take years. It had taken 14 years in court to settle the Bretons' claims against *Amoco Cadiz*.

The weather forecast for sea area Fair Isle on Sunday night would have been a news story in itself, even without an oil spill: 'South-westerly Severe Gale Nine to Violent Storm 11, occasionally Hurricane Force 12 for a time; wintry showers. . .' The lowest of lows was tracking 250 miles north-west of Shetland. The vicious south-east corner of the depression would hit the islands around midnight.

Dan Lawn, an Alaskan veteran of the *Exxon Valdez* disaster, looked into the dusk over Garth's Wick and said: 'We'll be damn lucky if she lasts the night.'

Soon after midnight the great storm shrieked in from the Atlantic. Blizzards moving at 110mph howled over the remains of the *Braer*, lit by the fitful glare of sheet lightning. Air, water, snow and oil were one, in a jetstream of greyish fog. Few dared go outside to watch. It was like standing in the firing line of a water-cannon. Car doors ripped off. Large vehicles blew off the roads. Power and phone lines were torn away. Even stone-built houses were creaking and shaking. Double-glazed windows warped in the force of a wind which blasted the paint from their frames.

At the Lerwick Coastguard station, lightning hit the main radio aerial, and then hit it again. The lights went out. Computer consoles flashed and went up in smoke. All the communication equipment was fused and most of it badly damaged. Reduced to hand-held portable radios, the duty officers had to ask Pentland Coastguards in Orkney to take over their round-the-clock radio watch while they tried to clear up the mess.

Not many slept well in Shetland that night. Islanders lay listening to the roaring violence of the storm, dreading what the helicopters would find in Garth's Wick at daybreak. This was the blackest night yet. It looked and sounded very like the end of the world for the islands at the bitter end of Britain.

# PETER POLAND, VOLUNTEER AT THE WILDLIFE RESCUE CENTRE

THE car was packed up and ready to go before they knew if the tanker had hit the rocks. Within a few hours Peter Poland and his friend Charlie were on their way to Shetland from Cornwall.

(Photo: Tom Kidd)

'I am not really a travelling person,' Peter confessed. 'I'd never been further north than York before, but Charlie had been here and was in love with the place. He was in tears when he heard the tanker had hit and was spilling oil.

'We drove overnight to Aberdeen, caught the ferry and by 8am on the Thursday we were in Shetland. I didn't have a clue where I was, but we just followed the road south to Sumburgh.'

Like many others, Peter, an unemployed graphic artist, had simply wanted to come and help. He had no idea what he could do, but was sure all hands would be put to use.

'We arrived and found lots of TV crews and photographers running around taking photos of people trying to catch birds on the beach and they weren't helping . . .' He shook his head, aghast at the uncaring attitude. 'There was this little oiled duck that I tried to get.'

He never caught it but he introduced himself to one of the volunteers and offered his assistance. 'He took us back to the hut at Boddam, kitted us out with oilskins and wellies and we were sent back out on the beaches.'

Peter knew very little about seabirds before he started. They were all 'seagulls'. He quickly learned to love them, especially the Shag 'with its immense feet'. That breed was the worst hit by the oil, with hundreds picked up dead. Gathering up the live ones, though, made it all worth while.

'To pick up a bird and tuck it under your arm and know that you might be able to save its life is a wonderful feeling. I was cuddling one Shag when it bit me.' He pointed out the small scar below his nose. 'It serves me right for not putting it straight in a bag.'

His enthusiasm was boundless, giving him a real zest for work, a feeling of doing something worthwhile at last. Being unemployed for more than a year and a half had left him depressed and with little self-esteem.

'This is probably one of the best things I have ever done,' he said. 'If I'd been at home and life was going on as usual I wouldn't have done a lot — maybe a bit of painting or listening to music . . . I certainly wouldn't have been walking.

'I suspect when I am home I will go out for a walk, sit on a rock by the sea and just bawl my eyes out.'

Peter's Cornwall home knows what it's like to face an oil spill. The tanker *Torrey Canyon* ran aground there in 1967. Some beaches were still oiled below the surface, he said.

He had a double reason for feeling angry about Shetland's oilspill. 'That tanker was there because it cost less. I hope the insurers have to pay the earth because that's what they've spoiled.'

He lit up a cigarette and sighed. 'The oil is there somewhere. I don't believe it when they say it's all over. At the end of the day 1,500 birds are still dead because of some fool.'

He had no doubt what the problem was: 'Oil is the root of all economics and economics is the root of all evil.'

In his three weeks on the islands, he met many people and felt the warmth of peat fires and whisky. He almost couldn't believe the kindness people showed him in the face of so many problems. He was housed, he was fed and he was welcomed. Of course, not everyone measured up . . .

Out scouring one particularly badly oiled beach on Burra Isle, he discovered a headless seal at the edge of the water. It didn't look as if it had been oiled, but he wanted to pull it up the beach and tag it for other team members to pick up.

Two men in clean oilskins wandered down the beach towards him. He enlisted one man's help in dragging the beast out of the sea. When the task was completed the man, who turned out to be from the Scottish Office, asked how long the seal would be left lying there. Not long, Peter told him. That was obviously not good enough.

'Don't you think it's a public health hazard?' the man asked with concern.

'I blew my top at him. I've never heard anybody say something so stupid. The beach was filthy with oil. "Have a look around," I said, "I don't think many people will be coming down here to sunbathe."'

Now his work was done. The final toll on the bird colonies will not be known for months, but fewer and fewer oiled carcasses or sick birds were being found.

'I really don't want to leave this place. I love it here and the people are fantastic. There's nowhere else like it.'

He paused and added sadly: 'I do have one regret — I'd love to have known what it was like before the *Braer* hit those rocks.'

# Chapter Six

# MOTHER NATURE'S MIRACLE

*George Sutherland said he'd just heard from the salvors that there was next to nothing left on board. Everybody felt hopeless and sad.*

MALCOLM GREEN, QUOTED IN *The Shetland Times*, 15 JANUARY 1993

The lightning picked a bad time to hit the Shetland Coastguards. They were very busy again. Another tanker was in trouble off the Fair Isle. At 1.23am on Monday, 11 January, they picked up a radio message from the captain of the 5,194-tonne Russian ship *Aleiska*. He was six miles south of Fair Isle, four miles off the mid-channel route recommended by the International Maritime Organisation's unenforceable guidelines. The ship was carrying 4,664 tonnes of jet fuel from Murmansk to Limerick.

The Russian captain wanted advice. He was making no progress against the south-westerly hurricane. Where could he shelter? The Coastguards suggested he make for Sinclair's Bay, on the east side of Caithness, or Winwick Bay, off South Ronaldsay, Orkney. But both were too far away, he said.

The *Aleiska* survived the storm and eventually found shelter in the lee of the Orkney island of Sanday. The Coastguards did not hear from the captain again after 6.37am. They had to take his word for it when he gave them his position. They still had no radar. All they could do was file a report to London for an official complaint to the Russian Embassy.

Coastguard headquarters could not see Monday's other rogue tanker either, but the people of Fair Isle could. That snowy morning the little island looked from the air like an iced Christmas cake, trailing a cloud of spume several hundred feet high and two miles long. At 10.15am at least eight of the Fair Islanders watched a large tanker with a red hull and a black smokestack steaming eastwards before the gale, through the south Fair Isle Channel between the island and North Ronaldsay in Orkney. Like the *Aleiska*, she was only six miles offshore.

Dave Wheeler, who monitors the Fair Isle weather for the Meteorological Office, said: 'It's absolutely amazing that they can be doing this when we've got a wreck on Shetland. There was a gale blowing, with gusts to storm

101

force, frequent heavy snow showers and visibility down to 600 yards at times. She had a fair turn of speed on and was shipping a lot of water over the bows, even though the wind was astern of her.'

Which meant that, like the *Braer*, the mystery tanker would not have been able to use her anchors if she had broken down.

Angus Hutchison, Principal Lightkeeper at the Fair Isle South lighthouse, said: 'Our reaction was just disbelief. In the weather we had this morning, if that thing had broken down she would only be an hour and a half off the beach.'

'That thing' was in ballast. Her tanks had oily water in them, not crude oil. But there was plenty of tarry muck in her slop tank and she would have plenty of heavy fuel oil and diesel on board.

We never found out the name of the ship, because she kept going east. She missed Fair Isle and escaped the notoriety of being the first tanker to desecrate a National Trust for Scotland property and a major bird observatory. In the continuing absence of action by the Government to monitor the Fair Isle Channel, islanders decided to do it themselves. An informal vigil was organised. They planned to report any more rogue tankers they saw.

The light was well up now. There were even glimpses of the sun between the snow showers. Fitful Head was occasionally visible from Fair Isle. Beneath the great headland, the storm had been too much for the *Braer*. As television viewers had watched her being battered to death during six days and nights, she had changed from being a novel object of horror into a familiar old lady, bravely fighting her last battle. Now she was going. The bows looked as if they were breaking adrift, as well as the stern. Only the bridge, the smokestack, the twin masts amidships and the bows were visible as huge seas tore across her decks. The masts were lurching from side to side, tearing up the plating of the deck.

The helicopter pilots could see at once that there was more oil in the water. Somehow it looked more menacing this morning, the brown stain in the sea contrasting with the snow on the shore.

There were hopes of salvage even now. Captain George Sutherland told reporters in the morning: 'There is no evidence to suggest that she is breaking up.' Soon after lunch, Geert Koffeman reported that most of the cargo tanks were open to the sea. The inspection hatches on deck, secured by heavy bolts, had been blown off by the pressure inside the ship. 'We can never be sure that we will not recover any oil,' he said, optimistic as ever. 'It's hard to say what exactly will happen next. The forecast is for hurricane winds and she may face more damage.' The salvage barge had been held up again by the weather and was not expected until Wednesday.

By mid-afternoon all hope disappeared. In the House of Commons at 3.30pm, Transport Secretary John MacGregor rose to make a statement on the *Braer* disaster: 'I regret to say that, in the past few minutes, I have heard that, owing to today's extreme weather conditions, very large additional quantities of oil are now escaping from the ship . . .'

That brown mist was blowing ashore again. The 'sniffer' instruments still showed that it was not dangerous. The scientists were now measuring the droplets of oil as well. There was no need to tell the Dunrossness head teacher, Audrey Mullay, to keep her pupils indoors. They were at home. Once again, all of Shetland's schools were closed because of the weather.

By evening the experts estimated that another 30,000 tonnes of oil had reached the sea, with perhaps as much as 20,000 tonnes still on board. The *Braer* had broken into three pieces.

Jim Wallace MP was not in the House of Commons to hear MacGregor's statement. His flight from Shetland was delayed by the storm which was bringing havoc throughout Scotland, closing roads and airports and making hundreds homeless.

MacGregor again paid tribute to the extraordinary efforts of the emergency team in Shetland; he praised the men who had risked their lives to save the *Braer*'s crew and those who had done the same to try to save Shetland in that last-minute bid to get a towline aboard; and he promised to publish the Marine Accidents Investigations Branch report 'in full'. Everyone who wished to give evidence would be allowed to do so. He did not specifically say he would publish all the evidence upon which the report would be based.

'The Government strongly upholds the polluter-pays principle,' he assured the crowded House. He said compensation would be available. He did not say that the first instalment of cash from the Government would be made available to claimants only through the *Braer* claims office in Lerwick. That would cause anger and consternation, until the insurers agreed to allow people to reserve their rights at law and not sign them away for an interim payment.

MacGregor firmly resisted calls for unilateral action to protect the British coast although, sensing the mood among MPs, he did not rule it out. They had to work through the International Maritime Organisation and the European Community, he said. He referred to recent discussion in Europe on 'a new directive on ships carrying dangerous goods and reporting procedures'. This would affect oil tankers, and had been under discussion already for about three years: 'We gave priority to getting the directive through and I am glad to say we got it through.'

Not soon enough to require the *Braer* to report her intended course, however, nor to have her movements monitored from the shore.

It was nearly five o'clock before Jim Wallace reached the House of Commons, exhausted and travel-weary. He was in time to hear Ian Lang, the Scottish Secretary, announcing his department's response to the disaster. It amounted to money and monitoring; money for interim compensation and the wildlife rescue efforts; more money on the way from the European Community as disaster aid; and monitoring of just about everything – human health, environmental damage, economic effects; the impression was given that no effort would be spared now that the disaster Wallace had predicted for so long had actually taken place. The Scottish Office being the Scottish Office, there would be a mysterious delay before the money for scientific monitoring studies became available.

Wallace did not launch the withering attack on the Government that many MPs had anticipated. Perhaps he was too tired or, more likely, he felt this was a time to concentrate on his constituents' immediate needs rather than making party political points about ministers' failure to guard the coast. In any case, Wallace does not have the political killer instinct. That is one reason why he keeps being re-elected in Orkney and Shetland, where fiery oratory is not generally favoured. He confined himself to a brief question about Lang's bridging fund, welcomed the Government action so far and asked Lang to express his confidence in Shetland seafood harvested from outside the exclusion zone. He got the replies he wanted. He had arrived too late to hear most of the very handsome tributes, from all sides of the House, to his tireless efforts on behalf of his constituency. The acclaim was deserved and gratifying but what he wanted most was some sleep.

Later he would remark, in his droll way, that perhaps other MPs now realised that it was not exactly a rural idyll, representing Orkney and Shetland. Apart from the punishing routine of weekly commuting on a round trip of over a thousand miles, the constituency was demanding in other ways. Wallace, his wife Rosie and their young family had just endured a formidable year because of the extra work for the MP in connection with an inquiry into notorious (and unproven) allegations made against some of his Orcadian constituents concerning ritual child sex abuse. The very last thing the Wallaces needed during the Christmas and New Year holidays had been a tanker disaster in the other half of the constituency.

At the emergency control room in Sumburgh staff watched the Commons debate on TV. There was not a lot else to do, now that all their efforts, so publicly applauded by the Government and MPs of all parties, had been in vain. The best organised, best equipped oil spill containment and clean-up operation ever put together at a major tanker wreck had been helpless because they had never managed to put the full plan into action. It was not their fault. It was the weather's fault. But that did not make them feel any better. For Malcolm Green and everyone else involved, Monday night was the lowest point in that frenetic, first week of the disaster.

The wind blew on and on, gusting to 100mph. Monday night was as bad as Sunday. A despairing gloom settled over the islanders as they waited for the worst, watching the TV bulletins in horrified fascination.

'She's gone!' The word spread quickly at breakfast time on Tuesday, New Year's Day, Old Style. Local radio news which, in a community the size of Shetland, exists mainly to confirm or deny rumours everyone has heard already, confirmed it.

Overnight, most of the *Braer* had sunk out of sight. The bows and stern were sheared off from the cargo tanks in the mid section. Ironically, the bow section was still partly above the waves, with the anchors that were never used pointing to the sky. The top of the smokestack was still visible, and the bridge – sitting on top of the main accommodation block, which had come loose from the deck. All the oil was in the sea; cargo, fuel oil, diesel, lubricating oil, tarry slops – the lot.

Captain Sutherland, succeeding as ever in keeping his emotions and his facts in separate compartments, simply told the morning press conference: 'She is now a total loss.'

Underwater, the hulk was still recognisable as a ship, but not for long. When salvage divers entered the water a week later they would find total disintegration, with huge pieces of steel scattered over the seabed. In the final collapse, the massive cylinder head of the main engine would be sheared off by the weight of the superstructure toppling into the engine room. The cylinder head had been secured by steel bolts the size of a man's arm. The extraordinary energy of the sea had snapped them like twigs, according to the salvage master.

Councillors were officially informed of the *Braer*'s end at their meeting in Lerwick Town Hall that morning. The Chief Executive told them: 'The effect on the community will be devastating in all sorts of ways that aren't expected.'

He reminded the councillors about the planned marine environment conference. Before the wreck, some of them had vigorously opposed a budget of up to £500,000 of public money for what they saw as a vainglorious publicity stunt: 'The agenda has never been more important than it is now,'

*'A constructive total loss'. Fitful Head, the legendary lair of Sir Walter Scott's witch, Norna, in* The Pirate, *glowers over the break-up of the* Braer
(Photo: Tom Kidd)

105

Green said. 'The Convener wrote to the Prime Minister before Christmas and there has been no reply.'

The mood in the council chamber, and everywhere else in Shetland, was strange. There had been doom and gloom for so long now that the awful news from Sumburgh brought something very like a sigh of relief. At least they knew the worst now. The mood manifested itself in a new determination to overcome the disaster.

A flurry of press releases landed on the newsdesks. There was confirmation of the £200,000 advance payment from the insurers, £250,000 from the European Community and a well-substantiated rumour that Ian Lang's bridging fund would start off with £1 million. That should be enough to meet immediate needs, unless the salmon farmers needed a lot of money very quickly – which they would.

Shetland Islands Tourism launched 'Operation Aurora' – a £500,000 international media campaign to fight back against the bad publicity. Tourism director Maurice Mullay knew he would have to be quick. After filming the last pictures of the *Braer*'s wallowing bows, the TV crews were crating up their satellite dishes and moving out, off to the next disaster, wherever it might be. Mullay had been on the beaches to check for himself. He faxed his customers, the tour operators and travel agents, telling them that the pollution was nothing like as bad as feared and it looked as if most of Shetland would be spared. He was ridiculed behind his back for being overly optimistic. Events would prove him right.

The fishermen and salmon farmers, equally determined to protect their image, had invited the media to the first Lerwick fish auction of the year and then laid on a splendid seafood banquet for them at the North Atlantic Fisheries College in Scalloway. The food was delicious and went down well, in every sense. The story made a useful new angle for reporters whose cynical old news editors were becoming tired of copy about anguished Dunrossness crofters and lobster fishermen. Perhaps to the regret of some news editors, none of their reporters was poisoned by tainted fish. The fish was perfect. These city dwellers had never tasted fish so fresh. If anyone became unwell, it was probably due to the liquid refreshments which followed.

Malcolm Green and Convener Edward Thomason were thinking positively, too. Both were keen amateur fiddle players with a love of traditional Shetland music. The music, not the money, had been what first brought Green to Shetland from a job in Manchester. They were both close friends of Aly Bain, the legendary Lerwick fiddler who had become Shetland's musical ambassador to the world. As the last of the oil was trickling out of the *Braer*, Green, Thomason and Bain laid plans for a series of 'Concerts for the Sea'. Bain would front the big-name events, to be held in cities around Britain, Canada and the United States.

The top two in the Town Hall saw the concerts as a way of raising consciousness as well as money. The cash would be used to fund a new Marine Environment Foundation, based in Shetland and making available grants for research and publicity projects to protect the global ocean from abuse by humans. The emphasis would be on getting the message through to younger people. Just as the fishermen had found that the way to journalists' hearts was through their stomachs, Thomason hoped the way to the youngsters' hearts would be through the music.

In the past decade Thomason's council had put a lot of money into saving the islands' traditional music from extinction – funding musicology projects and fiddle teaching in schools. The result had been a spectacular crop of young musicians, many of whom had taken traditional styles and mixed them with rock, country and western and jazz. The islands' annual Folk Festival and Fiddle and Accordion Festival were internationally famous – and major earners for the local tourist industry.

There were those who questioned the need to set up yet another environmental pressure group when the world already had a surplus of them. But this was hardly the time to say so in public. And few would argue with the idea behind the project – that if national governments had failed to protect the environment then it was up to local government to take a lead. Shetland Islands Council was already heavily involved in several organisations where local authorities from all over Europe campaigned against pollution. In the battle to stop nuclear reprocessing at Dounreay on the north coast of Scotland, the council had taken a leading political and financial role.

Thinking positively kept people's minds off the looming catastrophe. Most Shetlanders still had a mental picture of oil spreading all around the islands and ruining everything. There was certainly enough oil now to create an *Exxon Valdez* scenario, and worse, if the stuff was floating on the surface. But the body count on the beaches had still only reached 691 dead birds, two dead seals and two dead otters. That figure could only rise as the oil spread. The islands passed another night of anxious dread.

Not so long ago, a visit to Shetland by members of the British Royal family would have made the front page of the local newspaper. A report on the trip to Shetland by the Duke of Edinburgh and his son, Prince Charles, on Wednesday, 13 January, was relegated to page 12 of *The Shetland Times* that week (although it did make the front page of the staunchly loyal *Press & Journal*, published in Aberdeen).

There were good reasons for this editorial decision. It reflected a popular sentiment against monarchy. The Royal family had been going through a bad year. Appalling publicity about their private lives, rows about the cost of the Royals to the public purse (their yacht consumed £9 million a year for an average 37 days' use, for example) and in particular the satirical TV puppet show *Spitting Image* had so reduced the Royals' standing in the public eye that even Conservatives were talking about a republican system of government.

Prince Charles, well known and sometimes lampooned for his outspoken comments on the environment, had taken a keen interest in the spill. His father, although a keen participant in various bloodsports, had for decades been a major figurehead in international efforts to preserve rare wildlife.

All the popular press wanted to discuss with Prince Charles in Shetland was the publication, the day before, of a tape-recording transcript, in which

*Prince Charles (and minder) in Dunrossness to commiserate with oiled crofters, 13 January 1993*
(Photo: Tom Kidd)

he and one Camilla Parker-Bowles had allegedly exchanged intimate and saucy endearments over a mobile telephone in 1989. The press thought their interest was legitimate but the alleged extra-marital relationship had not been. As the future head of state, the domestic arrangements of the heir to the throne, recently separated from his wife, were fair game. The Prince glared at Brian McCartney, the Glasgow *Daily Record* reporter when, on the clifftop overlooking the wreck, he asked his future king whether the tapes of the conversation were genuine. There was no reply.

The Prince seemed grateful to escape from the tabloid pack asking about his troubles and talk to crofters, farmers and fish processors about theirs. He was very sympathetic. He said he was surprised how bad the land pollution was. He had oily mud all over his expensive shoes to prove it. Everyone else wore wellies. Offered a glass of orange juice at the Dunrossness Boating Club, he said he would rather have a whisky. He got it and promised to come back next year, when things would be better, he was sure. Those locals who like that sort of thing queued up to shake his hand, smile and exchange pleasantries. Then off the regal pair went, in a publicly funded aircraft of the Queen's Flight (which, unlike British Airways, had not yet been privatised by the Government).

BBC Radio Shetland also paid surprisingly little attention to the Royal visit. The truth was that the Royals were irrelevant, although some believed they had helped morale. There were much more important things to think about this morning.

'Where's all the oil?' asked one of the visiting experts when he landed in a surveillance chopper. 'Where is it? Show me the 20,000 tonnes. I just don't see that amount on the water.' It was an interesting question. The expected massive new oil slick was just not there. The sea had done with the second wave of oil just what it did with the first – mixed it with the sea itself. Even better, the wind was still, quite incredibly, blowing from the south-west. And it would do so for another week, to finish the job. Normally, depressions passing over the islands lead to sudden changes in the speed and direction of the wind every 12 hours or so. That was why everyone had feared that the slicks would soon be all around Shetland.

It was now clear that the pollution, bad as it was, was trapped in the triangle of sea between Sumburgh Head and the western edge of the Mainland of Shetland. The tide would carry it further, underwater, but a quick calculation showed that each cubic mile of sea contained over a billion US gallons of water (1,101,117,143,000 gallons, to be exact). This meant that the entire 24.6 million US gallons of oil in the *Braer*, mixed with just one cubic mile of ocean, would be diluted 44,761 times; that would be just 22 parts of oil per million parts of seawater. It was a concentration high enough to create a thin oil slick, but there were a lot of cubic miles of sea around Shetland to dilute it still further. In the fisheries exclusion zone alone, just five per cent of the Shetland fishing grounds, there were something like 18 cubic miles of water. That would dilute the oil over 800,000 times, to just over one part per million. The Sullom Voe terminal, after all, was legally

*Seaweed is normal winter fodder for hardy Shetland sheep. Hundreds had to be moved away from oiled shoreline and pasture*
(Photo: Tom Kidd)

allowed to discharge oil in water at up to 15 parts per million, although usually it managed as low as four. As that council official had said, 84,500 tonnes of oil was 'bugger all in the Atlantic Ocean'.

The problem was that the dispersed oil was not evenly distributed at one part per million. Wind, tides and geography had funnelled it into the narrow coastal strip between Sumburgh and Scalloway, where the sea had less room to dilute it. And there the damage would be concentrated.

Already the beige-coloured surf around Sumburgh was turning white again. 'We seem to have got away with it, so far,' Malcolm Green said. 'Shetland is fortunate. If the storm had been followed by calm weather, and if it had been heavy crude, we'd have been in a mess.'

The late afternoon surveys reported that the slicks were receding. Green was not the only one who found it hard to believe that the oil had just 'disappeared'. There would be worrying, sampling and scientific monitoring for months afterwards, trying to establish just how many parts per million remained.

The *Braer* was still a disaster for Dunrossness, and for the salmon farmers and fishermen around Burra Isle and Scalloway. The economic fallout would be a very serious problem for the whole of Shetland. The ecological effects

*A suitcase of personal possessions, belonging to a crewman from the* Braer, *washes ashore in the muck*
(Photo: Tom Kidd)

were completely unknown and probably unknowable. They might yet be serious. The bottom of the food chain had, after all, been assaulted. But the 'Shetland Disaster' had not turned into the Shetland catastrophe after all.

Mother Nature had helped to spill the oil. Now she was clearing it away. The miracle that the evangelical Christians and many others had prayed for had come to pass.

Shetlanders that night had confusing emotions: all were relieved; some were angry; some felt humble; and most felt determined. There was anger because each day brought new revelations which suggested that the wreck had been totally avoidable. Humility was appropriate because of the manifest inability of humans to stop the tide of oil, on and in the sea. And people were fiercely determined to do everything possible to make sure that nothing like this ever happened again, anywhere. If Shetland's disaster produced some action on tanker safety, then all the suffering might yet have some purpose, divine or otherwise.

Among some of the oil spill experts there was another kind of relief. They had been spared the public rows that would inevitably have followed if the weather *had* allowed them to get all that expensive kit in the water. Those who had studied the *Exxon Valdez* knew that the best oil spill containment and recovery equipment in the world does not work very well, even in ideal conditions. People would have expected them to clean it all up and would have asked very rude questions if they had failed, just as Exxon's three thousand million dollar, three-year clean-up had failed in Alaska.

On Wednesday afternoon, for the first time since the spill, Captain George Sutherland left work punctually and drove north to his home in Brae, in time for tea.

# JIM HARPER, OWNER OF THE MEADOWVALE HOTEL, SUMBURGH

THE LIGHTS of a helicopter appeared over the horizon of a field and buzzed over the Meadowvale Hotel before heading for the airport.

Inside, owner Jim Harper was finally relaxing after a freak boom in business. In common with every hotel and B&B within a rented car drive of Sumburgh, the place had been packed for almost two weeks.

His phone began to ring non-stop, hours before the tanker ran aground. Journalists wanting information. Journalists wanting accommodation. The Government marine pollution control team got there first, though, and booked the hotel out.

Jim (aged 74) and his 76-year-old wife Maggie would hardly expect so many guests in the peak of the summer season, let alone a bleak and windy January. They had to call in part-time help for some of the meals, but otherwise they coped alone.

Now Jim seemed unperturbed as he leaned back thoughtfully in his armchair. His life wouldn't change dramatically because of it, he said. A few less visitors perhaps . . .

Having lived by the airport for 30 years, Jim and Maggie are used to trouble. 'We've had a few accidents here . . . Dan Air crashed just at the end of the runway there,' Jim said, with a nod to the airport. 'Then there was the Chinook, with all that loss of life.

'This tanker created far more disturbance than those occasions when there were people killed. On this occasion there was no loss of life. We shouldn't forget that. It is hard to imagine that in that severe weather there were no accidents and no loss of life.

'But still the numbers of people that flocked into these islands . . . and there was nothing for them to see. But they had to get a story, they had to get something in the press.'

His thoughts on the media are not altogether kindly, although he remembers with pride how the first ever satellite transmission from the isles was made by ITN outside his hotel after the Chinook crashed. He first heard the tanker was in trouble on the radio. But it was obvious, to him, that the reporter didn't have much idea what was going on.

From the hotel he watched the tanker stumble across Quendale Bay, setting the facts straight with a live commentary to one radio station. Then it hit Garth's Ness. And life changed a bit.

'How could you feel? With the gales you got salt spray lashing across the island. Add to that crude oil and detergents. The waves hit the rocks and sprayed up the cliffs, where the wind caught it and carried it out.

'Whatever happens now, it was a disaster then and it will affect this end of the island, there's no question of that. The fish, the land, maybe the people. No-one knows what the long-term effects will be. Maybe there will be none.'

Jim looked more like a crofter than a hotelier, in his denim dungarees, body warmer and trainers. Unlike the crofters, though, he was able to keep inside when the poisonous oily air rushed across the land. He never bothered going for the health checks.

'I didn't think it would affect me,' he said, brushing off the question almost with indignation. 'I don't feel any different now than I did before.'

Maggie came in with a tray of coffee and biscuits and set them down with a smile, before returning to the kitchen. Soon after came the sound of her scrubbing the floor. She and her husband met in her home town of Fraserburgh, where he was a maintenance worker in a factory. Jim was born and brought up in the Ness so his return was probably inevitable.

For years after he came home he was a builder, before turning to the tourist trade. What will happen to that trade now, he cannot say.

'There are people now all over the world with more knowledge of Shetland, it was so much on the telly and the radio and in the press. But how that affects people in time to come is debatable.

'We don't know how people feel in Germany, Italy or Holland or the South of England . . . I would expect a drop in visitors to my hotel this year.

'The main reason people came to Shetland was because it wasn't polluted and not too commercialised. Most of it is still practically as it was before oil, and very few people come to Shetland to see Sullom Voe terminal.'

Visitors loved the contrast from other places, he said. 'It's a big, treeless island. If you get to the top of a cliff, there's nothing to stop you seeing 20 miles.

'If you go to the North of Scotland you can't see anything for trees. Unless you climb to the top of a mountain, and that's not always easy.

'If the tourists stay away because of the *Braer*, it's going to affect lots of people, not just the hotels.'

Money, he decided, was going to cause the big problems now.

'Insurance claims are going to be a lot of hassle. The people who have anything to do with the oil seem to be highly qualified. It's going to be hard for the natives to fight them.

'We're going to end up with a lot of people making a lot of money, and others who will make nothing. There are always problems when there's money involved.'

*Chapter Seven*

# GETTING IN ON THE ACT

*Can it possibly be true that the wireless operator on the* Braer *had an imperfect command of the English language?*

TAM DALYELL MP, HOUSE OF COMMONS, 11 JANUARY 1993

*Should we not ask ourselves who these flags are convenient for? They are surely not convenient for the Shetland islanders.*

ROBERT WAREING MP, HOUSE OF COMMONS, 11 JANUARY 1993

There is a convention in the House of Commons that an honourable Member does not ask the Government questions about matters concerning the constituency of another honourable Member. Strictly speaking, the wreck of the *Braer* was the business of the honourable Member for Orkney and Shetland, Mr James Wallace, Leader of the Scottish Liberal Democrat Party, and no-one else.

Wallace had plenty of questions. So did a lot of others. And on the afternoon of Wednesday, 11 January, the 'Shet-lagged' MP was happy to let them do the brawling for him, even after he arrived in the debating chamber. MPs queued up to ask questions, for the wreck had raised matters of national and international importance which had been on the back-burner for far too long. Everyone wanted in on the act. Politicians who had never heard of Shetland instantly became experts on the place, in their hurry to be wise after the dreadful events in 'the Shetlands' (as even the *Hansard* reporters described it).

Joan Whalley MP, Labour's spokeswoman on shipping, had been quick off the mark. Her hastily arranged visit to Shetland, soon after the wreck, had not achieved much but at least she had returned to 'the Londons' with enough information to brief her boss, Opposition Transport spokesman John Prescott MP, an altogether more formidable political animal. Whalley also managed to appear on TV from a Sumburgh beach, looking windswept and sounding genuinely distressed.

Prescott would arrive in Shetland eight days after the wreck, the day when Mother Nature's 'miracle' became apparent. Like Jim Wallace, Prescott had

*Jim Wallace, MP for Orkney and Shetland, at a Sumburgh Press Conference*
(Photo: Tom Kidd)

been wise before the event. As a former seafarer and National Union of Seamen organiser, the member for Hull East, knew his stuff. He was one of the few Labour MPs who knew anything at all about ships and the sea. There were many more knowledgeable nautical chaps on the Tory benches. They had yachts, or friends who did.

Long before maritime safety became a matter of even passing interest to governments of either party, Prescott was making abrasive, provocative, well-informed speeches about the decline of the British Merchant Navy, the collapse of crew training standards, the excessive pressure on master mariners, the punishing hours of overtime as shipowners cut back on wage bills and the growing scandal of ships flying 'flags of convenience'. In all the big maritime disasters, from the capsize of the *Herald of Free Enterprise* in Zeebrugge Harbour to the sinking of the trawler *Antares* by a Royal Navy submarine in the Firth of Clyde, Prescott had waded in with his steel toe-capped seaboots, kicking hell out of whichever hapless Tory happened to be in charge of shipping (one of the very lowest rungs on the ladder of ministerial promotion).

Prescott inspired fear and some loathing even in his own party. When the need arose, and sometimes when it did not, he could be suitably brutal. The Earl of Caithness, whose turn it was to be shipping minister when the *Braer* went aground, was quickly dismissed as an upper-class twit 'Bertie Wooster', Prescott called him, and thereafter completely ignored the hereditary peer whose namesake county overlooked the Pentland Firth. Prescott's target was the earl's boss, the elected politician John MacGregor, Secretary of State for Transport.

On 11 January, two days before he went to Sumburgh, Prescott laid into MacGregor in style. Jim Wallace was still making his weary way into central London from Heathrow after his delayed flight through snowbound Aberdeen. Prescott had the field to himself in the first debate on the *Braer*.

The House would welcome the fact, 'albeit with some suspicion', he leered, that Liberia, whose capital, Monrovia, was the *Braer*'s registered home port, had promised to hold an inquiry. Would the Secretary of State see to it that the Liberian inquiry was held under a British judge? It had been done before. He would not. Round One to the Hull Heavy-weight.

Did he agree that it was unacceptable for Britain to carry all the costs of the pollution and the accident investigation, while Liberia paid nothing? Did he accept that some countries 'prostituting their flags for a few pieces of silver' let shipowners run 'second-rate ships with second-rate crews'? Mr MacGregor thought crew standards would be a matter for the inquiry. Round Two to the HHW.

The 'flags of inconvenience', as a Liverpool Labour MP, Robert Wareing, called them, lost three or four times as many ships as 'traditional maritime countries', Prescott continued. The loss of 24 tankers in two years had killed 300 seafarers. There was less publicity for that than for pollution. Did blood wash away quicker than oil? The boot was in. MacGregor squirmed. Or maybe he was looking for his briefing notes. Round Three to the HHW.

Should those who sold their flags for short-term gain not pay the long-term costs of their irresponsibility out of their 'immoral earnings'? Did the Secretary of State accept that the loss of more than a thousand ships from the British register had contributed to these 'terrible tragedies'? Actually, Mac-Gregor ventured, 'the Liberian loss ratio is only half the world average' and Liberian inquiries were quite thorough. That round was a draw.

Why was there still no European Convention laying down standards and enforcing them on all ships entering British waters? Why were ships allowed to take dangerous routes to save money? Why was there still pressure on captains from their owners not to take tugs when they needed them?

There was more in the same vein. MacGregor repeatedly had to retreat into: 'That is for the inquiry to determine.' It was a virtuoso performance, with two mistakes: Prescott talked about 'the Shetlands'; and he made the unforgivable gaffe of saying, 'The rest of Britain will be affected by the pollution once it works its way through the food chain.' He meant that the North Sea was polluted enough already without having another 84,500 tonnes of oil poured into it. But his remark would be interpreted as inferring that contaminated fish from Shetland would find its way on to the fish-monger's slab. This would not go down well in Lerwick, where the fish-mongers and others had already taken stringent measures to avoid just that. But at least Prescott knew a haddock from a whiting. The big bruiser from the lower decks had won the match on points.

He made another point which would prove correct: '. . .the owners of the *Braer* will receive more compensation for the ship than it is worth on the open market.' He could have said 'scrap market'.

Local politicians in Shetland were also having their say. Councillor Leonard Groat, the Labour representative for Lerwick North, was a member of Lerwick Harbour Trust. He knew his boats. He knew that Lerwick Harbour Trust had, the previous year, spent about half a million pounds on a new, computerised radar system which, if the Government had installed one to cover the Fair Isle Channel, could have detected that the *Braer* was in trouble.

The day after the Commons debate, Groat demanded immediate action from the Government to stop the next *Braer* disaster: 'We don't need to wait for the results of the inquiries . . . to know that it could have been stopped if there had been an early warning radar to raise the alarm,' he said. 'A radar could be there by the weekend. The Royal Navy can send a ship to guard the channel until permanent radar stations are set up on the shore. If the Government act now they can stop the next one. As the incidents with two rogue tankers in the Fair Isle Channel on Monday show, there's no time to lose. The next disaster could happen tomorrow night.'

Wallace made a similar call the next day: 'My constituents are worried and deeply afraid . . . I am asking for a naval vessel to be sent immediately to patrol the waters between Orkney and Shetland. The ship would ask any vessel which appeared to be in difficulties, or straying from the tanker lanes, to identify herself,' he said. 'This breaks no international agreements. It does not pre-judge the inquiries into the *Braer* disaster. It is a practical measure which will give some reassurance to my anxious constituents.' Wallace said he hoped for all-party agreement on this.

Prescott was happy to provide it. He arrived in Lerwick on Wednesday morning and told the press about his solution to the problem. First, the Government could extend British territorial waters from three to 12 miles, under the Continental Shelf Act. This would not require international agreement and would allow them to control what happened in the Fair Isle Channel, north and south of Fair Isle. If he got his way, nothing would happen in the channel: 'It is absolutely clear [*that*] tankers should not come through this area under any circumstances,' he said.

He believed that a radar system could be set up on Fair Isle within three months, using the technology that Groat's harbour trust had already installed at Lerwick. Prescott also demanded that a salvage tug be stationed at Scalloway on the west coast of Shetland to deal with potential incidents which could not be reached by the tugs based at Sullom Voe.

The local Labour Party appealed to islanders to write to MacGregor demanding immediate radar coverage of the Fair Isle Channel and linking the scanners to the Coastguard station at Lerwick, as Prescott had suggested. 'It could happen again – tonight!' their notice in the local paper suggested, echoing Groat's warning. That was very near the truth, as events would show.

Isobel Mitchell from Whiteness, one of the scenic areas now lightly oiled, organised a protest meeting with her friend Paul Wood, for the public 'to express their anger and grief'. A lot of folk went along, despite the appalling weather. The strictly non-party meeting launched a petition that, within a month, would gather the signatures of a quarter of the islands' adult population. Scaled up, it was as if over ten million people had signed a national petition in the UK. Unthinkable. But these were unthinkable times.

The petition demanded: the Government should immediately underwrite the total costs facing islanders and their council; enforcement of tanker exclusion zones; a full and open public inquiry; unlimited liability for tanker owners; monitoring of tankers around the British coast; and 'an end to the whole flags of convenience scandal and the implementation of a global strategy for the safe management of tankers'.

The matter of liability had been taken up in the House of Commons by Robert Adley, the Conservative MP for Christchurch, Hampshire. With his much publicised love of steam railways and hatred for his own Government's plans to privatise British Rail, Adley had recently become a popular spokesman for the 'enough-is-enough' school of old-fashioned, 'one-nation' Conservatism.

In just under a minute, Adley ambushed the Transport Secretary with a very clever and hostile question. He asked MacGregor if he agreed that it was 'tragic that it takes a tragedy before he can set up the inquiries that he has announced'? He then dug up a very smelly old corpse from the last days of the last Labour Government in the summer of 1979, when Parliament had been briefly agitated about a recent oil spill in Shetland and the urgent need to do something about stopping the next one.

*In the port control room at Lerwick Harbour Trust, staff monitor a computerised radar system which could have given advance warning of the* Braer *wreck – if the Government had installed one to watch the Fair Isle channel*
(Photo: Tom Kidd)

The corpse was that of the Merchant Shipping Bill, in which the Government of James Callaghan (a former seaman) had sought to curb some of the more flagrant malpractices of the tanker industry. The Bill had died with the election which swept Labour from power, leaving Shetland Islands Council to draw up its own tanker safety scheme with the oil companies for the relatively small area of the Shetland coast that the council controlled, around Sullom Voe.

Adley recalled that he had proposed a new clause in the Bill, which had been accepted. The clause 'would have placed liability for pollution . . . on the cargo *owner* rather than on the carrier'. The MP explained that the thinking behind it was 'to prevent oil companies from chartering rotten ships with cheap crews'.

Callaghan, later to be Lord Callaghan and President of the Advisory Committee on Pollution of the Sea, had told Adley at the time that he was 'under enormous pressure from the oil companies' to remove the offending clause in the Bill. Would MacGregor 'stand firm against pressure from the oil interests', 14 years later?

With a final twist of the knife, Adley wondered if he 'would ask the inquiry to look into the links between oil companies and detergent manufacturers', by which he meant the people who made those controversial dispersants being used in Shetland with Government sanction.

MacGregor's reply is worth noting, if only for the record. He ignored Adley's question: 'It will be for the chairman of the inquiry [*Lord Donaldson*] to look at any aspect he wishes. My Honourable Friend will have noticed that the inquiry's terms of reference have been widely drawn and that it will be open for anyone to give evidence or to make recommendations.' Full stop. Thus do Ministers of the Crown debate the great issues of the day in the Mother of Parliaments.

Back in Lerwick, the Shetland Movement Party had a few well-chosen words of its own. The party, founded to campaign for more self-government in the islands, was the largest political grouping on Shetland Islands Council. Party Secretary David Hawkins wrote to John MacGregor that his apparent refusal to install radars around the British coast was 'extremely disappointing'. The level of traffic in Orkney and Shetland waters certainly merited the best technology to monitor tankers and more than justified the cost. That, surely, was self-evident.

'The principal duty of any government is to defend its people, not just from military intrusion but from all foreseeable catastrophes,' Hawkins said. Any government which failed to do this was 'guilty of an act of gross negligence'.

More home rule was also on the agenda in neighbouring Orkney, where *The Orcadian* reported the views of Councillor Howie Firth. Firth was worried that flag of convenience tankers would now avoid the north Fair Isle Channel and start going south, either close to the island of North Ronaldsay or down to the Pentland Firth between Orkney and Scotland. He said the Government had shown itself 'quite incapable' of looking after the environment in northern waters: 'We are going to have to do it,' Firth declared. He was right about that. Then he added: 'I think we should be looking at status under international law similar to the Isle of Man and the Faroe Islands.' This was an old chestnut, lovingly preserved by Councillor Firth over many years.

More immediate and practical measures had already been taken by Captain Bob Sclater, Director of Harbours for Orkney Islands Council. As with Shetland, Orkney's council runs a tanker harbour. Theirs is at Flotta, a small island in Scapa Flow and, as at Sullom Voe, there are sophisticated radars covering the entrance to the port. It came to light that Captain Sclater's radar could actually see most of the Pentland Firth as well. It was supposed to be used to assist port controllers bringing in tankers to Flotta, but there was no reason why it should not also do the Government's work for it and monitor the much larger volume of traffic on 'innocent passage' through the Pentland Firth. And that is what Captain Sclater started doing the Friday after the *Braer* wreck.

His officers sent a radio message to every large ship seen passing through the Pentland. All the Flotta-bound tankers answered, and so did all but two of the other 15 monitored in the first few days. They seemed quite happy to tell Orkney who they were, where they were going, what they were carrying and when they would be entering and leaving the rocky bottleneck of the Firth, only three miles wide at its narrowest point.

All but two. That was the problem. It only takes one to make a *Braer* disaster. Orkney was showing the Government that the system worked but also that it would not work properly until ships were required to answer the radiotelephone and until someone could be sent out to check on them when they did not.

'It's a pretty worrying scenario,' Captain Sclater told *The Orcadian*. Other folk in Orkney thought the same. Their councillors, who had decided as an economy measure not to attend that marine conference in Lerwick at the end of March, were asked to think again. Orkney and Shetland had fought together in 1974 to win special powers to control the oil industry on their land. They still shared an MP. Now they would have to fight together to win control at sea over the oil industry's unmuzzled Rottweilers, the tanker owners. The battle would have to be taken a lot further than Edinburgh and London.

The storm of public concern was attracting interest in Europe, where the Highlands and Islands' Member of the European Parliament, the veteran Scottish Nationalist Winnie Ewing, had tabled a resolution demanding higher safety standards for tankers. With an unerring talent for grasping the wrong end of a stick, Ewing said the destruction of the islanders' environment was 'exactly what they were promised would never happen when the oil industry arrived'. This entirely missed the point that the *Braer* was nothing to do with the oil industry based in Shetland. Tankers like her were passing Shetland in the night long before the first oil was found and would be passing long after Sullom Voe had closed down.

Never mind, Ewing meant well, if her grasp of detail in such a vast constituency as the Highlands and Islands was not always what it might be. And she had a bucketful of oily rhetoric to pour over the 'woeful' head of Lord Caithness, who had described the chances of a *Braer* incident as miniscule: 'To be complacent before the event is bad enough but continued complacency afterwards is ludicrous. It will not inspire the Shetlanders with confidence that Ministers are so obviously failing to grasp the gravity of the situation.' This was vintage Winnie – a good soundbite to hold the fort while she worked out just what was going on up there and what the line should be.

More detailed proposals came from a group of Socialist MEPs who drafted their own wordy but worthy resolution for their powerless parliament to debate. The resolution called for various bureaucratic measures to improve international shipping safety and demanded a ban on tankers over 15 years old from using European ports. People were too kind to point out that this would have the immediate effect of causing an oil famine throughout Western Europe.

They wanted to ban tankers without double hulls but, as Greenpeace had pointed out, fewer than five per cent of tankers had them, so this – although undoubtedly a good thing – would take rather a long time.

Next on the shopping list was a single language for safety purposes on ships – Basic Navigational English. This too was easier said than delivered.

Compulsory pilotage 'when routes pass the coast' was also somewhat ambitious but the MEPs did have some very sensible and practical measures which really could be put into effect quite rapidly – forcing tankers to use defined routes, improving crew training and inspecting ships more rigorously in European ports.

The European Commission was asked to help finance environmental studies on the impact of the spill, to set up a compensation fund for farmers,

*Rick Steiner, from Cordova, Alaska, briefs Highlands and Islands Euro-MP Winnie Ewing on his ideas for handling large oil spills: 'Don't let them happen in the first place!'*
(Photo: Jonathan Wills)

crofters and fishermen until their compensation claims were settled, and to hold 'a major conference on maritime safety' as a matter of urgency. Not another conference! Someone had not told them about the one already planned by Shetland Islands Council.

In the event, the European Commission proved to be extremely helpful and sympathetic, as did the Scottish Office, indeed. The big money took a while to arrive (particularly from the insurers, who wanted a lot of questions answered on those claim forms) and there were fights behind and in front of closed doors about who should get what, but that was normal after an oil spill.

The worries and rows got into the papers and the TV follow-up documentaries, prolonging Shetland's fleeting fame. For a month and more, these hundred or so little islands on the edge of Europe had been the centre of world attention. Politicians of all parties and many nations, environmental pressure groups in every hue of green and studios full of international media pundits had piled into the fray. The crescendo of condemnation, debate and demands grew and grew. The islanders listened to this worldwide frenzy of concern with a mixture of heartfelt gratitude, shy pride and wry amusement (and outright derision when patronising outsiders who had come to 'rescue' them sometimes made gaffes). But there was also a hope that grew slowly out of the despair – this time, surely, something good must come out of all the fuss?

'Save Our Shetland' had been a grand slogan for the successful campaign against the expansion of nuclear work at Dounreay in the 1980s. In the nineties it would come in handy again. As with Dounreay, the slogan was also 'Save Our Sea'.

*Chapter Eight*

# THE SPIN-OFF BEGINS

*I would like to express my personal regret and sorrow for the grounding of the* Braer *which has caused personal hardship to many of the residents of the Shetland Islands . . . this is a shipping man's nightmare. We are truly sorry to have had a part in it.*

MICHAEL S. HUDNER, LETTER TO *The Shetland Times*, 15 JANUARY 1993

*It's a bad accident but not a disaster, not a catastrophe.*

MAGNUS MAGNUSSON, CHAIRMAN, SCOTTISH NATURAL HERITAGE,
SUMBURGH, 8 JANUARY 1993

After the Dunrossness farmers, crofters and lobster fishermen, the spill's next victims were the salmon farmers in the 'Burra Triangle'. They were faced with ruin, literally overnight. They had over two million salmon swimming out there, south and west of Scalloway, worth around £10 million. The oily water had gone through their cages. Some of the fish proved to be contaminated when Government scientists did the first tests in the exclusion zone west of Scalloway. About half a million fish would have to be destroyed immediately − or rather, once the interminable paperwork was complete.

The same fate may await all the fish in the zone. At the time of writing, seven weeks after the wreck, a final decision had still not been made. One farmer, Stuart Owers, explained that what he was really doing was selling his fish stock to the tanker insurers. It would be up to them what to do with it. Regardless of whether salmon had actually been tainted or not, they were unsaleable to anyone else, simply because they came from the zone, which was later extended five miles to the west soon after the first test results came in. As the weeks went by, the tests showed a steady decline in the contamination, but it was above normal background levels for hydrocarbons in the zone almost two months later.

Salmon farmers were having difficulty arranging insurance for the baby salmon they would buy in 1993 to grow in the following year and maybe not harvest until early in 1995. The insurance companies (and the banks) were worried about long-term ecological damage to the farm sites, which could affect the young salmon. Moving the cages was no answer, because every-where on the south-west side of Shetland was now suspect. In any case, there were not enough spare sites to go round.

Without cash, the fish could starve to death before they were culled. The owners would not be able to feed them, nor even hire the labour to kill them, because the banks would not extend credit to fish farmers who looked like going to the wall. The cash did run out for one fish farmer, whose first compensation cheque arrived on the day the bank was due to stop his cheques. Form-filling for the insurance company had taken weeks and weeks, with lawyers haggling over every jot and tittle. The sum paid over was enough to keep him going for just one month, at the end of which he might have to go through the trauma again. All the time people were watching the cash draining out of their pockets and none coming in. In those first seven weeks it was estimated that the Burra Triangle farms had spent £2 million on feed, wages and other expenses just to stand still, without any guarantee of return.

There was a lot of anger and anguish among the salmon farmers, who had worked long hours for many years to build up their businesses and establish a reputation for carefully tended, high quality fish which attracted premium prices. The fish farm workers were even more worried. If their bosses went broke they could not see any other jobs to go to, certainly not in the rural areas – where fish farming was the ideal industry to retain population in remote communities.

The insurance fund agents and loss adjusters quickly realised that this was all much more complicated than it looked. You could not just mop up the mess with a bundle of £20 notes, say 'There – better now?' and go home. The *Braer* Claims Office might have to stay open on Commercial Street, Lerwick, for a very long time. Compensating a salmon farm for the loss of one season's crop was not the end of the matter. The effects of the spill would last for at least three years, because it had totally disrupted the highly seasonal cash flow of these very capital-intensive enterprises. Salmon farming in Shetland might have started as a part-time job for a few crofters who happened to live next to suitable bays, but by 1993 it was very big business, generating more income than the whole of the whitefish fleet.

Then there was the problem of a dozen or so small fishing boats from Burra and Scalloway who were now effectively locked out of their traditional winter fishing ground, the 'Burra Haaf', because two-thirds of it was in the extended exclusion zone. The boats were too small to go safely round the western and southern tips of Shetland in winter gales. And if they did move, they would only crowd out other boats on *their* home grounds. But how do you calculate the compensation for a fisherman who cannot fish? You know the cost of running the boat but the cost of the crew varies. Most Shetland boats are family-owned partnerships. The crew share in the proceeds from the catch, after the boat has taken her share. Incomes vary a lot – both weekly and seasonally. How could you work out which days the boats might have caught a lot of fish and which days they might have caught nothing? And how to estimate the price the catch might have fetched at market? It was an accounting nightmare, worse than trying to put a value on all those oiled Dunrossness cabbages which farmer Willie Mainland had been forbidden to sell to the public. As with the salmon farms, there were complaints about slow payment of compensation.

As the dizzying complexity of it all began to clog up calculators in the offices of the fishermen's selling agents, people wondered if the IOPC's limited liability compensation fund of some £58 million would really be enough. They concluded that it probably would not, when the knock-on effects on the economy of Shetland outside the exclusion zone were reckoned up.

The good news was that, after the first few weeks, it was clear that the insurers were not going to flounce off to the courts. They intended to stay in town for a while and do business, meeting their obligations as they saw them. In the first seven weeks the claims office paid out just under £300,000. Most of it was emergency hardship money for crofters, fish farmers and fishermen. Fodder for animals on oiled pastures was also being paid for through the *Braer* office, after the council handed over responsibility for it. An estimate of the cost of imported hay, beet pulp and concentrates for cattle and sheep was £200,000 for the first month alone. This sounded like a lot of money but it was noted, sourly, that Bergvall and Hudner had reportedly been paid their insurance claim on the *Braer*, in full, in only six weeks.

*The press were invited to see for themselves when the Lerwick fishmarket opened under strict quality control checks*
(Photo: Tom Kidd)

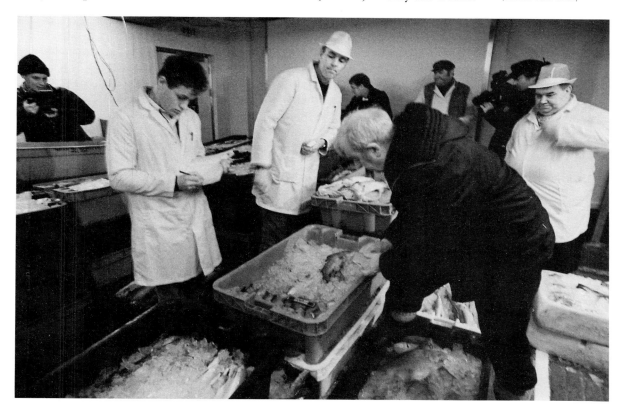

125

One of the difficulties for the *Braer*'s victims was that it was so hard to put a figure on the losses. Local solicitor Chris Dowle, a partner in the Peterkins firm, told *The Shetland Times* on 18 February: 'People are not yet sure what their losses are. Although it seems a long time since the tanker hit, it is not a long time in working out what your losses are. A lot of people are anticipating economic losses. There is no way people can say: "I know what my losses are, and that's it." '

This was particularly so in the tourist trade: how could a bed and breakfast operator know how much business had been lost until the 1993 tourist season was over? People in that situation could only register notice of intention to claim. The details – and the payout – would have to wait. The banks often would not.

Then there were borderline cases – what were Shetland angling enthusiasts to make of the threat from the Government that they would be fined up to £5,000 if they indulged in their hobby of catching trout in the burns and bays of southern Shetland? From the southern tip of Bressay right around to Skeld, including some of the best trout burns in the islands, trout fishing was banned until further notice. What compensation could an angler seek from the *Braer* Claims Office when he or she was unable to go fishing on 25 February, the opening day of the season? Would it be for loss of amenity or loss of a subsistence food supply? People in Alaska had received payment for that after *Exxon Valdez*, for several years in some cases. What price do you put on a three-pound Sea Trout? No wonder the Shetland Anglers' Association Chairman, Alex Munro, called it 'a serious blow'.

Sea anglers, fishing from small boats for Cod, Tusk, Ling, Haddock and Whiting, found some of their best sport fishing areas closed for the foreseeable future. Sea angling ('da eela' in local dialect) in Shetland is not just a sport. For many men, particularly, it is an obsession – their main recreation as well as a useful supply of wholesome food. The eela men were devastated. Apart from the indignity of having to buy fish from a van or a shop, their social life was affected: conversations tended to lag without the details of the day's catch to discuss. As Malcolm Green had said: 'The effect on the community will be devastating in all sorts of ways that aren't expected.'

There was some anger when one of the insurance men suggested that they might not automatically pay claimants' legal costs in cases settled out of court. Dowle gruffly reminded them that this was normal practice in Scotland. Another comment by Green, ten days after the wreck, had recalled similar worries over the *Esso Bernicia* compensation in 1979: 'I was involved in getting the money from the parties concerned,' he said. 'And we got it, plus interest, and interest on the interest. And we'll do it again.' Determined optimism like this was all many people had to sustain them as Shetland drifted through February and into March, with no end in sight to the wrangling and worry over compensation.

More good news: compared with the vicious bickering which followed *Exxon Valdez* in the small communities of Prince William Sound, there was remarkably little infighting and bitterness in Shetland. The credit for this rests partly with Lerwick solicitors who banded together to represent clai-

*Sonja Flaws leads her oiled Shetland ponies into the luxury of a barn. Usually they live outside in all but the coldest winter weather*
(Photo: Graeme Storey)

mants collectively, partly with the bodies representing the seafood, tourism and agricultural industries, and partly with the council. Between them, they managed to co-ordinate the compensation campaign rather well. In some ways it was an even bigger and more complicated job than physically dealing with the oil spill – or rather getting ready to deal with it but not being able to. Those of us who had often been critical of the council's dilatoriness, inefficiency and tendency to wanton extravagance were agreeably surprised. Those who felt that they had not been given the help they needed and deserved were not surprised at all, of course. But then they could believe almost anything of people they had known since they were at school together.

The children of Shetland watched the TV news like everyone else. They were upset. Birds and animals they took for granted as part of their world were being killed in front of their eyes. From Fair Isle to Haroldswick, Unst, all of Shetland's three dozen schools discussed the spill and what it meant. Teachers had been briefed by the educational psychologists about the emotional disturbance they might encounter in the classroom. That was how it had been in Alaska. And Shetland pupils were drawing pictures of the spill, startlingly like those done by the children of Valdez, Cordova, Tatitlek and the other little communities around Prince William Sound four years before. The difference was that in Shetland there was a brave helicopter rescue to draw and paint, as well as a wrecked tanker; a positive image to balance the negative, just a little. In Alaska a wicked captain off bridge and on the booze had been pinned to artroom walls. In Shetland the tanker captain did not seem to be such a hate figure.

To the children the spill was simple and straightforward, if horrible. There were goodies and baddies. The baddies had caused the trouble and were to blame for distressing their parents, who were too busy helping the goodies to read a bedtime story. Family life was under severe strain, and nowhere more than in Dunrossness.

School life was disrupted too. The primary school at Boddam was besieged, in the nicest possible way, by reporters and camera crews. Pupils saw themselves on TV when they went home. Outside Dunrossness, few Shetland youngsters actually saw the spill at its worst. In Hamnavoe Primary, Burra Isle, and Scalloway Junior High School they watched the sheens of oil and the frantic activity of the grown-ups, and saw the brown muck on the

*The wreck of the* Braer, *by Tom Wills (age 6)*

*A diver investigates
the wreck during a
lull in the storms
before the final
break-up of the ship*

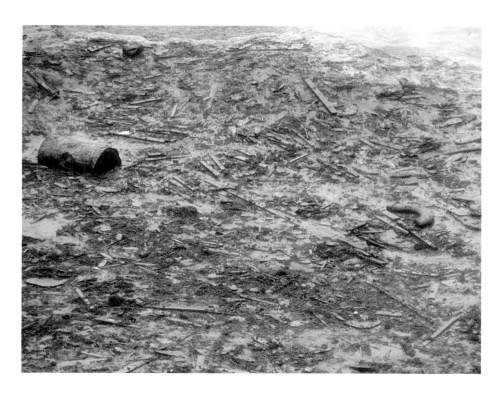

*Flotsam from the wreck*
(Photo: Tom Kidd)

*A common Guillemot, soaked in Gullfaks crude*
(Photo: Mike Wilkinson)

*Opposite:*
*Shag, Quendale Beach*
(Photo: Mike Wilkinson)

*The colours of oil*
(Photo: Mike Wilkinson)

*Previous page:*
*'She's gone': the*
Braer, *broken and*
*sunk after the*
*hurricane, spills the*
*last of her oil into*
*Garth's Wick*
(Photo: Tom Kidd)

*Ross Flett from Orkney Seal Sanctuary and a Cornish volunteer evacuate an oiled seal from the beach at Sumburgh. The seal was later moved to Hillswick for treatment*
(Photo: Tom Kidd)

*Local ornithologist Dave Suddaby brings in two more 'goners' from Quendale Beach, 7 January 1993*
(Photo: Mike Wilkinson)

*Traditional Dunrossness boats on a summer's morning at Spiggie Beach, before the oil*
(Photo: Jonathan Wills)

*The Gannet cliffs of Noss were spared — this time*
(Photo: Jonathan Wills)

*Muckle Flugga Lighthouse at the northern end of Shetland. A tanker broke down ten miles from here just 12 days after the wreck of the* Braer
(Photo: Jonathan Wills)

*The show must go on: lighting-up time for Lerwick's Up Helly A', fire festival, three weeks after the wreck of the* Braer
(Photo: Tom Kidd)

beaches. They could smell the oil, but it was not like the smell that made Dunrossness bairns and babies cough and cry in the oily night.

Although most youngsters experienced the spill at second hand, as a TV event, all of them feared for a week and more that the oil slicks would spread right around Shetland. Their secure little world suddenly seemed threatened in a strange, impossible and disturbing way. In trusting, rural communities where many people still did not lock their doors at night, it felt as if a violent and hostile prowler was out there in the dark. The door lock was rusted up and the bolt on the inside had been missing for years.

Convener Thomason recognised the anxiety and anger among the young. He told a Sumburgh news conference on 7 January (when 'disaster' was still the official word): 'Our economy and our society could be at risk . . . A younger person might begin to wonder if there is a future for Shetland . . . My message is that Shetland is still a good place to be and we can approach life with confidence.'

Bressay Primary's 24 pupils did not hear the Convener's message but they did have a visit from a man from Alaska. Scott Sterling, President of the Prince William Sound Regional Citizens' Advisory Council, told them all about the *Exxon Valdez* spill and brought them words of support and friendship from Mount Eccles Elementary School in Cordova. His buddy Rick Steiner brought a similar message across for Dunrossness Primary.

After Sterling's visit, the 24 pupils of Bressay began checking the shoreline on their way to and from school each day. They were ready to send in reports on the oil slick as soon as it showed its face. A few light sheens did reach Bressay Sound. They probably came from a fishing boat's bilges, not the *Braer*. There was an oiled Eider Duck, dead, and a Guillemot well enough to be sent off for cleaning, but the big spill never came.

The Bressay bairns really wanted to do something to help. They decided to write letters to the Prime Minister. The nice man from Alaska had told them that in America it really did make a difference if young people wrote to the President.

So Donald wrote to John Major: 'I am very furious with you because you should have sent us money to buy radars . . . The oil is drifting faster.'

Sean: 'I am very concerned. You should send us radars. The oil slick is growing bigger than ever.'

Tom wanted radars too, and quickly. He had heard his Dad going on about them: 'This will only take two months. You haven't seen the lovely beaches. Please do it. We are going to have to live with it.'

Lisa: 'If you threw toys in the sea they might be stuck with oil if you took them back. All the things in the sea are getting covered with oil. This makes me feel mad. I don't want them to spill oil again. A radar makes pictures to help us see the boats.'

Leighanne: 'We need lots of people to help make it all come beautiful again . . . we need you to help us because it's a disaster.'

Sara: 'Hurry up, we need your help.'

Hannah: 'The ship could have been saved if you had done something before. You could have made a law to stop ships going round that route.'

Major's secretary at 10 Downing Street replied that the Prime Minister thanked them for writing the letters and was most interested in what they had to say. That was all. He did not mention radars. It seemed that the man from Alaska had been wrong. Writing to the Prime Minister did not make much of an impact after all. But maybe it was different in America.

By the time Major's letter reached Bressay it was snowing. It does not snow very long or very often in Shetland. Some of the younger pupils had only seen a good snowfall three or four times in their lives. Oil spills were quickly forgotten as the school closed for the day. Sledges and snowmen suddenly became much more important than Prime Ministers, radars and tankers. But the oil spill was still there when they came in for tea and watched *Newsround* on Children's BBC. There was no getting away from it, however young you were.

Maybe it was just a bug, brought to the islands by those 600 globe-trotting reporters who had picked up who-knew-what infections from who-knew-where, or maybe it was the psychosomatic effects of the spill, but there was sickness in the air. Many adults felt rotten. A lot more bairns than usual seemed to be off school in late January, with symptoms like minor skin rashes, chapped lips and a fretty cold which left them listless and tired.

Some of the media celebrities they knew well came to the rescue, or tried to. Famous faces were seen in the streets of Lerwick. The bairns laughed at the jolly presenters of a popular Saturday morning kids' show when both of them blew over in the *Braer* wind, live by satellite from Sumburgh to the studio in London – and back to the sitting-room screen in Bressay.

For the grown-ups, there was the comic actor and broadcaster Bill Oddie, a fanatical birdwatcher and Shetlanditis sufferer. Bill wasted no time in countering TV's images of total catastrophe. Four days after the spill, he told listeners to BBC Radio 4's travel programme *Breakaway* that he would be going to the islands to watch the spring migration of the birds as usual, and taking his microphone with him: 'Shetland will be every bit as wild, every bit as magical, every bit as visitable as ever,' he chirped.

At the offices of Shetland Islands Tourism Ltd, publicity like that was manna from heaven. Tourism director Maurice Mullay and his assistant, Isobel Reid, were trying to raise more than twice their usual annual budget. They needed an extra £500,000 to promote Shetland holidays – particularly the growing market in wildlife tourism. The oiled corpses on TV were a tiny fraction of the hundreds of thousands of healthy seabirds who would soon return to the islands for the nesting season, but the average TV viewers on the mainland did not know that. They must be told. That would cost a lot of money.

To advise him on the fight-back strategy, Mullay had a visitor from Alaska. Stan Stephens had started in business in Valdez 30 years before, using a small boat with an outboard motor to show visitors the beauties of Prince William Sound and its wildlife. By the time the *Exxon Valdez* went aground, he had built up the biggest tour-boat business in the sound, carrying over 20,000 sightseers in a season. Stephens knew how it felt to be hit like this. In the 1989 season he lost more than half of his trade – and his end of Prince William Sound was completely unoiled. It took three years to build up again to the level of business before the spill.

Stephens told Mullay that, with heavy additional marketing, he might hope to sustain tourism business in Shetland as a whole, but he could expect a drastic affect on Dunrossness and other areas that had actually been oiled.

Offers of help came in from the tourist trade all over Britain. An Edinburgh design agency donated a logo for 'Operation Aurora' – a Killer Whale or Orca. The tourist board's usual logo was a Puffin, for the very good reason that Shetland was and is one of the best places in Europe to watch these delightful birds at close range. Only one Puffin had died in the spill so far but it was thought that something more dramatic was needed. Over Christmas a family of Orcas had spent 11 days in a little bay just north of Lerwick – Catfirth. The whales became a national sensation, appearing on TV and on the front pages of the London papers. Hundreds of delighted sightseers caused Catfirth's first recorded traffic jam, watching the whale family at a range of only a few hundred yards. It was a magnificent spectacle, rarely if ever seen before in Britain. The whales, at first thought to be trapped or ill, were just feeding. They departed as suddenly as they had arrived, just after a superb display of pink *Aurora Borealis* – the Northern Lights – had spread right across the winter sky. It was a joyful media occasion, unlike the one that followed a fortnight later. A few wondered in retrospect if the whales had come to warn Shetland of the impending disaster; and reddish aurora were traditionally supposed to be an ill omen of storm and disaster – normally the lights were greenish white.

So Orcas and Aurora it was. Never mind that the average summer visitor to Shetland is highly unlikely to see either of the two pods of Orcas known to frequent Shetland waters, nor that the Northern Lights are invisible in summer because it is light most of the time. In the circumstances there was unlikely to be any trouble with the Trades Descriptions Act.

Mullay believed in the direct approach. He was on the phone day and night to tour operators all over the world, telling and selling the good news. He wrote personal letters to every visitor who had left an address with the tourist centre, and to everyone who asked for a 1993 brochure, saying that the media reports of the damage from the spill had been 'sensationalised and grossly distorted'.

'One way you can positively help us after this incident is to come and see for yourselves how we have not been seriously affected and how we have encouraged recovery,' he wrote, '. . . very soon Shetland will be as beautiful, clean and dramatic as before.' He expected the seabird colonies at Sumburgh Head to be 'as impressive as ever' in the summer of 1993. Common sense said that he was probably right but there was no scientific basis for Mullay's optimism.

Seven weeks after the 'incident', the promised scientific monitoring of seabirds, the seashore and the seabed had still not begun in the area around the wreck. The much-heralded ecological monitoring group mentioned in Government press releases had not even held its first meeting. Members of the Shetland Bird Club were becoming restless about this. The club's own logo is a Black Guillemot or 'Tystie'. Over a hundred Tysties died in the first eight days of the spill. They were variously captioned as 'Ducks', 'Puffins' and 'Gannets' by the less ornithologically minded picture editors of the popular prints.

Other confidence-building measures were well under way. A team from the seafood industry set off for Boston, Massachusetts, to do a big promotion for Shetland fish at a major trade fair. They took evidence with them to prove that the islands were not as black as CNN and CBS had painted them. BBC Television came up from Bristol to make an entire programme devoted to Shetland's remarkable escape from the spill. It rated a full page in *Radio Times*.

'Sensational and grossly distorted'? That was a bit strong. Blaming it on the media was more than a little unfair.

Mullay had been optimistic from the start but some of the very people who had given doom-laden interviews to the TV cameras on Day One were telling a different story on Day 31. True, the story had changed, thanks to Mother Nature, but it was a little unrealistic to expect the national and international media to leave expensive camera crews waiting around in Shetland when there were other pressing matters claiming their attention – such as the continuing carnage in Bosnia, civil war and famine in dozens of other countries and, nearer home, the appalling murder of a Merseyside toddler and the continuing scandal of the British coal pit closures.

Shetland had been very important for a little while, a lot longer than Andy Warhol's maxim of 'famous for 15 minutes'. Now it was not so important. Life is like that. Those who took the trouble to read back over the disaster editions of the newspapers and look again at videos of the TV news coverage had to agree that Shetland had a very fair press during the second two weeks of January. There was some ignorance, to be sure, but not a lot of sensationalism. You cannot really sensationalise an already sensational event like the spillage of 84,500 tonnes of oil. Where there had been inaccuracy and overstatement it was usually a direct result of the refusal of the tanker owners and the authorities (the Government rather than the council, to be fair) to provide full and timely information to the press corps at Sumburgh. The vast majority of visiting reporters involved in Shetland's unprecedented media invasion were honest people trying to do a difficult job in extremely trying circumstances.

Now they were away. If the islanders wanted publicity for their miraculous delivery from disaster and their brave struggle to recover from the *Braer*, they would have to go out and fight for it. And that is exactly what they did. How successful they were, we will have to wait and see.

# JAN MORGAN, HILLSWICK WILDLIFE SANCTUARY

CANDLES flickered across the stone walls of The Booth – Shetland's oldest pub. Faces peered through the semi-darkness.

For Jan Morgan, a power cut was minor league compared with the previous six weeks. As well as owning the pub, she had been running the seal sanctuary next door.

She sat near the open stove fire, holding a glass of white wine and quizzing a man from the *Braer* Claims Office over what help they might expect. Legally, none, he told her, but the rules of the game were being changed.

The candles danced as the door opened again, and he left. She sat quite still, looking exhausted. Since the tanker ran aground she had been faced with the huge task of co-ordinating volunteers, fielding hundreds of phone calls, keeping tabs on administration and making sure the seals were being looked after.

Her garden had been completely turned over to the sanctuary. Special pens were built, each with its own pool, a sick bay was set up for the sickest beasts, and a quiet area at the back put aside for timid otters.

Jan had little time to help the animals. She had to cook and clean and house dozens of volunteers. Six weeks on, just a hard core of 17 helpers were left, but the house still seemed crowded.

'It's been a nightmare,' she said. 'One night I had to cook for 37 people. I've had to employ extra staff to work in the pub, and you wouldn't believe the amount of administration . . . It's really been a balancing act. I've not been able to get near a seal.

'It has been the goodness of people that has kept me going.' She took a sip of wine, and her eyes glistened with tears. 'It has been overwhelming. It gives you hope that there's all these people dotted around the world. I am knackered but it has given me inner strength.'

Jan was cleaning in the pub when she heard the tanker had hit the rocks. 'I put the phone down and started to cry, but I knew I had to just get on with it.'

133

(Photo: Tom Kidd)

A team of vets and helpers from Holland arrived at Hillswick, in the north Mainland of the islands, within a day of the *Braer* grounding. Hundreds more turned up over the next few days, from all over the country. More than 300 names of people who could be called on to help were filed away in a folder.

For the first week there were no seals. That gave the volunteers time to build facilities to cope with up to 30 animals. By the time five oiled seals had been gathered in, though, high tides and storms were back.

'A terrible storm came and gutted the sick bay, ripping the roof off,' Jan said. 'I remember this huge wave coming over and I was really scared for all the people working out there.

'The car park was two feet deep in shingle, so we got a JCB to clear it. But they reversed into a neighbour's gas tank, which fell over and ruptured. You've no idea what it was like. The fire brigade were here, the police were here . . . and we just had to get on with rebuilding the sanctuary.

'The nearest I can get to explaining how we felt is from stories my parents used to tell me about the wartime atmosphere. You're on this high and you just get above all the little problems in life.'

Six weeks on, the centre was caring for 24 seals, two of which were not oiled, and two otters. Three seals and one otter had died and seven seals had been released.

The patients included one rare Arctic Hooded Seal pup, which was picked up, weak, hungry, balding and riddled with parasites, on a beach on Unst. This breed is usually found far north at the edge of the pack ice. It is likely he was swept south when a chunk of ice broke free. The big worry for the volunteers looking after him now is that the situation will stress him so much he won't recover.

'They call him ET because he looks like an alien,' Jan said. 'He is eating fish himself now, so I hope he will recover. I would really love to release him back into the Arctic.'

Jan hoped that most of the seals would be released by late April. For the otters, however, freedom must come much later. The creatures are only around three months old, so they will have to be transferred to rearing pens for several months before moving into release pens. From there they can go and hunt for food, but still have the security of their pens to return to. Small amounts of food will be left for them there to stop them starving as they learn to fend for themselves.

Jan, a former social worker who moved to Shetland 22 years ago, knows that there has been criticism of efforts to save wildlife. Seals are commonly loathed by salmon farmers and fishermen for damaging stocks. Some people believe there are more important things to do than save a few animals. Particularly in this situation, where the relatively small numbers of oiled seals will have little effect on the growing populations around the isles.

'My argument is when you look at the rest of the world most big mammals are dying and it's time we recognised that. We ought to be proud of the fact that ours are increasing.' Viruses, illnesses and declining populations of creatures elsewhere were warnings from the animal kingdom, she said.

Jan has been running a seal sanctuary in her back garden for the last seven years. But it has always been her dream to set up a properly equipped wildlife centre. That looks like it may now happen as a result of the *Braer*. Work has started to convert a 350-year-old listed building into a special seal care unit, and plans are afoot to build a large pool with a water system linking it to the sea.

'It's a terrible way for it to happen, but it's great that there is something positive to come out of all this,' she said.

*Chapter Nine*

# 'WE TOLD YOU SO . . .'

*This accident raises wider questions about tanker movements around our coasts, as well as many other issues. I have therefore decided to commission an additional inquiry with the following terms of reference: 'To advise on whether any further measures are appropriate and feasible to protect the UK coastline from pollution from merchant shipping. Due consideration should be given to the international and economic implications of any new measures'.*

JOHN MACGREGOR MP, SECRETARY OF STATE FOR TRANSPORT,
HOUSE OF COMMONS, 11 JANUARY 1993

We have seen how it took 11 years for the British Government to take to the International Maritime Organisation a simple request for the tanker 'no-go' areas, pioneered by the council and BP back in 1979, to be marked on the nautical charts of the Shetland Islands.

Progress in other areas of tanker safety was equally slow. Captain George Sutherland and his predecessors in charge of the council-run harbour at Sullom Voe – Captains Bert Flett and George Biro – had consistently raised safety issues with the local harbour advisory committee, the oil industry and the British Government.

Being able to say 'We told you so' is usually more fun than most of us care to admit but after the *Braer* disaster there was no pleasure in it at all, least of all for Captain Sutherland.

In sorrow and justifiable anger, Willie Tait, the councillor for Dunrossness North, told the first council meeting after the wreck, on 12 January: 'It's a tragedy that it takes something of this magnitude for people to listen.' Tait (himself a crofter whose land had been sprayed with oil) recalled that in 1979 the council had urged the Government to enforce 'no-go' areas in sensitive parts of the UK coastline. They had no success. Tait believed that if the Government had listened then, the *Braer* would never have gone ashore.

The warnings were repeated, over and over again. They grew louder after the *Exxon Valdez* disaster. For, while it was true that *Exxon Valdez* would not have been wrecked if the port of Valdez had had the Sullom Voe system of tanker surveillance and monitoring, it was also true that Alaska was not the only place where big ships were allowed out on their own in dangerous coastal waters.

Captain Sutherland and Captain Dickson advised the Alaskans in 1990–91 on how to improve ship safety, using principles accepted by BP and Exxon in Shetland for a decade but still resisted by them in Prince William Sound, long after the *Exxon Valdez*. Their visits to Alaska were uncomfortable reminders of how vulnerable Shetland still was, even with the commercial sanctions imposed by BP to force their customers to obey the Sullom Voe rules. Captain Sutherland was to point out, yet again, that an estimated 1,000 large vessels a year passed close to Shetland without communicating with the shore. Several hundred of them were tankers. They were not going to Sullom Voe so the BP sanctions did not work. Alaska did not have that problem – nearly all the tankers in the north-east Pacific were headed to or from Valdez.

As in Alaska, most of the Shetland coast was unwatched. The network of Coastguard lookout stations, manned in bad weather by knowledgeable local men, usually retired seafarers, had long since been dismantled. The Department of Transport in London decided that even those paltry, part-time wage bills were too high. The old lookout cabins became derelict, their windows blew in and their timbers rotted in the winter gales. Only sheep used them now. The local Auxiliary Coastguard volunteers were still in place, but their job was to help with rescues, not to stand 'bad weather watches' to guard their coast against rogue tankers.

After the *Braer* disaster an Orkney councillor, Allan Taylor, commented: 'There has been a lot of talk of having a bigger radar survey, which is a grand thing at night. But there is nothing better than an eyeball picture to see what is happening . . . I don't think we have enough experienced men on the ground in the Coastguards now . . . A good pair of binoculars is very beneficial.'

It is difficult to argue with Councillor Taylor. He is a retired Coastguard with 30 years' experience in Orkney, Shetland and the English Channel.

The modern British Coastguard service has got rid of many of its most knowledgeable officers and replaced them with casual shift-workers – keen, committed, grossly underpaid people who, through no fault of their own, are less likely to have sea-going experience or detailed local knowledge of the shore. The Coastguards have been reduced to a dwindling network of hi-tech radio shacks, relying mainly on the radio to keep them informed of what is going on. In Shetland they do not even have a radar set.

Other watchers on the shore have suffered from Government parsimony. The lightkeepers at Fair Isle North and Sumburgh Head, who always kept an eye on the Fair Isle Channel, were made redundant by the Northern Lighthouse Board and replaced with robots – after complaints from shipowners about the cost of light dues. With the Department of Transport's blessing, the board intends to automate Shetland's last manned light, the Muckle Flugga off north Unst, in 1994–95. It could cost them a million pounds to install the equipment but that is capital, not wages, so it is no problem. The thought that three pairs of eyes on the northernmost lighthouse in Britain might be still handy for spying on tankers cutting corners has apparently not influenced the board's policy, despite the fact that lightkeepers have reported infringements of the 'no-go' zone on several occasions in the past 14 years. The automatic light will just wink at the transgressors.

Captain Dickson found that the *Exxon Valdez* had shaken up the US Coast Guards. Budget cuts during the Reagan years led to the closure of radars that might have seen the *Exxon Valdez* go off course. The oil companies and the ship insurers did not complain. Sophisticated ship-tracking systems like the one at Sullom Voe were just a dream. Underpaid and overworked, several senior US Coast Guard figures in Alaska gave up in disgust and went to work for the oil industry, whose interests Presidents Reagan and Bush nurtured so carefully. At the highest level, there were claims that the Coast Guard and the oil industry were too buddy-buddy by far. After the disaster, things had to change. But they changed very slowly. The US Coast Guard was given a budget to develop transponders to track tankers in Prince William Sound. It was a bit like re-inventing the wheel. Transponders already existed, as we discuss in the following chapter. But they came up with a workable system and it is soon to be installed.

The Alaskan oil companies may yet be persuaded to accept that they need highly manoeuvrable tractor tugs, with cycloidal propulsion, to escort tankers safely in the Narrows outside Valdez – a near disaster with the BP-chartered tanker *Kenai* in 1992 helped to concentrate minds. Sullom Voe has had tractor tugs for over a decade and they have prevented at least five *Exxon Valdez*-type disasters. The water in Sullom Voe is the same as in Valdez – wet and windy.

The US Coast Guard is also developing a tanker tracking system for the entire US coastline. It uses transponders, and a variant of the satellite navigation systems used by most large tankers (and even shipowners' pleasure yachts) to find their way around. Called the 'Differential Global Positioning System' (DGPS), this employs a shore radio station to eliminate the small errors in the radio navigation signals from satellites in stationary orbit above the earth. The accuracy is now down to 16 feet. In theory, the shore can tell which side of a tanker's bridge the captain is standing upon.

In the US Coast Guard headquarters in Washington DC, they have a map of the proposed DGPS network. It will cover the coast from Maine to Texas, from California to Alaska, and also the Great Lakes. Tankers will have to carry a DGPS set or not trade on the US coast. That means that ships carrying oil to US ports from terminals in Shetland, Orkney and Norway – and over a third of Shetland's oil goes that way – will have to have DGPS too, in the not too distant future.

Since 1988, the British Government has sent officials to four meetings with the International Maritime Organisation about transponders. As usual, the Government refuses to do anything about ship safety unless it can get agreement at the IMO. Unilateral action is frowned upon, just as it was when the US took unilateral action with the 1990 Oil Pollution Act, to phase in compulsory double hulls. A double hull might not have helped the *Braer* but it would reduce oil pollution from most slow-speed tanker collisions and groundings, according to the most authoritative survey on the subject, carried out by the US National Academy of Sciences two years ago.

The United States, condemned for going it alone by IMO members and shipowners' organisations like the International Chamber of Shipping, has shown that leadership involves unilateral action, not following the herd. The herd are now following the US example. The pity is that all the safety improvements which have been available for many years were not made law by the flag states of the IMO long before the *Exxon Valdez*, the *Aegean Sea* and the *Braer*.

On 13 April 1991 I wrote to my MP. I was not the only worried constituent to do so. Jim Wallace had been nagging the Government again to do something about the various sensible suggestions from Captain Sutherland and the councillors in Shetland. I thought Wallace might be interested in the views of someone who had given the subject a bit of thought over the previous 19 years. He was. Some of what I said was technically incorrect but my letter included three paragraphs which stand the passage of two years:

*'There is a large radar "blind spot" on the north-west coast of Shetland – perhaps the most dangerous area for a loaded tanker suffering a power failure in a gale at night (when spy in the sky helicopters don't fly). The surveillance problem could be solved by a new radar station at Eshaness, linked to [the council's] Sella Ness port control room by a landline . . .*

*'The Government argues that there are not enough ships to warrant such a system. But we only need one loaded tanker ashore on the Ve Skerries or the Muckle Ossa to devastate the entire coast of Shetland for many years . . . Exxon Valdez spilled only one-fifth of her cargo. It was blown over 500 miles and oiled over 1,000 miles of coastline . . .*

*'The answer to this problem [of sending a tug to the rescue in time] is to station an ocean-going tug in or near Shetland on a Government retainer all year round. The tug would be required to give priority to preventing tanker strandings but could also undertake other commercial contracts, perhaps ranging up to five hours' steaming time from Sullom Voe (more in favourable weather). As far as I know, this suggestion is not being considered. It has always been said that they could call on large oilfield tugs, such as those used for towing rigs, should the emergency happen. I do not believe this is fail-safe.'*

At the end of April 1991 Wallace wrote to Patrick McLoughlin MP, the then Shipping Minister, asking for unilateral UK action on double hulls, crewing standards and transponders. McLoughlin replied on 4 June, saying it was important to understand 'that most pollution incidents arise from human error and we need therefore to progress on a much broader front than tanker design'. This made unilateral action difficult to justify. Indeed, the minister believed, 'unilateral imposition of national regimes by a number of countries could be positively harmful if it led to inconsistencies in standards and to the development of a haphazard mosaic of competing national regulations'.

Double hulls were on the way, McLoughlin said, but they would take time: 'The technical feasibility, and its consequences for safety, are now being discussed by the technical sub-committee [*of the Marine Environment Protection Committee of the International Maritime Organisation*].'

In fact, the American experts' report, written in part by the US Coast Guard and the US Navy, had already dismissed the technical and safety arguments against double hulls – arguments which had been vigorously promoted by the International Chamber of Shipping, whose members would have to pay for double-hulled tankers.

Transponders were also being discussed, the minister assured Wallace, but again, 'Considerable technical work needs to be done before such a system will be available for use and once it is complete we will consider how best it can be utilised to improve safety around our coast.'

There was more in the same vein and the same dense, techno-camouflaged prose. Wallace sent copies to constituents who had asked him to take all this up with the Government. It was not an easy read. And then I came to the letter from a senior civil servant, Ms Z. Roberts. It was dated 9 July of the previous year, 1990. Roberts was the Secretary of the UK Safety of Navigation Committee, in the Marine Directorate of the Department of Transport at Sunley House, High Holborn, London.

This was the letter from the British Government to the IMO, asking them, at long last, to put the tanker 'no-go' zones ('areas of avoidance' in official-speak) on the nautical charts, as Shetland Islands Council had requested in 1979. Wallace had included it because he thought it might be interesting. It became even more interesting on 5 January 1993.

Roberts wrote:

> '*In considering the consequences of the grounding of the* Exxon Valdez *in Prince William Sound, Alaska, in 1989, and of other tanker casualties, the government of the United Kingdom is deeply concerned about the possibility of a major oil spill occurring off the Shetland coast . . .*
>
> '*. . . Shetland experiences a high frequency of gale force winds throughout the year, predominantly between south and west in direction. The coast in many places is "steep-to", making it possible for large vessels to drift close inshore before grounding. It is likely that tugs would have to travel a long distance to assist an endangered tanker. At this northernmost part of the United Kingdom it would take considerable time to mobilise and transport the resources necessary to deal with a major pollution incident.*'

Roberts must have had the Second Sight. For the Seer of Sunley House had just written an uncannily accurate description of the *Braer* disaster, two and a half years before the event. Now she can say 'I told you so' too.

She was only obeying orders. And her minister was jolly proud of himself. He had, after all, just persuaded the IMO to permit Her Majesty's Hydrographer of the Navy to draw some extra dotted lines on the chart, 'in order to avoid the risk of oil pollution and severe damage to the environment and economy of Shetland' – as that sadly prophetic letter had said.

Unfortunately, the new dotted lines were so drawn as to inform tanker skippers that they could come as close as they wished to the *eastern* shore of

*Bags of bird corpses are loaded into a freezer container at the Boddam Wildlife Centre. Over 1,500 birds died in the first three weeks after the spill*
(Photo: Tom Kidd)

Shetland, along the 40 miles between Sumburgh Head and Out Skerries. Incredibly, the famous National Nature Reserve of Noss island was thus excluded from the areas to be avoided. In theory, tankers could anchor in 16 fathoms right alongside the 600-foot-high seabird cliffs of Noss, while the crew watched 15,000 breeding Gannets all afternoon if they liked. But on the western and northern coasts of Shetland, they were 'strongly recommended' not to cross the dotted lines.

There was nothing on the chart, either, to prevent tankers from sailing within a hundred yards of Sumburgh Head and its colonies of Shags and Puffins – as long as they stayed east of a line drawn from the lighthouse to the north end of Fair Isle.

The breakthrough on 'no-go' areas was not a lot, but it was at least something. In Shetland, Wallace's constituents had given up hoping for a lot.

From July 1990 until January 1993, committees, sub-committees and technical working groups continued to meet in the Department of Transport and at IMO headquarters in New York. Reports were written, conferences attended. But for all the talk, not a single new measure was put in place by the Government to reduce significantly the risks of tanker disasters. But they did propose that British ships should no longer have to have British captains. British captains are still not as cheap as the shipowners would like.

Forty-seven days after the *Braer* disaster, the Department of Transport replied to a Parliamentary Question from Jim Wallace. He had noted that the Government set great store by sending their own inspectors aboard ships visiting British ports. Inspections in accordance with IMO rules were seen as a deterrent to sloppy maintenance. The official target was to inspect 25 per cent of tankers. Not a lot, but it would at least make shipowners realise that there was a one-in-four chance of being caught out.

The department told Wallace that in 1990 they had inspected 15 tankers at Sullom Voe. They said this was ten per cent of the tankers visiting the terminal. This was not true. In fact, 459 tankers docked at Sullom Voe in 1990, according to figures kept by Shetland Islands Council's Marine Operations Department. So the percentage was actually three, not ten. Someone at Sunley House had got their sums wrong.

The department's figure for 1991 was nine tankers inspected. They thought this was five per cent of the total. In fact it was only 1.9 per cent of the 467 tankers logged at Sullom Voe that year.

The 'statistics' were even more ludicrous for 1992. The department reckoned they had inspected two per cent, just four ships. Wrong again – their inspection rate was 0.77 per cent of the 517 callers. The figures for the Flotta terminal in Orkney were similarly inaccurate.

Perhaps it was just as well that the council's pollution control staff themselves inspected three-quarters of tankers in the Sullom Voe trade, and that BP, the terminal operators, made detailed checks on every ship before loading was allowed to begin. As the Department of Transport's junior minister, Steven Norris MP, said: 'The Directors of Marine [*sic*] at Sullom Voe and Flotta carry out their own vetting procedure of visiting ships and alert the department if they are concerned by the condition of a visiting ship.'

Alert the department? In fact, it was often difficult in those years to *find* a Department of Transport marine surveyor at Sullom Voe. The post lay vacant for months on end. The council tends to call in a Government surveyor only when they have found a real rascal and need a witness for a report to the procurator fiscal (public prosecutor). So much for the eagle-eyed Government and its desire to implement the IMO regulations.

Meanwhile, the Americans are going unilateral again. In February 1993 the US Coast Guard finalised details of the 'towing package' which every tanker will soon have to carry when entering US waters. There is now a specification for towing wires, attached permanently to tankers by heavy-duty bridles and fitted with shackles so that the towline can be grabbed by a tug even if there is no-one on board the disabled ship to make fast a messenger rope. The Americans intend to make each tanker carry two towing packages – one at the bows and one at the stern.

If the *Braer* had missed Shetland, Bergvall & Hudner would have faced a bill of up to $500,000 to fit her with a towing package if they had intended to make any more runs from Norway to New York. The towing kits cost that much because fitting them is a major structural alteration. The regulations say the wire must be attached to a stout, steel 'kingpost', fixed firmly to the keel and rising through the full height of the ship to the foredeck. Most tankers only have bollards welded to the deck, not kingposts. The US Coast Guard feared that bollards welded to the deck might not be strong enough in an emergency.

In Prince William Sound, sea trials of towing packages have been carried out by Arco, one of the companies running tankers to Valdez. There is still some argument about the details of the Arco towing package. But at least something is being done.

Over here, the Government is now, well, doing a lot of monitoring to find out exactly how bad the spill was. Oh, and the European Community gave £850 each to people in Dunrossness who had suffered from the spill. The European Environment and Fisheries Commissioner, Ioannis Paleokrassas, went to Shetland on 19 February to hand over one of the cheques in person, as a gesture of solidarity. Paleokrassas comes from an island himself. A Greek one. He got on splendidly with the Shetland fishermen and fish farmers. They were delighted to meet a Euro-commissioner who appeared to know what he was talking about. It was unkind and perhaps a little racist for a local cynic to whisper: 'I fear the Greeks, even when bearing gifts'.

# MARTIN THOMSON, NESS FARMER

A GIANT of a man jumped up and grinned. 'Sit down,' he beamed, gesturing to the extra-long sofa. Four weeks after watching the *Braer* career into Garth's Ness, farmer Martin Thomson was looking on the brighter side of life.

'We've just got to get on with things now. Our land doesn't look that different from normal,' he said. 'We've probably had about the worst wind and salt spray we could get — and that always makes the land look a bit brown.'

Martin, his family and their 670 sheep, 22 cows and 17 calves live at Exnaboe, just a wind's breath from the wrecked ship. They were dealing with the situation with optimism, even though they recognised problems could come later.

The morning it all happened they moved over 200 sheep, mostly in lamb, from the fields to the farm. The cows were all inside, but there was not enough room for the rest of his flock. They were still outside, in the lee of a hill, where Martin thought they would be protected from the oily wind.

'We phoned the vet and he told us to fill them up straight away with beet pulp and hay to stop them grazing. Although I don't know what we'll do if the land is not fit in the spring — no sheep will eat hay when there is new grass coming up.'

Shetland Islands Council stepped up fairly quickly to make sure crofters and farmers had the feed they needed for their animals.

'The Government was very lucky it was our council that had to deal with it because they are quite wealthy. The Government didn't do much at all . . . If it had happened in the South of England John Major would have had a canary . . .'

Feeding the animals has been taking the Thomsons more than two and a half hours a day — time which should have been spent mending fences and preparing for the busy springtime. But the extra effort should pay off.

'They are looking quite good now, but the thing is when they are stressed they can re-absorb their lambs. If there is a phenomenal amount of singles or no lambs, then maybe we'll claim compensation.' He looked doubtful. 'But sheep get stressed in this weather anyway.'

The first lambs should be appearing in the Ness around 13 April – about a month earlier than in the north of the islands. The area is renowned for its fertility. Now the big fear is consumers won't trust the goods, even if the soil gets a clean bill of health. 'Most of the tatties and vegetables come from here and we always try to get ours out first and get the big prices. Of course, there's no good in that if no-one will buy them.'

The door opened and Martin's four-year-old son David trooped in, clutching a bowl of chopped apples. He sat quietly with a book, eager to be allowed to stay up – at least until big sister Nicola (five) returned from the Girls' Brigade. Their lives, at least, were going on quite normally again.

He was reluctant to speak about much beyond his favourite *Thomas The Tank Engine* stories, but, according to mum Lesley, hadn't noticed anything amiss apart from the health checks offered to every family in the area.

'We were quite worried about the health business at first,' she

(Photo: Tom Kidd)

said. 'They said we were okay and everything was fine but then we were told not to go outside and the bairns were kept in at school at playtime.

'When they're at home they are used to a lot of freedom, but I wasn't keen to let them out. I did let them out to the byre at night though.'

Lesley admitted buying bottled water for the first few days to use for the children's drinks. And they did pick up a couple of masks in the local shop but they were so uncomfortable they got little use.

The worst day for the family was the morning after the tanker ran aground. When Lesley got up the stink of oil had already pervaded the house. The windows were smeared with oil and the concrete outside was running with the pollution.

The day before, Martin had been standing on the cliffs of Garth's Ness as the ship reeled ashore. As an Auxiliary Coastguard, he had been called out early on. But there was nothing any of them could do.

'The boat just came in quietly and began to leak oil,' he said. 'You would think there would be grinding of metal, but I suppose it was such a terrible day you couldn't hear anything.

'The stern was the height of a house out of the water. The next day the sea was washing over the decks and a few days later it was just the funnel left.

'I don't think the full extent of what was going to happen hit us that first morning. It was just another ship coming ashore. We just thought it would all be cleaned out quickly because of all the latest stuff we have here.'

By the time Martin arrived back home, the smell of oil was in the air. And the world's media were starting to arrive.

'We had John Craven here doing a special report and the bairns have had TV cameras in the school.'

Not everyone welcomed the invasion of furry microphones, cameras and Received Pronunciation. 'One old guy working with me saw a radio reporter coming and jumped over the dyke rather than be quoted,' Martin said, laughing at the memory.

'There was really enough to think about without all these extra people,' he said. 'Initially you wanted things to return to normal as quickly as possible. I still do.'

One of the biggest dangers for the Ness now, he said, was a split in the community. Some people stood to make a lot of money from compensation claims. Others didn't. 'Certain members of the community will play it all up. The more pessimistic they are the more they can hope to claim.'

Within a couple of weeks of the incident communities had already begun squabbling over European humanitarian aid. The council decided it should be shared out amongst families in those areas they considered to have suffered most. But not everyone was happy. Some places were getting more than others, prompting grumbles in homes lower down the list.

'These EC payments have caused a lot of stress, but you have got to draw the line somewhere,' Martin said. 'If you are on one side of the line and getting different from your neighbour then there can be ill feeling . . . and that will go on for years with the compensation claims.'

Martin looked gloomier than he had done all evening. But it was a brief relapse. 'Things aren't as bad as all that . . . all we need now is some fine weather.'

*Chapter Ten*

# WHODUNNIT?

*Will my Right Honourable Friend [the Transport Secretary] ensure that the possibility of ship traffic control, like air traffic control for aeroplanes, is considered? Such a system would enable there to be a round-Britain network. It would be possible to know the position of all ships by the use of computer screens.*

ANTHONY STEEN, CONSERVATIVE MP FOR SOUTH HAMS, DEVON,
HOUSE OF COMMONS, 11 JANUARY 1993

Act of God, misadventure or negligence? Those are the choices of verdict in the case of the *Braer*. In the court of public opinion are the British Government, the tanker's owners, the insurers, the skipper and the ship's engineer officers.

There are three inquiries under way. One is being held by the Liberian authorities. The British inquiry by the Department of Transport's Marine Accidents Investigation Branch (MAIB) began on the day of the wreck. The MAIB is a branch of the UK Department of Transport, whose failure to ensure adequate surveillance of the Fair Isle Channel was one of the causes of the wreck of the *Braer*.

At the time of writing, evidence to the MAIB is being heard in secret, apart from some snippets which have found their way into the hands of reporters – such as Captain Gelis' statement to MAIB investigators on 15 January. An interim report has been made to the Secretary of State for Transport but is unlikely to be published. We have been told by the Department of Transport press office in London that the final report is unlikely to be published before January 1994.

Not even factual details – such as what was written in the *Braer*'s deck log by her Second Officer at 0040 hrs, 0330 hrs and 0400 hrs on 5 January – will be entrusted to the public before then. We were told that the regulations do not permit the Secretary of State to publish the interim report unless it contains specific and urgent safety recommendations. Apparently (and incredibly) the interim report on the *Braer* did not contain any such recommendations. This hardly inspires confidence in the final report.

There is no guarantee that the evidence taken by the MAIB will ever be published in full. That is the British system, in a maritime state which meekly tolerates having an unelected member of the House of Lords appointed as its shipping minister. Our American friends, who live in a country where the Government treats people as grown-ups, find this hard to believe or understand: 'How on earth do you guys in the British press do your job?' one US claims lawyer asked us. 'With great difficulty,' was the reply.

Lord Caithness, the shipping minister at the time of the disaster, purports to know a great deal about radar, and its drawbacks when you try to use it to follow tankers carrying oil past our coast. What Lord Caithness did not know, until he was corrected in public at a press conference in Shetland on the day after the wreck of the *Braer*, was that there is not and never has been any shore-based radar coverage of the channel between the Fair Isle and the parish of Dunrossness in Shetland. Nor is there any between Fair Isle and North Ronaldsay, the northern tip of Orkney.

The absence of radar and other electronic surveillance on most of the British coastline will be an important topic for the third inquiry, to be held in public (but in London) by the respected (but English) judge, Lord Donaldson. Lord Donaldson's task will be to find out how a carbon copy event can be prevented in future. The fear in Shetland, Orkney and the Western Isles, to say nothing of the Isles of Scilly, off Cornwall, is that there will be another *Braer* on someone's rocks long before either British inquiry has time to report.

There may yet be a fourth inquiry, in the form of a hearing in the United States, either in Congress or in the courts during pollution compensation claims by Shetlanders. A brief, preliminary hearing was held by a Congressional sub-committee in Washington DC a month after the wreck. Unlike the Liberian and MAIB investigations, a Congressional inquiry would be held in public, except when witnesses cited the Fifth Amendment to protect themselves from incrimination. That is the American system.

The 'Act of God' theory does not bear examination. The weather was severe but winter storms of Force Ten and more are commonplace in these waters. The *Braer* left Norway in a gale. Perhaps she should have stayed in port. Any schoolchild looking at the isobars on the TV weather chart could see that a big one was on the way. The lines marking the pressure gradient around the Atlantic depression looked like a giant thumbprint. There was no prospect of the weather easing before the ship reached the Fair Isle Channel. And the storm did not reach its full ferocity until after the *Braer* had gone ashore. Then, indeed, it became a 'hundred year storm' – the longest southwesterly storm in living memory.

The master of the *Braer* had two choices as he finished loading in Mongstad; either he could delay sailing until the weather eased or he could steam a hundred miles or so off the Norwegian coast and then heave to, to wait it out. The third choice, to press on, risked damage to the ship even if he had not suffered engine trouble. The storm might have been an Act of God. The decision to sail through it was an act of man. To go on, and increase speed, when the master already knew there were loose pipes rolling around next to the deck vents on his fuel tanks was, well, 'incomprehensible' is the kindest way to put it. It only becomes comprehensible if, as Hudner suggested on 25 January, ten days after Captain Gelis' own account to the MAIB, he did not know – or if he was too tired to think clearly. And Captain Gelis, by doing his duty as he saw it, had become very tired indeed. Other officers may have been equally tired and overworked.

Misadventure is the charitable view of the loss of the *Braer*. In extreme weather, even the most well-found vessel can be overwhelmed by the sea. In mid-ocean there may be an excuse when a ship is suddenly damaged by freak waves. But Captain Gelis was not in mid-ocean. And he had available to him, in his copy of the *North Coast of Scotland Pilot* book, a detailed description of the horrendous seas likely to be encountered when wind met tide in a storm in the Fair Isle Channel. The description was based on the accumulated experience of mariners over hundreds of years, and hundreds of wrecks. The area ranks with Cape Horn, the Bay of Biscay and the Cape of Good Hope as a place to avoid if possible in very severe weather, or at least to take extra precautions.

Captain Gelis, as a qualified master mariner with qualified navigating officers, also had easy access to full information on the speed and direction of the tides, hour by hour, in the Fair Isle Channel – in the form of the Hydrographer of the Navy's *Tidal Stream Atlas* for the Shetland Islands and the tidal predictions for 5 January, which gives not only the exact minute of high and low water but also the expected height of every tide, to within a tenth of a metre. On the day after the wreck, Michael Hudner, the ship-owner, told a press conference at Sumburgh Airport, in answer to a question from one of the authors, that the *Braer* did carry on board the charts for the Fair Isle Channel, the *North Coast of Scotland Pilot*, the *Tidal Stream Atlas* and the tidal predictions.

The line between misadventure and foolhardiness is a thin one. Misadventure implies excusable ignorance. The only possible excuse for ignorance in this case is that Captain Gelis was too tired out, in the service of Hudner's delivery schedules, to make sense of the information available. Perhaps he was too tired even to look it up. He had been through The Hole four times before, while on charter to Exxon. Perhaps he thought he knew it well enough.

In Chapter One we examined the spiral of mechanical problems which led to the breakdown of the *Braer*. The question Captain Gelis must answer is – at what point in that spiral did he become aware of the seriousness of the situation? Was he awake when the auxiliary burner failed and they had to switch to diesel fuel for the main engine? If he was, he should have known about it. Someone should have told him. He may say that he was asleep. Like Exxon's Captain Joseph Hazelwood of the *Exxon Valdez*, he had every right to be asleep, as long as there was a competent officer of the watch on the bridge. Captain Gelis says he left detailed instructions with his subordinates to call him if anything serious went wrong with the ship. The inquiry has yet to determine fault but, like the commanding officer of a military unit, a ship's captain is ultimately responsible and can be held legally accountable for everything that happens on board, whether he knows about it or not.

This is not always fair but the buck does stop with him.

Even without heavy pipes loose on your deck, it is unwise to sail on into very heavy weather in a tanker powered by heavy fuel oil, when a potentially crippling fault had developed – such as a defect in the steam boiler which makes that heavy fuel oil usable and keeps the ship alive. It is doubly unwise if what lies ahead is not the open ocean but a notoriously dangerous channel between two rocky islands, where the known, predictable tides are likely to carry the ship very quickly towards the shore.

Negligence implies neglect. From Captain Gelis' account, someone neglected to raise the alarm as soon as the steam boiler was having trouble, some time between eight pm and midnight on 4 January. Someone neglected to call him when they had to switch to diesel 'shortly before midnight', and again at 2.30 am when they found water in the fuel. The shipowner says the captain was 'eventually' advised by the chief engineer to alter course and seek shelter. Captain Gelis says no-one woke him until 4.10 am, when by his account he had been in bed for over two hours, sleeping through the crisis in the engine room.

Captain Peter Hilding, one of Captain Gelis' predecessors, told reporters after the wreck: 'The Chief Engineer should have reported back to the Captain by three am. If there was even a possibility the engines would fail, the first thing to do by standard marine convention is to contact the Coastguard and owner and order a tug – even if it stayed on standby half a mile away, you have it there just in case.'

This raises the question of exactly when one of the officers realised the danger. No-one can decide individual responsibility until all the evidence is published to resolve the apparent inconsistencies. Unfortunately, the shipowner has, at the time of writing, not yet published the engine room log of the *Braer*.

Whenever Captain Gelis did become aware of the faulty boiler, the switchover to diesel for the main engine and the discovery of water in the diesel, it is surprising that he did not immediately call out a tug and inform the Coastguards. But the shipowner said on the day after the wreck that he was very pleased with Captain Gelis, who had done 'an outstanding job of trying to maintain the ship' which was 'completely seaworthy' when she encountered extremely bad weather.

The problems continued, even after the Coastguards were belatedly informed. After the Engineering Superintendent (not the Captain, note) had spoken to the shipowners, the *Braer* did not call out a tug immediately. Even at that late hour, *Star Sirius* could have reached her in time. Then Captain Gelis did not leave a towline hanging over the stern when he abandoned ship – because earlier someone had omitted to ensure that there was a heavy-duty towing wire stowed at the ship's stern. The mooring ropes attached to the stern winch when Captain Gelis released the winch brakes and left the ship were not strong enough to tow her from the stern in heavy seas. Gelis knew that. Also still unexplained is the delay of almost an hour in taking a salvage crew back to the ship as soon as she had drifted past Horse Island at 10.03 am. Not that it would have helped, because of the missing towline.

Captain Gelis has taken a lot of stick since his ship was lost. He was in charge, so that is his lot. The 'Old Man' carries the can. But was he really in charge? Here we have no firm evidence, only questions. What exactly was the role of Mr Khan, the Engineering Superintendent from the shore side, during the *Braer*'s brief and miserable final voyage?

One former ship's officer who sailed for years with other companies told us that having 'a man from the office' on board is always stressful for the officers of a ship, particularly for the master. A superintendent, whether he be from the engineering or deck departments, is a very powerful figure. He is, in fact, the boss while he is on the ship, even if the nominal boss still has to bear the responsibility without enjoying all the power. If Superintendent X says: 'Let us sail, Captain Y,' and Captain Y refuses to sail because he thinks the weather is too bad, Captain Y can very quickly find himself packing a suitcase and leaving down the ladder with the pilot, with another officer taking his place on the bridge.

In practice, the company's representative may have unusual influence aboard a ship. Having the ear of the office, he can tell them what he likes, knowing that they are more likely to believe him than a captain. If there is engine trouble, the engineers may talk directly to the omnipotent 'Super' and assume that he will be telling the 'Old Man' on the bridge about it. Deck officers will tend to raise their concerns with the Super if he is up and about – as he probably will be – while the Old Man is having some well-earned rest.

Even so, when a ship breaks down it would be normal for the Old Man to talk directly to the office, not the Superintendent, who is a passenger, however well-regarded he may be by the office. It would be normal for the Captain to be advised by the responsible officer, the Chief Engineer, about the desirability, for engineering reasons, of seeking shelter – not by a Superintendent Engineer who happened to be on board.

So, the floating can of worms that used to be the *Braer* has given the Marine Accidents Investigation Branch plenty to keep itself busy, in secret. In Scots law there is no justification for this secrecy. Until a charge is laid against a person or persons by the procurator fiscal (public prosecutor) at Lerwick, in whose jurisdiction the wreck occurred, there is nothing to stop public discussion of the facts of the case. All the evidence can and should be made public immediately.

Complaining of 'much speculation and misinformation' in the media, shipowner Hudner on 25 January published what he called a 'Casualty Synopsis', giving facts as he said he knew them. The facts were not *sub judice*. Although it appears that legally he could have done, he did not release all the relevant information. He may not have had it available. On 28 January we wrote to Hudner, thanking him for publishing the information and asking for more. Our questions included the following:

*What was the average speed of the ship, as logged by the* Braer's *navigating officers during each four-hour watch between leaving the Fedje pilot station and losing all power in the Fair Isle Channel?*

*Michael S. Hudner*
(*The Scotsman*)

153

*How many nautical miles were logged between leaving the Fedje pilot station and the loss of all power at 0445 GMT on 5 January?*

*At what time, precisely, did the engineers fire up the auxiliary boiler . . . after leaving Norway, or was the diesel-fired boiler working throughout the voyage until the 2000–2400 watch on 4 January? At what time, precisely, during that watch, did the watch engineer shut down the boiler?*

*What was the 'routine adjustment' the watch engineer performed at that time?*

*What was the ship's latitude and longitude at that time?*

*What was the ship's latitude and longitude at 2300 hrs and 2400 hrs GMT on 4 January, and at 0100 hrs, 0200 hrs, 0300 hrs and 0400 hrs on 5 January?*

Hudner declined to publish these simple facts. We asked the questions because the public does not know where the *Braer* was during those crucial hours. There is no independent verification even of the tanker's position when Hudner and Captain Gelis say she finally lost all power 'ten miles south of Sumburgh Head'. The Department of Transport was not interested in paying people to watch tankers passing Fair Isle. They should have been, and they knew they should have been, but they were not.

Could surveillance, advice and traffic control from the shore have given advance warning and prevented the loss of the *Braer*? Lord Caithness and his boss, Transport Secretary John MacGregor, want us all to be patient and wait for the results of the inquiries. We cannot and need not wait for either British inquiry before taking some common-sense action to prevent another *Braer* disaster.

Lord Caithness, after admitting that there was no radar coverage of the Fair Isle Channel after all, said it would not have helped anyway. Here he was wrong again. Radar would have told the Coastguards that there was something out there which had been moving but had stopped and appeared to be drifting shorewards. To find out what it was, in the dark, they would have had to send a radio message. If there was no reply, there was a helicopter they could send to investigate. The helicopter's searchlight would at least have shown them that the object was a laden tanker stopped in the water and that her name was *Braer*. They could have then found out who owned the ship and asked them what was going on. It would have given them a head start of at least an hour, enough to summon a tug to reach the ship before she was abandoned.

There is another way of identifying an unknown ship which shows up on the radar. A simple device used to track commercial aircraft could have given advance warning of the *Braer*'s difficulties. It is called a transponder.

On 2 February, exactly four weeks after the wreck of the *Braer*, Air Traffic Control radar at Gander, Newfoundland, picked up a blip some 150 miles out over the Atlantic, at a height of 35,000 feet. The blip was

*Transponder on
flight deck of Boeing
747*
(Photo: Jonathan Wills)

approaching from the north-east at over 500 mph. Air traffic sent a one-word radio message: 'Squawk', followed by a number code.

On the flight deck of the Boeing 747-136 aircraft G-AWNB, Captain Graham Gilbey punched his allotted number code into the transponder, a grey box on the instrument panel above his head. Then he pressed a button: The transponder transmitted the code back to Gander and told the ground that this was British Airways Flight 223 from London Heathrow to Dulles International Airport in Washington DC.

Just to make sure, air traffic radioed back: 'Squawk, ident.' Captain Gilbey pressed the button again. The identification of the plane was confirmed. For the remainder of the flight down the east coast of North America, 'Speedbird 223' would be continuously watched and would automatically identify itself. It was a useful precaution in a crowded airway. It meant that if anything should go wrong, someone on the ground would know, as well as Captain Gilbey and his First Officer, Peter Walmsley. Indeed, someone on the ground might see a problem before they did and alert them to it.

Several thousand feet below us, an Air India Jumbo Jet was on the same course, clearly visible from the flight deck of G-AWNB. It too was 'squawking' to the ground as the planes flew over the loose pack ice east of Newfoundland. Neither of the two flight deck crews felt that their airmanship was being questioned. Air traffic control, surveillance and transponders were part of a team – the normal, sensible way of doing things.

Without transponders, commercial aircraft are not allowed to fly. Aviation authorities worldwide would forbid them to take off, as would the owners and insurers of the planes, whether carrying passengers or cargo.

The transponder is a very ordinary piece of radio equipment. A top of the range model costs well under £5,000. It does not require satellite navigation. As soon as it is within range of a shore-based radar, it tells the people watching the scanner what it is that they can see. The radar has already worked out the position, course and speed of the target.

Captain Gilbey and First Officer Walmsley could not see why transponders would not work on ships. On the flight back from Washington, we happened to sit next to a man from the multinational electrical and electronics company, Lucas. He was on his way to Slough. Slough is famous for producing more chocolate than the whole of Switzerland. It is not so well known that the town next to Heathrow Airport produces Lucas transponders. The man from Lucas could not see why they would not work on ships. Nor, indeed, can anyone else, except shipowners who, ever since the invention of the lifeboat and the watertight compartment, have moaned and whined about the expense of simple safety devices. Not surprisingly, very few ships have transponders. Another reason is that the marine insurance industry does not insist on them.

Five miles below us, tankers steaming through the fogs and icebergs of the Grand Banks of Newfoundland were not being watched by the shore. There would have been no-one to watch the *Braer* if she had made it across the Atlantic and started to pick her way through the sea ice in the Gulf of St Lawrence, with just an inch or so of steel between the oil and the ice floes. Radar coverage on the North American coast is limited mainly to harbour areas like New York and Boston. There are only four civilian shore radars to cover the entire coastline of the United States, outside harbour limits.

The reason for this strange state of affairs is partly historical. Civil aviation is relatively recent. Traffic control and safety advisory services were designed from scratch, mostly after the Second World War. But sea transport has evolved over many centuries during which the only feasible way of ensuring the safety of a ship was to trust the captain. Compasses, sextants, charts, lighthouses, radio beacons, radar and even satellite navigation were all developed to help mariners find their way around, not for landlubbers to keep an eye on them.

Not until the 1950s were radars used by the authorities on shore to monitor the movement of vessels, and then mostly in harbours or in very busy, narrow channels such as the Dover Straits. There is still a feeling of resentment among some master mariners (and shipowners) at the suggestion that they might be 'spied upon' by the shore. There are commercial reasons for this – a ship may not wish everyone to know where she is at all times, particularly when she may suddenly receive new orders to sail for a port where there is a better price for her cargo, when she cuts a corner to save time and money on a voyage, or when she makes a surreptitious rendezvous with another tanker to trans-ship some oil in, let us say, an unorthodox transaction. And sanctions busters bound for Serbia have an obvious fear of surveillance. This is not to suggest that the intended voyage of the *Braer* was anything other than lawful and innocuous.

The whole idea of being watched and advised, let alone controlled, from the shore is anathema to some captains. They have been trained to be independent and they see themselves as experts against the might of the sea – proud, competent men who alone can decide what is best for the safety of their crew and cargo. The master is sovereign on his ship. There is more than a little machismo in this. Admirable in the days of the tea-clippers, perhaps, but increasingly dangerous in crowded seaways where enormous ships carrying vast cargoes of toxic, explosive substances mean that even a single mistake can cause deaths and environmental disaster.

The purpose of the journey to Washington was to be present at the two-hour Congressional hearing into the wreck of the American-owned *Braer*. The US House of Representatives Committee on Natural Resources (formerly the Interior and Insular Affairs Committee) was taking evidence, in a sub-committee hearing, from Malcolm Green, Chief Executive of Shetland Islands Council. The committee chairman, Congressman George Miller, is a Californian Democrat who once did a student job as a deckhand on a Chevron oil tanker. He conducted one of the first inquiries into the *Exxon Valdez* disaster and has been a consistent critic of the oil industry, the tanker owners and the US Coast Guard.

Congressman Miller listened carefully to Green's account of the *Braer* disaster and the council's response to it. He was told of the need for better surveillance, better ship inspections and tanker-free zones, which the council had been campaigning for since 1979. Miller had already received an invitation to the conference on tanker safety which the council planned to hold in Shetland at the end of March. He said President Clinton would be told what had been said at the hearing.

Green's recommendations were detailed and had a familiar ring about them to the Congressman:

1 *Ships carrying oil and other hazardous cargoes should be required to file voyage plans, just as planes file flight plans, and to communicate with traffic controllers in their area before deviating from their agreed route;*

2 *When sailing in coastal waters, tankers should be monitored on radar by people who know the local waters, hazards, currents and tides;*

3 *Mandatory traffic separation lanes should be established in environmentally sensitive areas where there are a lot of ships passing;*

4 *Tankers should be registered and crewed in the same country where the owner is based, to ensure that there is a common language between the owner and the crew, and proper training of crew members;*

5 *International conventions and regulations governing the operation of tankers should be strictly and uniformly enforced by all nations.*

Green's evidence aroused some interest and sympathy, but the main action of the day came when the US Coast Guards' Rear-Admiral Arthur G. Henn admitted that they had not yet carried out all the instructions they were given by Congress in the 1990 Oil Pollution Act, passed in the wake of the *Exxon Valdez* disaster.

Detailed plans for monitoring tankers in confined waters were not ready; specifications for double-hulled ships had not been drawn up; radar cover of the US coast was rudimentary outside harbours; plans for tug escorts were incomplete; and progress on defining no-go areas for tankers had been slow. Without being asked, the US Coast Guard had evaluated the 'cost effectiveness' of vessel traffic services. They had been asked to say how vessel traffic services could be put into effect, not how they would affect the commercial interests of shipowners.

Admiral Henn's response to these detailed criticisms, made in *Safety at Bay*, a report to Congress by the US Natural Resources Defense Council, was to say: 'We are aggressively implementing our myriad new taskings and we continue to evaluate risks to further identify weak points and options for improving the US spill-prevention infrastructure.' In other words, the coastline of the USA was just as much at risk as Shetland's.

Speaking to the same hearing, Scott Sterling, President of the Prince William Sound Regional Citizens' Advisory Council, said his experience in Shetland during the *Braer* disaster had taught him something: 'We need to ask ourselves whether we are vulnerable to the same scenario . . . In Alaska, the answer is clearly yes. Many of us believe that the sequence of events – bad weather, loss of power, tanker on the rocks – will account for the next big oil spill there.'

Exxon, BP and other partners in the Alyeska Pipeline Service Company had people at the hearing. They were taking notes. So were men from the insurance companies. They had a lot to learn.

The system of Protection and Indemnity (P&I) Clubs operated by the tanker insurance industry ensures that the costs of a wreck like the *Braer* are spread very widely and very thinly. No single insurer will face ruin as the result of a single incident. In one way this is good because it means that claimants are more likely to get their money, eventually. But it also has the effect of diluting and dissipating the interest of individual insurers in promoting safety measures which could save them all a lot of money in the longer term.

If you drive a car without brakes and have an accident, the loss adjuster from your insurance company will make a large deduction from the payout. If negligence is established, you may find yourself uninsured and bankrupt after a serious crash, particularly if a third party is injured or killed.

In theory, the insurers of the *Braer* could have refused to cover her for a midwinter voyage in high latitudes – particularly if they knew in advance (as they should have known) that she had no way to anchor if broken down in heavy seas – no 'brakes', in other words. Indeed, it can be argued that they should not have offered cover and that it was rash of them to do so. It may also have been unwise to insure a ship which had no duplicated fuel system for the main and auxiliary engines, and no standby generator with its own fuel supply. But, if that were the case, very few tankers would be plying for trade today. Or rather, they would be, but with a different and less reputable insurance company taking the risk, probably in a Third World country where American and European ship safety standards are unknown.

A case can be made that a prudent insurer should not cover a ship unless satisfied that the officers and crew can communicate with each other, and with the shore, in a common language. In practice this means basic navigational English, as in international aviation.

Insurers who want to avoid expensive payouts might also pay some attention to the increasing problem of polyglot crews with unsuitable or inadequate training, not to mention the practice of many shipowners of leaving ships short-staffed and paying overtime. It was, after all, the Institute of London Underwriters who warned in 1989: 'Manning levels, and the quality and skills of officers and crew, need the most careful monitoring – particularly where flagging out has taken place.'

Despite this pious exhortation, not much has been done. Workers' representatives such as NUMAST, the union for British merchant marine officers, have been warning of the dangers of flagging out for many years. The union, along with the International Transport Workers' Federation, has been demanding better training and the implementation in all member countries of the International Maritime Organisation's 1984 'Standards of Training, Certification and Watchkeeping Convention'. NUMAST has repeatedly warned that there are so few British citizens now being trained as seafarers to British standards that a 'generation gap' is developing. Even if the decline in the UK fleet is reversed, there will not be enough British sailors to run the ships. This situation is likely to persist beyond the year 2000.

The warnings by knowledgeable and concerned seafarers have been to little or no effect. Flagging out is endemic. More than two-thirds of the British merchant fleet has either been scrapped or registered in flag-of-convenience countries since 1979. Since 1975, when there were more than 1,600 British-registered merchant ships, the decline has been even more dramatic. In 1993 there are fewer than 300 ships still flying the Red Ensign. Shetland Islands Council, with its fleet of car ferries, actually ranks as a major British shipowner, with about five per cent of the 'Red Duster' fleet. If there were another Falklands War or similar conflict requiring transport back-up by merchant ships, the UK would have to hire them from other countries.

The Americans call flags of convenience 'run-away' flags, for the very good reason that if you register a ship in Liberia, for example, you conveniently run away from both American and Liberian tax liability (even though the Liberian ship registry is actually administered from offices in New York and Reston, Virginia – just across the Potomac River from the US Coast Guard headquarters).

The insurance industry is the key to making immediate improvements in ship safety because it is the only body with the commercial power to enforce higher standards. Governments say they can only make improvements through international legislation, which takes years. They could, of course, hire enough enforcers to implement existing regulations but that also takes time – and cash. All the insurers have to do is get together and agree not to cover high-risk ships. A lot of insurers have gone out of business in the recession. A very few major underwriters now have the market, and the power, concentrated in their hands. As Roger Nixon of the Institute of London Underwriters told the press in February 1993: 'We are in a position to be incredibly ruthless.'

Respectable underwriters do not cover high-risk aircraft. They would object if airline captains were regularly forced to work for 38 hours without proper rest, as Captain Gelis was. In the air, under-staffing, poor maintenance, polyglot crews and fail-dangerous designs are the exception. On the sea, they are the rule.

The statistics of the world tanker fleet are a scandal. It is estimated that one-fifth of the world's 3,200 tankers are unfit to be afloat, let alone put to sea. More than half of the ships are over 16 years old. Although many older tankers are well maintained and managed, three-quarters of all those lost in 1991 were built before 1976. And ships like those still get insurance, unless they are trading on the American coast, where the Oil Pollution Act has introduced the spectre of unlimited financial liability where negligence or criminal action can be proven. The US is not a signatory to the convention which limits a tanker's liability.

Until recently there was little sign of concerted efforts by the insurance underwriters to enforce higher standards. But the massive and still unquantified insurance liabilities floating around four years after the *Exxon Valdez* disaster, followed by three disasters within a month – the *Aegean Sea*, the *Braer* and the *Maersk Navigator* – appeared to have concentrated minds wonderfully. On 12 February 1993 the *Wall Street Journal* carried an interesting article whose timing could not have been more apt (or significant). All of a sudden, the oil companies and the insurers were ready to talk, and boast, about their plans to make the global ocean a safer and cleaner place. The article began by telling how BP, Shell and other oil majors were increasingly rejecting the tonnage offered to them on charter to carry their oil.

Instead of relying solely on reports by the ship classification societies like Det Norske Veritas and Lloyds, oil companies were sending their own inspectors to work over the ships before they hired them. What they found was horrifying, the *Wall Street Journal* said. BP alone rejected 30 per cent of the tankers it inspected in 1992. Shell failed 20. The French company Elf, which operates the Flotta oil terminal in the Orkney Islands, found that *three-quarters* of the ships it was offered were sub-standard. It is strange that this was not widely publicised earlier. If the newsdesks would not touch the story, the companies could always have slipped it into their advertising copy.

The paper found that, belatedly, insurance underwriters were taking a similar line. In 1992 the Institute of London Underwriters refused to insure a quarter of the 133 ships it inspected, after finding serious structural problems. Most of the shipowners found someone else who would offer cover. Even the classification societies are getting the message. Their ship inspection standards are slowly being improved. But what were they doing before the *Exxon Valdez* and the other disasters hit the headlines?

Governments are neither powerless nor blameless. They have the power, or could quickly obtain it, to withdraw licences for insurance companies to operate in their countries unless and until they use their financial muscle to make the shipping industry shape up. The immediate result of such action would be to put up insurance premiums and freight rates. Higher freight rates are what shipowners' organisations such as the International Chamber of Shipping have been demanding for years. They argue that this is the only way to pay for rebuilding the global tanker fleet to acceptable safety standards. Current day rates for chartering a 250,000 tonner are around $30,000. Fleet managers estimate that they would need between two and three times that figure to finance replacement ships built to the standards of the US Oil Pollution Act of 1990. Not surprisingly, not many keels have been laid recently. Good ships would not make money in today's market. But it is the oil companies who are driving freight rates down by hiring cheap and nasty old ships.

With a world glut of tanker tonnage, rates for hauling oil are likely to stay low. Unless maritime states force shipowners to scrap obsolete ships, that is. Then the shipowners will want subsidies to build new vessels. This is anathema to market-worshipping Conservative governments like the present British administration but it may be the price taxpayers have to bear. Unfortunately, the cult of the unfettered market has led to the closure of most of the British shipyards which could have built new, safer tankers. The work is likely to go elsewhere.

The rot has gone so far that there would not be enough tankers to carry the world's oil if proper safety standards were to be phased in even over ten years. The ships that the Glasgow *Daily Record* called 'coffin boxes' on the day after the *Braer* disaster are going to be with us for a very long time. Which makes it all the more important to improve surveillance and control in coastal waters.

With complaisant insurers, shipowners have continued to make money out of old tubs. Bergvall & Hudner, who owned the *Braer*, have based their entire commercial philosophy on buying up older tonnage ever since they startled the Wall Street shipping community in the 1980s with their new ideas on ship-financing.

Starting with bulk carriers of between 15,000 and 24,000 tonnes deadweight, and trading in dry cargoes such as grain, sugar, fertiliser, steel, coal and ores, they brought to shipowning the real-estate techniques which Hudner, a former lawyer, had learned during many years in the property business. By January 1993 they owned 47 ships. In March 1988 the magazine *American Shipper* interviewed Hudner for an article quaintly entitled 'The Homely Ship May Be the One That Makes Money'. The wonder-boy was in expansive mood.

'A ship is like an office building,' Hudner said. 'You rent out the space. The big difference is that shipping is a lot more volatile. It's like the owner of an office building has to go out and find a new tenant every month.' B+H Bulkcarriers Ltd, in association with Commodity Ocean Transport Corporation (run by a partner of Bergvall and Hudner) had bought a fleet of eight old, cheap ships. Their earnings and costs were pooled and the profits distributed to the investors in the fleet. There was little or no provision for retrofitting old ships or building new ones. When they were no longer profitable, the hulks were scrapped or sold. The idea was that the company would be a 'self-liquidating entity' – after seven years or so it would be wound up and all the proceeds would be distributed to the shareholders.

This method of ship financing was so successful that by 1988, only ten years after Bergvall and Hudner started in business together, their group owned and/or managed more than 40 vessels. In April that year they had bought 14 ships from the former Canadian Pacific fleet, including their first six tankers, carrying refinery products. The tankers were to be operated in a pooled fleet like the first batch of dry-bulkers. Again, as reported by *American Shipper*, the new venture was set up as a self-liquidating entity 'intended primarily to generate cash return for the investors and for the managers'. Some of the cash for the Canadian Pacific deal came from the Bergen Bank, reflecting the Norwegian origins of Hudner's partner, the shipping expert Arvid Bergvall.

From the start, B+H ships have been supplied with crews by crewing agencies using low-wage seafarers from China, the Philippines, Korea and Indonesia. Filipino crews cost between a quarter and a third of the wages for British seafarers. B+H normally fly the flags of Panama, Liberia and Singapore.

At first the bankers and institutional investors were suspicious but, as *American Shipper* noted, they were won over when 'Hudner stressed over and over again . . . that the vessels would be paid for at low prices. There would be almost no leverage [*debt*] and, as a Liberian corporation, [*it*] would not be subject to taxation either in the United States or Liberia.'

In other words, Hudner persuaded investors to put their money into elderly ships with cheap, polyglot crews in the hope of a quick return and a tax shelter. The way Hudner preferred to put it was that the 'shipping business is 20 years behind the real estate business in terms of the depth of the capital markets and lack of sophisticated financing techniques'.

There is nothing inherently wrong with a shipping company being 'intended primarily to generate cash return for the investors and for the managers', as long as enough of the profits are put aside to ensure that the ships are maintained, managed and crewed to the best international standards. Hudner referred repeatedly to the *Braer* and her officers and crew as 'first class'. There is one good reason to suspect that something was not first class. It is the crumpled wreck of the *Braer*.

Total power failure on large oil tankers is increasingly common, world-wide. What happened in the engine room of the *Braer*, some time between eight pm on 4 January and 4.40am on 5 January 1993, was fairly routine in the elderly ships which now carry most of the world's oil, even if the immediate cause was weather damage to the air vents. It cannot have been a surprise to the shipowner, who could have ensured that his tanker was equipped to deal with such problems. The *Braer*'s sister ship, *Celtic*, broke down in the Atlantic a week later.

The shipowners knowingly sent this ship and crew to sea without a back-up fuel system and generator to use in an emergency, and with anchors that could not be used at all in heavy weather. In that respect they were no different from most other owners of large oil tankers, but that does not excuse what happened. The emergency equipment which should have been the first resort was inaccessible in heavy weather and, to all intents and purposes, had been designed out of the ship long before she was built in Oshima, Japan, 17 years before. Even so, Hudner could have insisted that a heavy duty towing wire was kept at the stern of the ship, where it would have been accessible even when the lines at the bows were not.

Hudner regarded the passage through the Fair Isle Channel in midwinter as 'routine'. At the press conference at Sumburgh on 6 January, reporters asked him if he would send a ship through there again in the same circumstances. He at first said: 'I expect so.' Later in the conference, after intense interrogation about the last hours of the ship, he was asked that question again. 'Circumstances would dictate what would be the correct thing to do. I would have to think about it,' he said. Legally, there is nothing to stop him.

Sitting at the same table was Sir Hector Munro MP, the Scottish Office Minister for Agriculture and Fisheries. Sir Hector, a wartime air veteran, said: '. . . as one who has been interested in the sea all my life and flew in flying-boats in this part of the world for many years, I would think twice about taking a heavily laden tanker through the strait in the conditions that have been prevailing for the last 36 hours . . . It certainly was a hazardous thing to do . . . I know it was probably a thousand-to-one chance that his engines would fail, but having failed it showed the risk he took in going through the straits.'

Sir Hector was not the only one to think that. Captain Eivind Johanson, the Swedish master of the ship when she crossed the Atlantic in February 1992, told *The Sunday Times*: 'The most natural thing in the prevailing wind would have been to sail north of Shetland. I would not have gone that close to land in bad weather.' Another former skipper, Captain Hilding, said he had commanded the *Braer* on two transatlantic voyages in 1991, when he chose to go through the English Channel rather than around the north of Scotland. He said Captain Gelis took 'an unnecessary risk' by sailing close to Shetland: 'In the summer the Shetland route is viable but not in winter and especially not between the islands. Anything can happen if you take this route in winter.' Captain Hilding told the Swedish newspaper *Expressen*: 'You can always expect unfavourable conditions in the Shetland Channel, which not only increases the risk of an accident, but also the wear and tear on the ship.'

To be fair to Hudner, this is common practice. The *Braer* was not the first tanker to attempt the Fair Isle Channel, the Pentland Firth or the Minches in such weather, nor was she the last. But all the others had got away with it. Their skippers took a calculated risk, betting Fate and the insurance companies that they would get through without total engine failure. And as long as they won their bets, no one on shore was any the wiser, least of all some shipowners who rewarded their captains with bonuses when they arrived on time, despite 'stress of weather'.

The quickest and therefore the cheapest route from Mongstad to Quebec is through the Fair Isle Channel. That is why the *Braer* was there, like so many before her. Captain Gelis could have gone south, through the English Channel. That would have added two days to his journey, he said. Or he could have passed around the north of Shetland. That would have added a few dozen miles and delayed his arrival at Quebec just a little. It would also have taken him into an area where several other large tankers were lying hove-to, up to 50 miles offshore, waiting for the weather to ease so that they could go into Sullom Voe to collect their cargoes. There was a risk of collision. Not a large risk, but a risk, nonetheless.

If he had sailed from Mongstad around the north of Shetland, his route would have taken him close to several large oilfields – another source of danger. A loaded tanker hitting an oil production platform is perhaps the ultimate marine catastrophe still waiting to happen. The inescapable conclusion is that a more prudent navigator would either have headed south for the English Channel or stopped his vessel, however large and 'completely seaworthy', and waited on the sheltered, eastern side of Shetland until the weather improved. There may be explanations but there are no excuses.

For the British Government, there are no excuses at all. They were repeatedly warned, for 14 years, about the dangers of the radar blind spots around Shetland – and even admitted the danger themselves, three years before the wreck; they were told, by experts, how to minimise the danger with radars, transponders and more resources for the Coastguards; they were pleaded with to do something to enforce the Sullom Voe surveillance system on ships within the UK Government's coastal jurisdiction and to implement a traffic advisory scheme like the one they already had in the Dover Straits; they were told by Jim Wallace MP and others about the lessons from *Exxon Valdez*; and their own publications specifically described the dangers of the Fair Isle Channel.

For 14 years the Government did nothing – except, after a delay of 11 years, to put an unenforceable, advisory no-go area for tankers on the Shetland charts. They did attend a lot of international conferences and help to draw up well-meaning conventions, but the net result was less than nothing – matters actually became worse.

If this does not amount to gross negligence, the phrase has no meaning. No wonder that the Marine Accidents Investigation Branch is holding its inquiry in secret. No wonder that there is not to be a public inquiry held before a Scots Sheriff (judge) or a Commissioner of Wrecks. No wonder that the Government did not dare to hold the Donaldson inquiry in Shetland but found lodgings for it in London, where few Shetlanders can afford to attend. No wonder that ministers did not welcome the Shetland Islands Council conference on Managing the Marine Environment and, even after the *Braer* was lost, intended to stay away. Not until six weeks after the disaster did Lord Caithness and Scottish Office minister Lord James Douglas-Hamilton MP (one of Britain's few elected lords) agree to come. Hardly star material but they will have to suffice.

At least the *Braer* reminded John MacGregor to look through his in-tray.

A week after the wreck he announced that substandard shipping was 'an international disgrace'. This may have been news to MacGregor. It was not to Jim Wallace MP, John Prescott MP, the seafarers' unions, the environmental pressure groups and Shetland Islands Council, who had been telling the Government exactly that for so long.

A month after the disaster, the newly green-minded MacGregor announced a 'voluntary code', agreed with the tanker owners' representatives, to avoid the use of the Fair Isle Channel and other dire straits in bad weather. He had to do something because of the bad publicity, but his code will be unenforceable. It is most likely to be flouted by those ships most likely to get into trouble – the tankers whose skippers have instructions to follow a course, regardless of weather. They will just make sure that they go through the straits unseen – at night or in fog. To misquote President Reagan – 'Trust, but don't bother to verify.'

Details of the code, announced seven weeks after the wreck of the *Braer*, show that it will allow tankers to sail within 2.5 nautical miles of the southern tip of Fair Isle, just a mile from a shallow patch with only 55 feet (16.8 metres) of water above it at low tide. That shoal would have put the *Braer*'s keel within 20 feet of the seabed (in 30 foot waves!) and would tear the bottom out of a fully-laden 300,000 tonner. Large tankers will also be allowed to sail within five miles of the notorious shoals off North Ronaldsay, on the southern edge of the Fair Isle Channel.

MacGregor proposes a 'traffic separation scheme' for the area between Orkney and Shetland. West-bound ships will be advised to use the north channel between Fair Isle and Sumburgh, while east-bound vessels will be encouraged to use the south channel between Fair Isle and Orkney.

The west-bound lane passes just 3.6 nautical miles north of Fair Isle, 6.4 miles closer to the island than the existing mid-channel route recommended for tankers bound to and from Sullom Voe.

While exposing Fair Isle and its seabirds' cliffs to more danger than at present, MacGregor's scheme does extend the 'area of avoidance' on the west side of Shetland to take tankers at least 15 miles clear of the outlying island of Foula – if they pay attention to the new recommendations. A similar extension is proposed for the north of Shetland and an entirely new 'please-don't-go' area covers the east coast – but still allows large, loaded tankers to pass half a mile from the internationally important seabird colonies on the cliffs of Noss.

A Government press release on 25 February said the scheme (which also bars tankers from the Minch and establishes areas of avoidance on other parts of the UK coastline) will 'recommend to shipmasters and shipowners provisions to reduce the risk of pollution caused by grounding of large tankers around the UK coast and stresses the importance of':

- *'Passage planning' – where captains tell the shore authorities where they plan to go, before they sail;*

- *'Compliance with internationally agreed routeing schemes';*

- *Telling the authorities in the country where a ship is registered if she is in difficulties which could lead to pollution;*

- *Asking captains to report their position when in the new areas of avoidance – and 'precautionary areas' in the approaches to anchorages;*

- *Keeping enough sea-room to fix broken-down engines before drifting ashore [which is what prudent mariners do already];*

- *Testing that essential gear on board is working;*

- *'Satisfactory towing arrangements on tankers';*

- *'The right of masters to exercise their discretion in particular circumstances.'*

The let-out clause comes last.

Even this meagre effort, with all its stressing, recommending and encouraging, will not be put on the charts until the IMO agrees it. A committee meeting is scheduled for May 1993, when the MacGregor code is due to be tabled 'as an information paper', not a demand.

There is another snag: the traffic separation scheme for the Fair Isle Channel cannot be put on the charts until the area has been fully surveyed – which it never has been, despite being used for decades by enormous tankers. A full hydrographic survey can be expected to take the Admiralty at least one season, delaying the printing of new charts until 1994 or possibly 1995.

It will no doubt be of great comfort to the people of Fair Isle to know that, even in the present emergency, Britain has at least managed to avoid taking unilateral action which might have upset the flag of convenience states who have a majority vote on the International Maritime Organisation.

Nowhere in the press release about the voluntary code was there any mention of radar surveillance, interception of rogue ships, or the banning of miscreants from British ports. But a sign that the Government was at last beginning to understand the problem was the phrase used to describe the 'now-please-behave-yourselves' code: 'interim measures . . . pending the introduction of measures within the organisation' (the IMO). Whether these 'measures' will be bottle messages or transponders remains to be seen.

The voluntary code, pathetic though it is, is at least a move towards regulating shipping in the same way that aviation is managed and controlled, although it is likely to be used as a further argument to delay the installation of shore radars – until the next unwatched tanker causes a disaster. MacGregor may have changed course but he is on the wrong tack.

The code is, however, a tacit admission of the Government's guilt after the years of inactivity which made MacGregor's Department of Transport an accessory to the wreck of the *Braer*. It reminds some people of what Congressman George Miller had said after the Bush Administration and the tanker owners suddenly, in the summer of 1989, agreed to look into ship safety in Prince William Sound, Alaska: 'Where were they in the decade before? Where *were* they, the *day* before the *Exxon Valdez* went aground?'

Even President George Bush finally accepted the inevitable. After years of pussyfooting around with the totally ineffective International Maritime Organisation ('organisation' is perhaps not the right word for a committee controlled by the very flag of convenience states it seeks to influence), the United States at last lost patience and went out on its own to legislate for better ships, better crews and better traffic control. The US Coast Guard may not have finished the job yet but at least it has begun and, under the Clinton Administration, it will probably be forced to deliver the goods.

Contrast this with the bleating of MacGregor in the House of Commons on 8 February 1993 about the impossibility of taking any enforcement action against tankers without the agreement of the International Maritime Organisation, and you begin to understand the exasperation and bitterness of Shetlanders who have seen their islands despoiled to make a fast buck.

It came as no surprise to Shetland when the Transport Secretary rejected Jim Wallace's sensible, short-term solution to the problem – sending in the Royal Navy to patrol the Fair Isle Channel and to escort and advise tankers there until such time as shore radars and transponders could be installed. Oblivious to the opinions of those who knew much more about the sea than he did, he told the House of Commons: 'Radar surveillance all round our coast would be extremely expensive. We must, therefore, carefully consider the cost benefits.' What will he say when he sees the estimates for salvage tugs to escort tankers?

No-one yet knows what the cost of the wreck will be. But B+H have made an estimated $1.4 million out of it.

Six weeks after the *Braer* grounded, they were paid $9.525 million by the London insurance underwriters who covered three-quarters of the risk on the tanker *Braer*, by then declared a 'constructive total loss'. Hudner expected to get $19 million from insurers, he had told the *The Advocate* newspaper in Stamford. But B+H only had the *Braer* covered for $12.7 million, London underwriters said, on a policy which was due to run out on 19 January, two weeks after the wreck.

Even so, they walked away from the disaster with a nice surplus. The insurance payout was between three and four times the scrap value of the *Braer*.

The ship's cargo, and third-party liability for compensating Shetland islanders for pollution, were covered by separate insurance policies. The cargo was valued at over $11 million. The compensation bill could reach $100 million.

B+H bought the *Braer* and her sister ship *Celtic* in 1989 for a combined price of $31.6 million. Hudner said there was a $20.8 million joint mortgage outstanding on the two tankers. The *Braer* insurance cash of $12.7 million reduces the mortgage on the remaining tanker to around $9.1 million, after fees of about $1 million have been deducted. That could leave B+H with some $1.4 million on the black side of their balance sheet. There is a risk, of course, that it could all be swallowed up in higher insurance premiums.

At the time of writing, they still have the *Celtic* earning money on charter.

She was detained in Quebec by the Ultramar oil company the day after the wreck, as security for Ultramar's cargo lost on the *Braer*. B+H paid over a reported $20 million bond immediately, allowing the *Celtic* to leave port. Several days later *Lloyd's List* reported her broken down in mid-Atlantic. Power was restored and she was later seen at anchor in the Mediterranean, off the coast of France. The French coast is covered by shore radars to help tankers if there is any sign of trouble.

Messrs Bergvall and Hudner and their shareholders had lost little, except some sleep during the two weeks when the disaster 'dominated our lives totally', as Hudner told *The Advocate* reporter. The paper printed a picture of Hudner, looking sad, tired and concerned at his office desk in 'Clearwater House', 2187 Atlantic Street, Stamford.

The people of Shetland will be paying for the disaster, in one way or another, for years to come. You do not have to be a betting man, or even a marine insurance underwriter, to calculate that the expense of shore radars to cover the Fair Isle Channel, the Pentland Firth and the Minches would be much less than the price of this single 'accident'. And the Royal Navy, which ought to be patrolling these waters, is already being paid for by the taxpayers.

The British Government should be ashamed but, as Jim Wallace MP said to us in February this year: 'This Government has no shame.'

# NEIL SMITH, SHELLFISH FISHERMAN

THE broken lobster pots were piled up at the side of the white cottage. Their coloured ropes creaked as the wind licked round the frames.

(Photo: Tom Kidd)

'I really should get them fixed,' said fisherman Neil Smith as he closed the door, 'but to tell the truth I don't have any enthusiasm.'

He paused and smiled sadly. 'There's nothing to go and catch anyway.'

Neil, aged 36, should have been out catching sharks close inshore at Sumburgh Head. He's been chasing these fish for eight years . . . but he does not yet know if he'll chase them again.

He brought out a book of photographs and pointed proudly to snaps of large, bloody beasts on the deck of his boat *Crystal Sea* (an unfortunate name now).

'In our first year we caught nine sharks in three hours. The biggest we ever landed was 32 and a half stone.' He talked about his fishing experiences with the air of one contemplating The Good Old Days.

'I'm usually at the sharks until about March, and the lobsters and velvet crabs start up about April. The West Voe of Sumburgh is where you get the better quality of lobster because it's not been fished all winter. It's a bit of a race to get there first . . . . usually.'

Through the spring and summer, the *Crystal Sea* moves slowly up the west coast, as far as St Ninian's Isle. For the second half of the year, they make their way up the east coast, past his home in Levenwick, as far as Bressay.

Neil's patch is bang in the middle of the fishing exclusion zone. His father, a few miles up the coast at Cunningsburgh, is also a shellfish fisherman.

'I've been at the fishing since I left the school,' Neil said. 'Apart from eight years out where I worked at Sumburgh Airport. But I had to get back to the sea. Its something that seems to be in your blood. It's an incurable disease.'

He got up and switched the telly off. Outside, the three o'clock sky was already getting dark. He was at a loss for things to do since the *Braer* hit. Even his compensation claim was being dealt with by Shetland Fishermen's Association.

But the prospect of money in his hand wasn't enough to lift the gloom. 'What can compensate for losing a way of life? There's no job satisfaction with getting a cheque through the post every month. The lawyers have told me to take another job if I get the chance. Or move to another area.

'But that's not the answer. Shetland has been saying for years that there are too many fishermen. If I move to someone else's patch, they are going to be affected. Their grass has to go down for mine to go up.'

The *Crystal Sea* remains tied up at the Pool of Virkie, Sumburgh. Neil's fear is that with nowhere to keep her, or the lobster pots, under cover, the weather will take its toll.

'I don't know what I'll do if they say we can't fish this year. But I'm going to try and get work with the fisheries department, taking samples. That'll maybe keep me going a bit.'

Neil is not bitter. He is angry, maybe, that the tanker hit Shetland. Angry at the irony that brought a ship not bound for the islands ashore that Tuesday morning.

'I was on my way to Lerwick and heard about it on the radio. I turned around and made straight for Sumburgh. When it hit I wasn't sure what was going to happen. I knew there were rocks on one side, but I knew there was also a sandy bottom there. I never really thought it would break up.

'I walked over the hill to Garth's Ness just after it happened and you could smell the oil. Within an hour you could see the effect on the seals there. I'm not a seal lover because they play havoc with my lobster pots, but it's a very undignified way for any animal to die.'

For the next few days he didn't know what to think. 'It's difficult to apportion blame,' he said. 'The old Ness men say you never go ashore on Horse Island . . . but of course the tanker skipper didn't know that.'

Despite the threat to his own future, Neil was adamant that the exclusion zone should stay in place for as long as was necessary. 'There's no point in lifting it until you know everything is clear.

'I hope in April I'll be off to the lobster fishing, but I just get this gut feeling . . .

'The thing about oil spills in other places is there's a period that the seabed may be sterile, but in the end it comes back richer and better.'

He didn't look convinced of his own words. But he needed to believe something good would come of it. He smiled as if he suspected he was being too naïve, too trusting that Nature would sort the sea out.

'To be a fisherman you have to be an eternal optimist,' he said.

*Chapter Eleven*

# NEVER THE SAME AGAIN

*Mother Nature sent the* Braer *as a warning. I think I can hear what she's saying to us: 'People, stop doing this to me!'*

DANIEL J. LAWN OF VALDEZ, ALASKA, SPEAKING IN SHETLAND,
12 JANUARY 1993

*Radar surveillance all around our coast would be extremely expensive. We must, therefore, carefully consider the cost benefits.*

JOHN MACGREGOR MP, SECRETARY OF STATE FOR TRANSPORT,
HOUSE OF COMMONS, 8 FEBRUARY 1993

Twelve days after the *Braer* was wrecked, the Norwegian-registered tanker *Ambra Dolphin* broke down twice while fighting yet another hurricane, ten miles west of the Muckle Flugga Lighthouse. She was in ballast, waiting to go in to Sullom Voe. The seas were so huge that her propeller was coming out of the water and racing, causing governors to cut in and stop the engine. A Sullom Voe tug was put on alert until the ship regained power an hour or so later. The tanker had difficulty raising enough compressed air to start her single main engine. Like the *Braer* and most other tankers, she had no clutch. The propeller shaft was connected directly to the crankshaft of the engine.

Later, in port, a member of the *Ambra Dolphin*'s crew told shore workers that he had never seen such waves, in 30 years at sea. It was worse than Cape Horn. So why was the master of the *Ambra Dolphin* there in the first place? He had been obliged to report his speed, course and position to Sullom Voe Port Control, run by Shetland Islands Council, when he was 200 miles from the pilot station. That is what the Sullom Voe Port Information Handbook told him to do, anyway. Why was he not advised to stay on the sheltered, eastern side of the islands? Councillors in Lerwick Town Hall were, after all, urging the Government to adopt the Sullom Voe rules for the coastline under London's control. Was the pot calling the kettle black? The best-laid schemes can gang agley.

Three days later, the Finnish-owned tanker *Bonny*, bound for Sullom Voe in ballast from Hamburg, went through the Fair Isle Channel in a near-hurricane, or tried to. The seas were so violent that she could make no

171

headway. Her skipper had to do a U-turn and go back round the east side of Shetland for shelter. He could not keep the *Bonny* outside the 'area of avoidance'. He came within two miles of the wreck of the *Braer*.

The day before the *Bonny*'s adventure, Captain Sutherland had addressed councillors. His theme was 'Where do we go from here?' One thing was sure: '. . . the status quo cannot be an option . . .' He was not talking about double hulls. His prescription was based on what was possible in the immediate future:

- *Defined 'areas of avoidance' and, possibly, compulsory traffic lanes for tankers;*

- *Power to make tankers and other large ships report to the shore their position, course and speed, when steaming through certain waters;*

- *A surveillance system that worked;*

- *Local control by properly qualified staff;*

(Photo: Tom Kidd)

- *Enough money to do the job.*

Captain Sutherland also suggested that it would be desirable to send a plane or helicopter to keep an eye on passing tankers. Last, but not least, it could be useful to have legal powers to 'intervene' if a ship looked like colliding with another ship or with the rocks.

That was what *he* wanted to talk about at the forthcoming conference on the sea. At the time of writing, we still do not know whether senior Government ministers and oil industry executives will accept their long-standing invitations to join that public debate in Lerwick at the end of March.

Most of the oil has gone now. But where has it gone? Perhaps a third of it is in the atmosphere, evaporated as the experts said it would. Some people wish it was all up in the sky. Bombs have got a lot smarter since 1967, when the RAF tried to set fire to the *Torrey Canyon*, to save Harold and Mary Wilson's holiday beach in the Isles of Scilly. It might just be an idea to open up the deck of the next one with some high explosive and burn the lot with napalm.

Huge amounts of oil must have blown on to Dunrossness during those days and nights of the brown wind, probably a lot more than has been realised. If the 15 square miles known to have been affected received an average 'oilfall' of even a tenth of an inch, that would account for 96,000 tonnes – more than all of the *Braer*'s cargo and bunkers. The average oilfall was a lot less than that, because much of the oily spray carried right across the southern tip of Shetland and fell into the North Sea on the other side. But it is possible that another third of the oil went into the air as droplets, in addition to the third which evaporated. A reasonable estimate would be that between 5,000 and 15,000 tonnes actually fell on the land and stayed there. It was not possible to plough it into the soil in January, as some 'experts' suggested, because Shetland fields are usually too wet to plough until late April.

So the remaining portion of the oil, at least 30,000 tonnes, must still be in the sea, somewhere. What is it doing? A man called Donald Button thinks he may have the answer. It is not very encouraging.

Button is Professor of Marine Science and Biochemistry at the University of Alaska in Fairbanks. He has been studying oil in the sea for over 20 years. Until recently, he did not have much luck securing research money.

In Professor Button's terms, the *Braer* was a small oil spill, a very small one compared with all the oil that we wash into the global ocean every year. It just added to the long-term damage caused by millions of tiny trickles every day – from road drains, oil terminals, factories, garage workshops, planes, helicopters, tanker ballast water tanks, all ships' engine rooms, and most ferries, fishing boats and sea-anglers' dories. Not forgetting leaky tankers like Shell's 319,000 tonne *Lampas*.

The *Lampas* is one of the few tankers still flying the Red Ensign. She is registered in Douglas, Isle of Man. She is more than three times the size of the *Braer*. She sailed from Sullom Voe on 15 December 1992 with 200,000 tonnes of oil for China. We have to presume that she leaked oil for eight weeks, half-way around the world, before she discharged her cargo and headed for dry dock in Singapore to have a crack in her hull fixed. The leak was detected while she was finishing loading at Sullom Voe. Divers went down and found the oil weeping from a crack in the ship's bottom. She was single-skinned. It is possible to weld under water but it is not advisable if there are 200,000 tonnes of oil above your head, on the other side of a 1.5-inch thick steel plate. The *Lampas* could have been unloaded again and taken straight to a dry dock in Europe for repairs. But that would probably have meant bringing an empty tanker into Sullom Voe and pumping across the leaking tank's contents before she sailed. All very expensive, not least because she was blocking a loading jetty that another ship needed. So she was allowed to sail as she was and become someone else's problem. Perhaps she should be re-named *Nimby*.

That streak of oil from the *Lampas* and the slug from the *Braer* will be around for a while. Professor Button estimates that it takes a hundred years before half a gallon of every gallon spilled can truly be said to have 'disappeared'. Part of the oil left after evaporation on the surface washes ashore as visible pollution. The rest is dissolved and oxidised in the sea. The bugs that plankton eat will react with the oil. Some bacteria eat and excrete it, some combine chemically with it.

What is left after these complicated and little-understood reactions are new substances which can be more poisonous and persistent than the oil. They are called amphipathic compounds — amphilites, for short — and no-one really knows yet just how harmful they are. It takes a long time before natural biological processes can recycle them. And while that is happening the amphilites are changing the bugs that are changing them. The sea's chemistry is altered in a way that Mother Nature did not intend. What happens then is anyone's guess. Professor Button's research is trying to put numbers on it. Even without numbers, common sense tells us that putting oil in the sea is a bad idea.

We know that most of the oil produced from the world's oilfields eventually ends up in the sea, in one form or another, through the global cycle of exchange between air, land and water. We know that in seven years or so a cubic mile of mid-ocean water can find its way to the North Pole. We do not know if, or for how long, the sea can accept and deal with all this carbon which Mother Nature had locked up in coal deposits, gas wells and oilfields over hundreds of millions of years — and which we have released in just two centuries.

The sea's chemistry is changing, that is for sure. The change can cause sores and cancers in bottom-living fish, as it has done in the Baltic and the southern North Sea. We can avoid eating sick fish by throwing them back over the side. As long as the damage goes no further, things may be all right. But scientists like Professor Button think that we may be approaching a biological threshold, when the world's ecosystem will change irrevocably, in a way that has not happened before. It is like carrying out an uncontrolled experiment in the chemistry lab, not knowing if it will blow up.

When you live in a 60-mile thick bubbleskin of air, water and soil, wrapped around a ball of warm rock 7,926 miles across and whirling through the cold void of space at 66,597 miles an hour, it is a pretty good idea to take care of the bubbleskin – particularly if you do not know how to make another one. That is why even little oil spills like the *Braer* matter a lot.

That is why all those Alaskans were in Shetland in the second week of January.

I still feel a bit guilty about Joe Hazelwood, the Captain of the *Exxon Valdez*. He ruined Prince William Sound for a while and I joined in the chorus of his critics. We were right, but Joe did me a good turn. Because his ship ended up on Bligh Reef, I made some very good friends. I also met Alaska, one of the most beautiful wild places left in our mucky old world. If I had not gone to Cordova and Valdez the month after the spill (and if Harold Evans had not put up the money for the fare) I would never have known Don Button, David 'Indiana' Grimes, Brenda Guest, Chuck and Kathy Hamel, Dune Lankard, Dan and Patti Lawn, Vince Kelly, Johanna Munson, Riki Ott, Rick 'Crocodile' Steiner, Stan Stephens, Scott Sterling, Mayor Kelly Weaverling or any of my other dear Alaskan friends. And I would never have seen Meteorite Mountain, Power Creek, the Copper River Delta, Robe Lake or that Black Bear – or heard the Sandhill Cranes whooping it up over Cordova. Oil spills can bring compensation more valuable than any insurance claim.

When the *Braer* impaled herself on the pointed end of Shetland, I knew we were not alone. We had friends who had gone through all this before. If the worst came to the worst, there would be some big shoulders to cry on (and there were quite a few grown men in Shetland who wept on the morning of 5 January 1993, me included). I faxed the news to Valdez at 7.15am – 10.15pm the day before, Valdez time. Within 12 hours Dan Lawn, Stan Stephens and Scott Sterling were on a plane for Sumburgh, via Seattle, Los Angeles, London and Aberdeen. A week later, Rick Steiner followed them.

They said they came as 'observers' for their citizens' advisory council, set up after *Exxon Valdez* and modelled on Shetland's Sullom Voe Association, but (alas) without its legal powers. Dan later told *Scotland on Sunday*: 'We did not come to advise but to observe and learn. That probably made us more acceptable because with the Alaskan spill we had way too many instant experts giving advice and telling us what to do. I had a preconceived notion that the Shetland Islands Council had the management system in place that could respond well to emergencies. My feeling was confirmed.'

Dan Lawn was the first person from the shore to board the *Exxon Valdez* after she grounded. He took notes, made a video and asked why no-one was breathalysing the captain. He was checking up. That was his job, as Superintendent of the Valdez District Office of the Alaska State Department of Environmental Conservation. For seven years he had been the eco-policeman at the oil terminal. He repeatedly warned his superiors that a disaster was waiting to happen. When it did, he exposed the people who had caused the disaster and failed to clean it up. He came to Shetland and discovered that many of the improvements he wanted had been in place here for years. That got right up the noses of BP, Exxon and the other five owners of the Alyeska Pipeline Service Company which ran the Valdez terminal. An Alyeska official

*Dan Lawn, the man who warned of the* Exxon Valdez *disaster and lost his job when he exposed the causes of it*
(Photo: Graeme Storey)

175

called Dan Lawn 'a jerk and a hard ass'. The State, which relies on oil dollars for 80 per cent of its income, obligingly took him off the case. They transferred one of the world experts on oil pollution prevention to inspecting septic tanks and domestic water supplies. Dan's union appealed and won. The State refused to reinstate him. Now the dispute is in court.

'Observers' Dan and his friends may have been when they came to Shetland, but they did give advice when asked and it was good advice too. Everyone who met them at Sumburgh and elsewhere during the *Braer* emergency benefited from their wisdom and warmth. At a bad time, it was good just to have them around. At the Bressay office of the Shetland News Agency, they cheerfully acted as my unpaid filing clerks, domestic skivvies, child-minders, telephonists, researchers, tea-boys, technical consultants and stress counsellors during the tempestuous early days of this book.

Since the *Exxon Valdez*, 'our' Alaskans have become regular migrants to Shetland and a few of us have had the privilege of flying back to Prince William Sound. Air fares being what they are, these have been business trips of necessity. When we meet, we talk mainly of oil spills and how to stop them. But we have also had a lot of fun. One day, perhaps, we shall hold a reunion and just go fishing – or maybe whalewatching off Bligh Reef, or birdwatching at Sumburgh Head. If we mention oil spills at all, I hope it will be just as a bad memory from very long ago.

There is no better way to end this book than to quote a few words from the Alaskans.

Scott Sterling, the President of the Prince William Sound Regional Citizens' Advisory Council, faxed his first report to them from Shetland on 8 January:

> *'There seems to be a high level of co-operation between the local authorities and the national government. The media is overplaying the immediate damage while not doing enough to discuss the long-term impacts. Local residents are, of course, heartsick and afraid, but are facing the tragedy with courage and determination. The political climate does not seem overly adversarial.'*

After his return to Valdez, Stan Stephens, the tour boat operator, wrote to the Alaskan Republican Senator Ted Stevens, a long-term supporter of the oil industry:

> *'I am an environmentalist and a realist. What is real is that we can no longer ignore the damage being done . . . by the oil industry when there is technology to protect the environment and still have a very profitable industry . . . Complacency has never been the central problem. The central problem is outright greed, a search for profit by any means.'*

Dan Lawn told *Scotland on Sunday*:

> *'Prevention is the only answer, not more equipment to mop up spills or technology that puts double hulls on tankers. We have got to stop them*

*landing on the beach. If you do not protect yourselves, no-one else is going to do it. We have got to quit talking about it and get on with doing it. Shetland is in a unique position to make it happen. JFK said we are going to the moon, handed over to the technical experts, and we went to the moon. If politicians make the statement that we are going to solve the problem, it will be solved. I'll keep pushing for that.'*

Rick Steiner, the University of Alaska marine biologist who advised the Prince William Sound fishermen after the *Exxon Valdez* said: 'Your lives will never be the same again.'

## Postscript

In the Valdez City Museum and Art Gallery there hangs a collage sculpture by an Alaskan Aleut artist. The centre of the piece is the face of a greedy European, disrupting the traditional patterns around him. The work is called *The White Man Came, and He Hung Around, and He Hung Around.* If we are to hang around much longer, we had better get this little planet neat and tidy again. The Alaskans have a word for it – 'Skookum'.

*A local checks the state of the beach at St Ninian's Isle*
(Photo: Tom Kidd)

177

# DEBBIE AND DAVE HAMMOND, SHETLAND SMOKEHOUSE

THE sweet aroma of smoking fish wafted into the office. Debbie Hammond came in, dressed in her working uniform of white wellies, hat and apron over a bright, red boilersuit. Her hair was tucked, EC-hygiene-style, neatly into a net.

Her husband Dave was busy with paperwork. There was a bit of catching up to do since the oil spill. Dave had spent the first days and weeks trying to retain their customers, as reports of the disaster flashed around the world.

He faxed the latest information, drew maps of the oiled areas, and went out to look at beaches himself so he could send first-hand news.

For most of their buyers in Belgium, France, Holland, Italy, Switzerland, the USA and the Caribbean, this was enough to instil confidence in the continuing quality of the Shetland Smokehouse products. But they couldn't promise that their customers in turn would support them.

'A few asked us not to put "Shetland" on the label,' Debbie said. 'That was kind of painful after spending seven years building up your label and keeping it apart from Scotland.

'I think we could go back to using "Shetland" now, but we've got all these other labels to use up first . . .'

But even that didn't satisfy the ultra-sensitive Japanese market — orders for February were postponed. Business for the first two months was way down on last year and the Hammonds fear it will be some time before the true effect of the oil spill on their carefully nurtured image will be known. Let alone the effect on the living sea.

'If the oil does spread through the food chain it won't just be Shetland that suffers, but the whole of the north of Europe,' Dave said. 'But I have a gut feeling that one season's biological action on this crude will get rid of it — and I don't think that's just wishful thinking.

'The power that blew the tanker apart and dispersed the oil was the same power that makes our fish great.'

The Hammonds have been smoking fish out at Skeld on the west Mainland of Shetland for the past seven years. They arrived independently in Shetland in the early Seventies. Debbie discovered the islands during travels to escape the heat of her Florida home and medical studies. Dave, from Edinburgh, worked for a time on pilot boats at Sullom Voe.

The business started out as experiments in a kiln in their garage. Now they employ seven other people full-time and five part-time, and smoke their way through 80 tonnes of salmon every year, along with smaller quantities of herring and mackerel.

Before the *Braer* came ashore, plans for a new state-of-the-art factory, double the size of their current premises, were well in hand, with building work due to start in March. As 'an act of faith' the expansion will continue. Shetland Islands Council will own the factory and lease it to the company.

'After the oil spill, we thought about whether we would be in business by the time the council built the new factory,' Dave said. 'We even thought we'd have to mothball this factory and offer it to the council as a canteen for workers cleaning up the oil . . . We've dodged the bullet really.'

'That was the first image we all had – of black tar everywhere like *Exxon Valdez*,' Debbie added, in her Shetlandic/American drawl. 'For me, the business wasn't the main concern – it was a big concern, but not the main one. I live here for a reason, and it is not just the work.'

While the visible signs of the disaster, six weeks on, were not as bad as they had first feared, they had been through plenty of frustration, anger and tears over the havoc being wreaked on their adopted home.

*Salmon processor Dave Hammond walks away from the beach at Scatness after seeing the brown sea*
(Photo: Jonathan Wills)

'Even when the tanker hit, nobody knew what it meant,' Debbie said. 'When the oil began to spill there was a kind of numbness. Then there was that slight exaltation when we thought these amazing Dutch salvors would get the oil out. And everybody held their faith.

'After that it was just storm after storm after storm.'

The height of Debbie's anger came while listening to Transport Secretary John MacGregor speaking in the House of Commons: 'It was MacGregor who broke the news that the tanker had broken up and I will never forgive him for that. I didn't want him to be the one to break the news to the world. We should have been told first . . . I was livid.' She still fumes at the memory.

'A customer phoned from Switzerland asking what was going on and Dave went berserk,' she said. 'He told them to call up the British Embassy in Switzerland to say information was being withheld from us, and to get them to make a formal protest to the House of Commons.'

Dave laughs with delight: 'They actually did it — we've seen the faxes. They sent a protest to the Commons.'

It may not have achieved much, but it was a gesture against injustice. Next stop, compensation.

# CHRONOLOGY OF EVENTS

The exact details of what happened and when will have to be established by the Marine Accidents Investigation Branch inquiry, but enough is known to construct a draft chronology of events.

All times are Greenwich Mean Time (GMT). The source of the information is given in italic script. Coastguard messages and information are from the published log of HM Coastguard's Marine Rescue Sub-centre at Lerwick, unless otherwise stated. Some of the radio conversations were overheard and carefully logged at the time by an experienced radio operator on shore who does not wish to be identified.

WEDNESDAY, 21 DECEMBER 1992

> *[Captain Gelis' statement of 15 January 1993]*
> *Braer* loaded full bunkers of diesel oil and heavy fuel oil at New York, the last time fuel was taken on before she was wrecked.

SUNDAY, 3 JANUARY 1993

0737 *[Captain Gelis' statement of 15 January 1993]*
Finishing loading 84,413 tonnes of crude at Mongstad oil terminal, Norway. No bunkers loaded.

Norwegian press reports of difficulties caused by leaking steam. This meant that not enough 'inert gas' – boiler exhaust – was being produced to pump into the cargo tanks and keep the oxygen level low enough to prevent explosions. Loading delayed after repairs and safety checks.

1110 (approximately) Left Mongstad for the Ultramar Refinery in Saint Romouald, Quebec. The weather forecast was for Force Eight to Force Ten south-westerly gales in sea area Fair Isle.

1210 *[Axel Sundøy, as reported by Norwegian press]*
Dropped pilot off Fedje pilot station. Wind southerly, Force Nine.

*[Captain Gelis' statement of 15 January 1993]*
'Sailed at 1200 GMT. Set course of 243° True' for Sumburgh Head with manual steering and satellite navigation checks on position. Heavy seas between 25 and 30 feet high were breaking green over the decks as soon as the ship entered the open sea. Ship rolling about ten degrees. Making way at reduced propeller speed of 90 revolutions per minute ('full ahead manoeuvring' speed). Captain Gelis remained 'mainly on the bridge' until the evening of

4 January, 'except for the occasional trip to my cabin to make some coffee and to have some food and rest'.

1500 *[Captain Gelis' statement of 15 January 1993]*
*Braer* only 13 miles out from Fedje pilot station.

2000 *[Captain Gelis' statement of 15 January 1993]*
*Braer* 25 miles out from Fedje pilot station.

2300 *[Captain Gelis' statement of 15 January 1993]*
*Braer* 36 miles out from Fedje pilot station.

*[B+H Ship Management Press Release, 25.1.93]*
At some point 'just after the ship left Norway', a rack of steel pipes 16 feet long was seen to break loose on deck, possibly damaging air vents for the diesel fuel tanks. Weather was so bad that crew was not sent on deck to secure the pipes. Vessel did not heave to and secure the pipes.

## Monday, 4 January 1993

*[Captain Gelis' statement of 15 January 1993]*
Wind southerly Force Ten, all day until evening when it abated to Force Nine.

*[Captain Gelis' statement of 15 January 1993]*
'I was informed by the Chief Engineer on the morning of 4th January that the pipes [stored on deck] were loose and rolling around on the port, aft deck *[back left-hand corner of the ship, behind the superstructure]*. Unfortunately, it was too dangerous for anyone to be allowed to go out on deck to resecure the pipes.'

1100 *[Captain Gelis' statement of 15 January 1993]*
*Braer* still only 60 miles out from Fedje pilot station, less than one-third of the way to Shetland, giving an average speed of only 2.5 knots.

2000 *[Captain Gelis' statement of 15 January 1993]*
'. . . it had become possible to increase speed again to 107rpm at 2000 [hrs] because the sea conditions had improved slightly.'

2000 *[B+H Ship Management Press Release, 25.1.93]*
'During the 2000 to 2400 [hrs] watch . . . the watch engineer shut down the ship's [composite] boiler to perform a routine adjustment.' The boiler would not re-start.

2345 Fishing vessel *Stephens* passed a large ship heading west, midway between Fair Isle and Sumburgh Head. Shortly afterwards the crew of another fishing boat, the *Sean Pol*, saw a similar vessel under power in the same area. A Force Eight south-westerly gale was blowing, gusting to Storm Ten, and rising to Hurricane 12.

## Tuesday, 5 January 1993

0001 *[B+H Ship Management Press Release, 25.1.93]*
'Shortly before midnight' the engineers switched the main engine to diesel fuel when the fuel oil became too sticky to run the engine.

0200 *[Captain Gelis' statement of 15 January 1993]*
Captain Gelis went to bed, 'unaware of any problems in the engine room'.

0230 *[B+H Ship Management Press Release, 25.1.93]*
Chief Engineer Ionnis Vloutis called to engine room when water found in diesel fuel service tanks. He 'eventually' advised the Captain to head for the nearest anchorage.

0410 *[Captain Gelis' statement of 15 January 1993]*
'I first became aware of a problem at 0410 on 5th January when Mr Khan [the Superintendent Engineer] came to my cabin. I had already been woken by the Second Officer, who was on bridge duty, a few minutes earlier to report a reduction in the engine revolutions . . . Mr Khan . . . reported a problem with the generators. He had found water in two diesel oil service tanks.'

0430 *[Captain Gelis' statement of 15 January 1993]*
*Braer*'s position 'fixed by the Chief Officer from a radar bearing from Sumburgh Head'.

0436 *[Captain Gelis' statement of 15 January 1993]*
'I laid off a course and at 0436 I ordered a change of course [for the Moray Firth]. At that time we were in position 59° 41.5'N, 001° 13.7'W which was fixed from Sumburgh Head, about 10.5 miles distant. The weather at this time was south to south-west Force Nine, with nine metre [30 feet] seas. The anemometer showed wind speed of 55–60 knots with gusts in excess of this figure. After the alteration of course I went back to my cabin to change from my pyjamas into some day clothes.'

0436 *[B+H Ship Management Press Release, 25.1.93]*
*Braer* altered course to the south, heading for anchorage in the Moray Firth. 'Moments later' the main engine stopped.

0440 *[Captain Gelis' statement of 15 January 1993]*
'A few minutes after our alteration of course when I was still in my cabin, the vessel's main engine stopped and a short time later we suffered a blackout at 0440.'

0445 *[B+H Ship Management Press Release, 25.1.93]*
Electrical power lost 'by' this time. 'Calculating that the vessel would slowly drift clear of the land out into the North Sea, the master did not immediately require tug assistance.'

'about 0500' *[Captain Gelis' statement of 15 January 1993]*
Captain Gelis asked his radio operator to contact Mr Makrinos, B+H Technical Director, in Connecticut, 'and advise him generally of our difficulties'.

'about 0508' *[Captain Gelis' statement of 15 January 1993]*
The *Braer*'s radio operator called Aberdeen Coastguards via Wick Radio.

'about 0513' *[Captain Gelis' statement of 15 January 1993]*
Contact made with Makrinos in Connecticut. Khan, the Superintendent Engineer on the *Braer*, spoke to him. Captain Gelis could not hear what Makrinos said. 'The call lasted only a few minutes. Mr Khan said he was going back to the engine room to re-assess the situation and was to call Mr Makrinos again in about ten minutes. He left for the engine room. The meantime I was called by Lerwick Coastguard on VHF, Channel 16. This was about 0519. I advised them of our position and the power failure.'

0519 Tug requested, according to Hudner.

185

0519 *[Published log of HM Coastguard]*
Shetland Coastguard received first information about the *Braer*'s problem, 109 minutes after the serious fuel problem was discovered, 69 minutes after Captain Gelis says he was told about it, and 39 minutes after the power blackout aboard the *Braer*. The message was relayed via Aberdeen Coastguard who had received the message through Wick Radio. Position given was ten miles south of Sumburgh Head, at 59° 41' North, 001° 17' West. Fix reported by the *Braer*, not confirmed by any independent sources.

0530 *[Captain Gelis' statement of 15 January 1993]*
'At about 0530 Mr Khan returned to the bridge. He told me there was little prospect of restarting the engine and the water problem in the diesel was very serious.'

0531 Crew of Coastguard helicopter *Rescue 117*, operated on contract by Bristow Helicopters Ltd, put on alert at their base in Sumburgh Airport.

0536 *[Captain Gelis' statement of 15 January 1993]*
'With the radio operator's help, Mr Khan was again connected to Mr Makrinos [in Connecticut]. This was about 0536. I was in the radio room for this second call to Mr Makrinos but again I could not hear what Mr Makrinos was saying. Mr Khan told me that Mr Makrinos was going to arrange for salvage assistance but had suggested we seek assistance from the local Coastguard.'

0539 *[Published log of HM Coastguard]*
*Braer* tells Coastguards she has contacted owners but 'am having language problems' and asks if they will speak directly to the owners. Passes over telephone number in Connecticut.

0545 *[Captain Gelis' statement of 15 January 1993]*
'I contacted Lerwick Coastguard again at 0545. They advised me that it would take about five hours for a tug to reach us. I asked them to despatch a tug urgently. Shortly before the call I had heard a local fishing vessel [the *Philorth*] report our position to the Coastguard by VHF. I had been unable to plot our position because the radars and satellite navigation were not working without the power . . . The Second Officer plotted the position reported by the fishing vessel. It was clear that we had drifted northwards by about two miles in the hour since the power failure. If continued, the course of the drift would take us on to the southern coast of the Shetlands.'

0550 Harbour tugs at Sullom Voe alerted, according to press reports.

0553 *[Published log of HM Coastguard]*
Coastguards ask Captain Gelis if he wants them to arrange a tow. Gelis says he will speak to the insurance underwriters and get back within five minutes.

0556 *[Published log of HM Coastguard]*
Lerwick Harbour port control asks Coastguards if *Braer* requires a tug. Coastguards reply that they are waiting for a decision from the master/owners of the ship.

0600 *[Published log of HM Coastguard]*
Shetland Coastguards requested assistance from RAF Search and Rescue station at Lossiemouth on the north coast of Scotland.

*[Captain Gelis' statement of 15 January 1993]*
'At 0600 I spoke again to the Coastguard at Lerwick and discussed evacuation of 16 non-essential crew.'

0604 *[Published log of HM Coastguard]*
Lerwick Harbour port control tells Coastguards that the tug *Star Sirius* is in Lerwick and may be available from her charterers, Shell UK Expro.

0609 *[Published log of HM Coastguard]*
*Braer*'s owners asked Coastguards to arrange a tow, 24 minutes after Captain Gelis says he asked the Coastguards to despatch a tug 'urgently'.

0610 *[Captain Gelis' statement of 15 January 1993]*
All *Braer* crew woken up and told to assemble on the bridge in life-jackets.

0611 *[Published log of HM Coastguard]*
Coastguards told Captain Gelis he should declare a 'Pan'. This prefix to a radio message means, in the Standard Marine Navigational Vocabulary, a 'very urgent message to transmit concerning the safety of a ship . . .' It is one stage lower in urgency than a 'Mayday' – which means that a ship is in grave and imminent danger and requires immediate assistance.

0617 *[Published log of HM Coastguard]*
Coastguards ask helicopter *Rescue 117* to start evacuating crew from the *Braer*.

0626 *[Published log of HM Coastguard]*
*Braer* broadcasts a 'Pan' radio message, 64 minutes after first contacting the Coastguards.

0630 Shetland Towage Ltd report that tug *Swaabie* is preparing to leave Sullom Voe and her estimated time of arrival at the *Braer* is four to five hours on.

0632 *[Published log of HM Coastguard]*
*Braer* asks Coastguards to arrange for 20 of her 34 man crew to be evacuated, as 'this is dangerous'.

0634 Lerwick Harbour port control reports tug *Star Sirius* is getting under way and will leave port in 30 minutes at 0704.

0639 *[Published log of HM Coastguard]*
Coastguard helicopter *Rescue 117* on scene above the *Braer*. Position 6.7 nautical miles from Sumburgh Head.

0650 Lerwick Lifeboat *Soldian* launched and left for the scene.

0652 *[Published log of HM Coastguard]*
Coastguard asks Shetland Towage Ltd if the tug *Swaabie* has left yet. Reply: 'Now departed'.

0654 *[Published log of HM Coastguard]*
Coastguard helicopter *Rescue 117* started to winch crew up from deck of the *Braer*.

0720 Tug *Star Sirius* passed South Ness light in Lerwick Harbour, heading for the casualty.

0734 *[Overheard radio message]*
*Star Sirius* tells Coastguards that her estimated time of arrival at the *Braer* is 2.5 hours.

0738 *[Published log of HM Coastguard]*
RAF helicopter *Rescue 137* arrives on scene.

0741 *[Published log of HM Coastguard]*
RAF helicopter *Rescue 137* reports *Braer* now 2.5 nautical miles from land [Sumburgh Head].

0805 *[Overheard radio message]*
Shetland Coastguard tell Lerwick Lifeboat that Coastguard helicopter *Rescue 117* is winching up crew from the deck of the *Braer*.

0807 Helicopter *Rescue 117* reports to Coastguards '16 lifted'.

0811 *[Published log of HM Coastguard]*
RAF helicopter *Rescue 137*, hovering over the stern of the *Braer*, asks what are the Captain's intentions. *Braer* reports 18 persons still on board.
Coastguards ask *Braer* if she intends to abandon ship. RAF helicopter *Rescue 137* suggests all extra crew should go to the stern of the tanker now as there is little time.
*Braer* reports ten crew now [ready to be lifted].

0815 *[Published log of HM Coastguard]*
RAF helicopter *Rescue 137* reports no crew on deck of tanker and helicopter running low on fuel.
*Braer*: 'They are going now.'

0815 *[Captain Gelis' statement of 15 January 1993]·*
'At 0815 I decided that in view of the helicopter pilot's strong advice I would have to abandon the ship.'

0818 *[Published log of HM Coastguard]*
RAF helicopter *Rescue 137*: 'Sea is getting bad. You must get all on deck.'
*Braer*: 'This is second mate. Will call you back.'

0823 *Braer*: 'Master asks if you can wait longer.'
RAF helicopter *Rescue 137*: 'No, you must abandon now. It will take us all the [time/fuel] left to lift off the crew.'
*Braer*: 'I will tell the Captain.'

0825 *Braer*: 'Is it possible to leave eight persons on board? I intend to anchor.'
RAF helicopter *Rescue 137*: 'There is a rock close to the starboard side. It will take one hour to winch.'
*Braer*: 'We abandon. Eighteen persons on board.'
RAF helicopter *Rescue 137*: 'Commencing to winch.'

0827 *[Overheard radio message]*
'18 still on board.'

0841 *[Published log of HM Coastguard]*
Position of *Braer* one mile south of Sumburgh Head, bearing 240°.

0845 *[Overheard radio messages]*
Wind at Sumburgh reaching 60 knots, direction 220°–240°.

Coastguard helicopter *Rescue 117* returns to Sumburgh to land 16 rescued crew and refuel.

RAF helicopter *Rescue 137* reports running short of fuel and insists all crew leave the *Braer* as there is a risk of the ship going ashore before *Rescue 117* can return to the scene. Position of *Braer* 0.75 miles off Sumburgh Head, bearing 260°.

*Braer* radios that there is no time to drop anchor. RAF helicopter *Rescue 137* insists that all crew leave now as the rocks [of Horse Island] are very close and *Rescue 137* is unable to remain on station because of shortage of fuel. Captain Gelis agrees when proximity of rocks pointed out [by Coastguards].

0846 *[Overheard radio message]*
RAF helicopter *Rescue 137* reports 'Fourteen [*Braer* crew] onboard, four to lift.'

0850 *[Overheard radio message]*
'Two still to lift'

0850 *[Captain Gelis' statement of 15 January 1993]*
'I was the last man to be winched off, together with Mr Khan, at 0850.'

0854 *[Published log of HM Coastguard]*
RAF helicopter *Rescue 137* reports all 18 remaining crew of the *Braer* have now been taken off. Position: 0.75 nautical miles, bearing 260° from Sumburgh Head.
The *Braer* is on her own.

0856 *[Overheard radio message]*
Coastguard helicopter *Rescue 117* back on scene above the wreck and radios: 'Will monitor drift'.
Position of *Braer* 59° 49.9′ North; 001° 18.3′ West.

0858 *[Overheard radio message]*
RAF helicopter *Rescue 137* tells Coastguard helicopter *Rescue 117*: 'Across to Bristows [helicopter hangars at Sumburgh Airport] for refuel, skinwash [of salt from helicopter fuselage] and refreshments'.

0900 Capt. Jim Dickson, Oil Pollution Control Officer for Shetland Islands Council, on scene in helicopter.

0905 *[Published log of HM Coastguard]*
Coastguard helicopter *Rescue 117* reports *Braer* drifting west of Sumburgh Head.

0910 *[Overheard radio message]*
[Coastguard helicopter *Rescue 117*] reports *Braer*'s position now 59° 49.7′ North, 001° 18.4′ West.

0918 *[Overheard radio message]*
Coastguard helicopter *Rescue 117* reports position as 3.02 miles from VOR beacon at Sumburgh Airport. Bearing not heard.
*[Overheard radio message]*
Coastguard helicopter *Rescue 117* reports *Braer*'s position as 59° 49.9′ North, 001° 18.7′ West. Drift since 0920 0.75 miles, direction 327°.

0930 *[Captain Gelis' statement of 15 January 1993]*
'At about 0930 I received a call from . . . the Lerwick Coastguard asking if I

189

would go back to the vessel to attempt to drop the anchors . . . I immediately agreed to return with a boarding party to assist the two pilots he [District Coastguard Controller Ken Lowe] said were coming from Sullom Voe . . . Between the time I received the call from the Coastguard at about 0930 and 1030 when the taxi arrived to take us to the helicopter base, we were awaiting the arrival of the marine pilots from Sullom Voe. I was told by . . . Lowe of the Coastguard that they were travelling by road.'

0935 *[Overheard radio message]*
Suggestion from Coastguard helicopter *Rescue 117* [to Coastguard station at Lerwick]: There is just a possibility of putting a *Braer* crewman on to the fo'c'sle [bows] to drop anchor. This would mean putting helicopter captain into left-hand seat.

0936 *[Published log of HM Coastguard]*
Tug *Star Sirius* reports that she is 0.5 nautical miles from the *Braer*. Gives *Braer*'s position as 1.4 nautical miles from Sumburgh Head, bearing 215°.

0938 According to press reports, Mr Barry Cork, an official of the company owning the *Star Sirius*, said the tug reached the *Braer* at this time, 43 minutes after the crew abandoned ship.

0940 *[Overheard radio message]*
Coastguard helicopter *Rescue 117* reports *Braer* now 1.7 miles from Sumburgh Lighthouse.

0942 *[Overheard radio message]*
Coastguards speak to Sullom Voe tug *Swaabie*, which reports that she is an estimated 4.5 hours from the *Braer*.

0944 *[Overheard radio message]*
Tug *Star Sirius* reports water depth at 50 metres and says no green water breaking over bows or stern of tanker. Suggests that, as the tanker is abandoned and has no power, the tug will have to pull cable off the *Braer*. Asks if men could be put back aboard to retrieve a rocket-fired line and let go the clutch on the mooring cable drum.

0950 *[Published log of HM Coastguard]*
*Star Sirius* reports *Braer* now 0.8 nautical miles from Horse Island, bearing 200°.

0952 *[Overheard radio message]*
[Unidentified speaker] says Coastguard helicopter *Rescue 117* 'can put seamen on to stern [of *Braer*]'. Suggests getting the 'alert crew' ready at Sumburgh Airport to do this.

0954 *[Overheard radio message]*
Local fishing boat *Sette Mari* of Skerries, which had been standing by the tanker, is released from the scene by Shetland Coastguards but remains in the area.

0958 *[Overheard radio message]*
*Star Sirius* reports position as 0.6 nautical miles from Horse Island, bearing 240°.

1000 Weather at Sumburgh Airport: wind blowing 37 knots, direction 190°.

1004 *[Published log of HM Coastguard]*
Position of *Braer* 0.65 nautical miles from Horse Island, bearing 070°.

1010 *[Overheard radio message]*
Position of *Braer* three nautical miles south-east of Fitful Head, bearing 168°. Drift in past hour: 3.2 kilometers [1.99 statute miles].

1015 *[Overheard radio message]*
*Star Sirius* reports position 0.7 nautical miles from Horse Island, bearing 100°. Shetland Coastguard asks for half-hourly position reports, 'though appreciate *Star Sirius* is busy'.

1016 *[Published log of HM Coastguard]*
Coastguards tell pilot of helicopter *Rescue 117*: 'Police will deliver five crew plus two [marine] pilots to be taken to the vessel.'

1022 *[Overheard radio message]*
*Star Sirius* asks Shetland Coastguard if the seamen are 'out' [in the helicopter over the *Braer*?]. Coastguard replies that helicopter *Rescue 117* is refuelling.

1024 *[Overheard radio message]*
Coastguards ask *Star Sirius* how far she is from Lady Holm. Reply: 0.68 nautical miles, bearing 029°.

1030 *[Overheard radio message]*
Position of *Braer* 0.53 nautical miles from Lady Holm, bearing 040°.

1035 *[Overheard radio message]*
Position of *Braer* 0.44 nautical miles, bearing 053° and drifting 350°.

1036 Local man with detailed knowledge of the area reports that the *Braer* is now out of the west-going tide and setting into Quendale Bay. Hopes rise that she may ground on sand, well-sheltered from the swell.

1042 *[Overheard radio message]*
Bristow Helicopters report to Coastguards that the *Braer* crew who are supposed to be flown out to the tanker have not arrived at the helicopter yet.

1045 *[Overheard radio message]*
*Braer* now 0.9 nautical miles from Lady Holm, bearing 090°.

1051 *[Published log of HM Coastguard]*
Captain Gelis, Engineering Superintendent Khan, *Braer*'s Bosun and Captain Jim Dickson depart from Sumburgh Airport in Coastguard helicopter *Rescue 117*.

1052 *[Overheard radio message]*
*Star Sirius* estimates that the tanker will be aground in 20 minutes.

1055 *[Overheard radio message]*
*Star Sirius* reports *Braer*'s position 0.65 nautical miles from Garth's Ness, bearing 010°.

1100 *[Published log of HM Coastguard]*
Coastguard helicopter *Rescue 117* hovering above the *Braer*, winching down Mr Khan, the *Braer*'s Bosun, Captain Jim Dickson and Bristow Helicopters' winchman Friede Manson. Captain Gelis remains aboard helicopter.

1107 *Star Sirius* fires a rocket line on board the *Braer*. It misses. A second line is fired and caught by Captain Dickson and Friede Manson but is torn from their hands seconds before the tanker grounds.

1113 *Braer* grounds on rocks in Garth's Wick.

1115 *[Overheard radio message]*
Shetland Coastguard to helicopter *Rescue 117*: 'Vessel aground. Take the crew off.'

1119 Coastguards confirm *Braer* aground.

1120 Weather at Sumburgh Airport: wind gusting to 47 knots, direction 210°/235°.

1121 All salvage crew taken off *Braer*.

1122 Coastguards report black [fuel] oil leaking from the stern of the wreck.

1155 *[Overheard radio message]*
Coastguards on shore at the scene of the wreck report 'very little oil from stern . . . most from around the bow . . . blowing on to shore . . . some to sea, round Fitful Head . . . nothing into Quendale [Bay] . . .'

1500 *[Overheard radio message]*
Coastguard on scene reports: '. . . oil now into Quendale [Bay] . . .'